# EYE ON THE FLESH

**CULTURAL STUDIES**
*Series Editor*
**Richard Johnson,** *University of Birmingham*

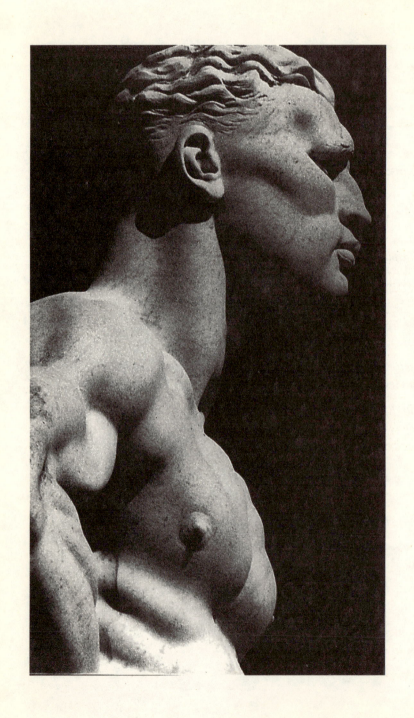

# EYE ON THE FLESH

## Fashions of Masculinity in the Early Twentieth Century

### MAURIZIA BOSCAGLI

**WestviewPress**
*A Division of HarperCollinsPublishers*

*Cultural Studies*

Frontispiece photograph: *The Boxer,* Foro Italico Stadium, Rome, © George Mott, Wessel O'Connor Gallery, New York

Copyright © 1996 by Westview Press, Inc., A Division of HarperCollins Publishers, Inc.

Published in 1996 in the United States of America by Westview Press, Inc., 5500 Central Avenue, Boulder, Colorado, 80301-2877, and in the United Kingdom by Westview Press, 12 Hid's Copse Road, Cumnor Hill, Oxford OX2 9JJ

Library of Congress Cataloging-in-Publication Data
Boscagli, Maurizia.
   Eye on the flesh : fashions of masculinity in the early twentieth
century / Maurizia Boscagli.
      p.   cm.—(Cultural studies)
   Includes bibliographical references and index.
   ISBN 0-8133-2726-1 (hc).—ISBN 0-8133-2727-X (pbk.)
   1. Men's clothing—Europe—History—20th century.   2. Men's
clothing—Europe—Psychological aspects.   3. Costume—Symbolic
aspects—Europe.   4. Masculinity (Psychology)—Europe.   5. Body,
Human—Social aspects—Europe.   I. Title.   II. Series.
GT720.B67   1996
391'.1'0940909—dc20                                                                    95-46430
                                                                                              CIP

The paper used in this publication meets the requirements of the American National Standard for Permanence of Paper for Printed Library Materials Z39-1984.

10      9      8      7      6      5      4      3      2      1

"You've not changed," he said—the face he meant.
A plain face scarcely changed; whereas beautiful
faces wither. She looked neither young nor old;
but shabby; and the room, with the pampas grass
in a pot in the corner, was untidy. A lodging-
house room tidied in a hurry.

   "And you—" she said, looking at him. It was as
if she was trying to put two different versions
of him together; the one on the telephone perhaps
and the one on the chair. Or was there some other?
This half knowing people, this half being known,
this feeling of the eye on the flesh, like a fly
crawling—how uncomfortable, he thought; but
inevitable after all these years.

**—Virginia Woolf, *The Years***

*Per Villelmina Maurizio e Anna*

# Contents

# Figures

# Acknowledgments

Several people have helped and sustained me at different stages in the planning and writing of this book. I would like to thank Robert Scholes, Ellen Rooney, and Neil Lazarus at Brown University for encouraging and enthusiastically supporting my early forays into the territory of corporeality and gender. Drafts of two chapters were presented at the Pembroke Center for Teaching and Research on Women at Brown University and at the Wesleyan University Center for the Humanities, and I would like to thank the directors of those centers, Elizabeth Weed and Richard Ohman, for inviting me to speak. Khachig Tololyan gave me important suggestions for Chapter 3, and Christina Crosby's reading of the entire manuscript energized me to write a better version of it. Brenda Silver's friendship and interest in my project have sustained me throughout. Kathleen Woodward, Gabriele Schwab, and Lindsay Waters encouraged me to consider what a feminist critique of modernist masculinity might imply. The late Allon White's teaching represented one of the most powerful points of origin of my interest in gender and sexualities, critical theory, and modernism; his classes marked, early in my career as a graduate student, an exhilarating and most meaningful intellectual experience. I would also like to thank my colleagues in the English Department at the University of California, Santa Barbara, for providing me with the intellectually stimulating environment in which this book was written. Special thanks to Christina Nelson, who worked out my schedule in a way that gave me the material time to complete the writing. My editors at Westview Press, Gordon Massman and Connie Oehring, have been extremely helpful in guiding the book toward publication, both in its early and late stages. Enda Duffy was there from the beginning, in different countries. To him I owe my greatest debt of thanks and much more.

*Maurizia Boscagli*

# INTRODUCTION

THIS BOOK IS ABOUT a new representation of the male body that took shape in early twentieth century European culture. The type of masculinity inscribed by this body commands attention from the feminist critic of gender: The marks of eroticism and desire that it bears contradict its claim to phallic plenitude and rather present an image of dispossessed masculinity that gestures toward gender instability and abjection.

Between the turn of the century and the 1930s, a period that in western Europe witnessed a crisis of bourgeois models of masculine subjectivity and male authority, the male body was brought to the fore as a model of ideal masculinity and, literally, changed shape. The characteristic male body of the turn of the century was that of the unassuming "black-coated clerk"—of the diffident Leonard Bast in *Howard's End,* the shop boys of *Punch* cartoons, T. S. Eliot's "young man carbuncular." By the 1930s a whole new order of flagrant male corporeality had been put on show in spectacles as varied as Johnny Weismuller's Tarzan, the self-conscious nakedness of the male characters of D. H. Lawrence's late fiction, or the brutalist musculature of fascist statuary displayed around the new Foro Italico stadium in Rome. Muscular, tanned, and either uniformed or unclothed, this novel twentieth century western male body no longer signified the propriety and the sense of measure that had characterized the subject of late Victorian bourgeois rectitude but rather was displayed as a spectacle of untamed natural strength and controlled gestures of rebellion.

This newly visible male body responded to a range of cultural imperatives from mass consumerism to a new economy of gender. Through the new corporeality, the western male subject was deftly inserted into the new circuits of commodity culture and consumer desire. Above all, however, this shocking new corporeality, by which men displayed themselves as women had been displayed, became the site upon which gender relations were configured and sexual identities tested at the moment when the hegemony of males of every class was being threatened. To map the emergence of such a spectacle of masculinity is to trace the arrival of a New Man, a figure that on the one hand corresponded to the more familiar New Woman and on the other reacted to the dangerous and anxiety-producing gender transgression performed by the aesthete. The aesthete, like the New Woman, appeared as one of the key figures in the cultural disorder of the fin de siècle;[1] Oscar

Wilde's trials ended in 1895, and with them ended the possibility for the aesthete to dissimulate and elaborate homoerotic desire through the alibi of aestheticist taste.

In the early twentieth century the authority of the male bourgeois subject came under siege: Social, economic, and cultural changes corroded the authorial and authoritative position to which he had risen during the nineteenth century as paterfamilias, public man, or entrepreneur. In literature these threats were registered in the vehement renunciation of the elders by the self-professed "young generation" in, for instance, texts as different as Samuel Butler's *The Way of All Flesh* (1903) and Stephen Spender's *The Temple* (drafted in 1929). Franz Kafka's own life had the effect of destabilizing and contesting paternal authority. Another attack upon bourgeois male authority came from the class-transgressive petty bourgeois clerk, whose massified taste seemed to threaten the system of social barriers and exclusions through which the middle class guarded its cultural territory. In turn, just as the male subject from the established bourgeois class was threatened by the rise of the suburban clerk, the clerk himself, imitating his betters, was nervous before the rise of modern mass culture and the invasion of public spaces by women. Between the 1890s and the First World War, office and factory jobs were increasingly occupied by female workers, as were the streets by female protesters demanding universal suffrage. At the same time, working class socialism as well as signs of right-wing nationalism threatened the frayed political order of liberalism. The troubled cultural imaginary of the period was exemplified in the social analysis of such bourgeois conservative critics as Adolf Loos castigating ornament, Max Nordau fearing degeneracy, and Gustave Le Bon's warning of the dangers of the crowd and, more generally, fearing the "Asian" and "African" peril; in critical accounts such as these the perceived dangers of social change were often conflated with the masculine fear of losing one's ego boundaries and one's individuality to the feminine and irrational masses. In this historical scenario the image of the New Man, flexing his muscles in order to reinforce his ego boundaries (a veritable attempt, to paraphrase T. S. Eliot, to "shore fragments" against one's own ruin), assumed an apotropaic value; it marked a struggle to resolve phantasmatically, at the level of bodily representation, a moment of crisis of legitimacy and social power.

The vitalistic modern male body represented fetishistically a coherent visual signifier of masculinity without a referent. It made available to modern men the means to fabricate a gratifying specular image of themselves and thus reclaim as natural and innate a wholeness that appeared under threat but that had never been theirs. As a signifier of vitalism and renovation, this modern male body found its structuring trope in the corporeality of the Nietzschean superman. Nietzsche manufactured a new image of the male body as "blond beast of prey" through a bravado manipulation of gender categories: In *On the Genealogy of Morals* (1887) and in *Thus Spoke Zarathustra* (1892) he repositioned the instincts, traditionally stigmatized as female, as a symptom of virility, whereas reason and morals, the classical virtues of masculine order, were degraded by their association with women, priests, and the masses. The novel version of gender identity encoded upon the Nietzschean body relied on two fundamental qualities: its phallic plenitude and its anti-Cartesian materiality, according to which the body was no longer regarded as the demonized other of the spirit but as itself, the sine qua non of a new masculine identity. The image of the Nietzschean "blond beast of prey" in possession of the leonine animality of the superman radically subverted the hierarchical relationship between body and spirit predicated by western rationalism: The armorlike body of the superman, offered in countless replicas to a mass audience as the physique of the modern athlete at the revived Olympic Games of 1896, for example, was not simply a receptacle for the softness of the flesh. Its polished and hard surface heralded a new version of male subjectivity that wanted to abolish any opposition between inside and outside, interior conscience and exterior will. Beyond good and evil and no longer encumbered by the imperatives of bourgeois morality, Nietzsche's superman stood as an absolutely modern image of intelligent materiality, representing a subject that did not have to renounce his body in order to gain a self but rather inscribed his selfhood in his musculature.

By virtue of its attack on bourgeois authority *and* on bourgeois decadence, Nietzschean vitalism was seized upon to give expression to two very different impulses: the desire to dissolve the structures of rational masculine identity (an impulse to loss) and the opposite desire to reinforce them, to strengthen the boundaries of the body to preserve the masculine ego. On the one hand, the Nietzschean ideology of the body fueled the fin de siècle aestheticist revolt, led by Walter Pater in the 1870s and by Oscar Wilde, Aubrey Beardsley, F. Holland Day, and others in the 1890s, who deployed the aesthetic values of Hellenic paganism to foreground homoeroticism. On the other hand, it also directly influenced the fashion for a "manly" ideal of pure and healthy masculinity, a fashion taken up by the newly enfranchised bourgeoisie and impersonated by the ascetic and desexualized body of the young athlete-soldier who volunteered for the First World War. In Edwardian England eugenicist polemics on "national efficiency" and the paranoid fear of "racial decay" gave a new impulse to mass sports, personal hygiene, and practices that could fortify the body of the nation and make it fit to fight in war. This drive to have the national body, coded as male, transformed from a "narrow-chested" weakling to a muscular fighter began with the setbacks in the Boer War and reached a crescendo with the start of the First World War in 1914. With figures such as Rupert Brooke in England and the writers Ernst Wünsch and Walter Flex in Germany, the ephebic and upper class body à la Dorian Gray was transformed into a mass image of "authentic" manliness in which rebellion and wartime sentimental rhetoric of self-sacrifice became incorporated and dissolved into the image of the newly efficient warrior's body.

In this particular figuration of Nietzschean vitalistic masculinity, the potentially rebellious, antibourgeois bodiliness of the New Man was transformed into a means of interpellation into the ideology of nationalism and social obedience.

This is not the only case in which early twentieth century hypermasculinity was called to function in support of the political and cultural hegemony of the time: The desire for a strong and spectacular male body, and the body's own desires, were foregrounded at the time when monopoly capitalism called modern individuals to consume en masse. Although my contention throughout the book is that this new male body in fact short-circuited its hegemonic function by continually gesturing toward the dangerous space of loss, expenditure, and femininity (the space that until the early twentieth century had been occupied by the "effeminate" aesthete), its significance as *also* a hegemonic medium of mass interpellation must always be assessed within the historical conditions of its production. During the early twentieth century the flaunted male body, from being conceived as a covert vehicle of scandalous sexuality by the aesthetes and as an embodiment of a utopian return to nature by a new petty bourgeoisie, came to represent a means of modern discipline. The novelty of this disciplinary meaning of the body lies in its functioning as a pleasure device in the new spaces of modern leisure: In these years the modern subject is produced not primarily in the traditional spaces where, as Foucault has demonstrated, the discipline of the body gives shape to the self (the prison, the asylum, the hospital) but also in the gym, at the seaside, and in the newly multiplying spaces of "free time" in general. The spaces and time of leisure—the afterhours of the employee—were the result, in turn, of Taylorist organization of labor and its newly orchestrated rhythms.

The powerful male physique that in the new century invaded the beach, the gymnasium, the sports tabloid, the cinema, and the national military parade marks a crucial epistemic break in the history of the embodied subject and the modern representation of gender. This physique was no longer the well-trained classical body studied by Norbert Elias and Mikhail Bakhtin,[2] a trope of transcendental individualism through which the modern subject was civilized and subjected to reason; nor was his virility the regulated masculinity of the bourgeois producer, whose self-denial Max Weber recognized as the propeller of the spirit of capitalism. The new masculine identity of the early twentieth century was predicated on physical prowess rather than on the priority of the spirit and reason, and as such it appeared as a return, to use a Bakhtinian term, to the grotesque body, the heterogeneous, premodern flesh whose exclusion had made possible the recognizable identity of the bourgeois individual. Reclaimed from the marginal position to which the Cartesian systematization of corporeality had confined it since the seventeenth century,[3] the newly excessive male body now flaunted its existence in its own right: It no longer appeared as the despicable other of the soul. A modern culture of the body solidified around this subject: Sports, sunbathing, hiking, nudism, and vegetarianism developed mass followings in the early years of the twentieth century as modern body technologies, practices through which the body could be maintained young, beautiful, and efficient. The same aim was pursued through the advertisement of commodities: Cosmetics, vitamins, and sports equipment similarly promised physical health and beauty to the consumer.[4]

Brought to the forefront of early twentieth century culture, this body and its desires could no longer be ignored and excluded; rather they were understood and appropriated by state power as a form of interpellation aimed at securing the state's own hegemony. The new bureaucratic state apparatuses instituted between the two great depressions of the 1880s and 1929[5] were designed to forestall unrest and control "deviance" by catering to the citizen's bodily welfare. Given the enormous expansion of the lower middle class, the entry of women into the public sphere, and the new class consciousness of the proletarians, the first two decades of the twentieth century were characterized by attempts on the part of established regimes to reabsorb and keep under control any potential explosion of the masses. Posed in Althusserian terms, the question was how a potentially rebellious subject could be transformed, once again, into a good one that would work by its own initiative. The bourgeois denial of the body for the positivity of the spirit had served this aim effectively at least until the end of the nineteenth century but was rapidly losing its legitimating role. In order to create consent among politically rebellious social groups—workers, petty bourgeois employees, militant women and nationalist minorities—these subjects needed to be interpellated exactly in the terms in which they had organized their protest. At the historical moment in which the "grotesque" corporeality of dissident social groups (women, homosexuals, "others" identified as a danger to the bourgeois polity) was being shrilly presented by eugenicists and imperialists as a metaphor of subversion capable of compromising a whole cultural order, power had to argue *in favor* of the body in order to make it its prop. This was a strikingly new way of managing the individual and his divided condition: The gap between the grotesque carnality of the body and the proper, rational inner self was no longer kept open by arguing that the opposition between body and spirit was natural or part of a divine design but rather, as Nietzsche taught, by assuming that this gap no longer existed. This perfect seamlessness between the natural body and the individual self, which defined the hypermasculine identity of the superman, sanctioned a return to phallic masculinity and its denial of castration, loss, division.

At the same time, because of its structural ambiguity, evidenced by the effort to redefine masculinity through the "feminine" flesh, the Nietzschean body was always an unsutured and castrated body opening onto the abyss of the libidinality that had until then been excluded, and it was articulated through a double moment of excess and spectacularity. The key irony that undercut the spectacular male corporeality of the superman in his early twentieth century reembodiments was the fact of its excessiveness: That is, this new corporeality appeared at precisely the moment when bodily strength was no longer needed in the majority of people's work. The new male muscles were of no use to the employee, whose working activity involved sitting at a desk. The contradictory character of the modern male body, the fact that its larger-than-life natural qualities appeared at the very moment when they were being rendered obsolete by technology, is a nodal point for my argument of the transformation of the body into a spectacle.

Eccentrically clad as the fin de siècle aesthete and the 1920s dancer (Oscar Wilde and Vaslav Nijinsky), turned into a music hall show of virile power (the Edwardian strongman celebrity and bodybuilder Eugen Sandow in William Sarony's photographs), chastely uniformed to signify national health and self-sacrificial purity (Baden-Powell's Boy Scouts and the British popular icon of the First World War, the poet Rupert Brooke), these bodies gestured toward a symbolic economy that foregrounded excess, desire, sexuality, and the exhibitionist pleasure in being seen rather than the phallic propriety that had characterized the middle class male body in the nineteenth century. As a signifier without a referent, this body was a semiotic object continually encoding contradictory meanings. As a fetishized spectacle, it could take on a life of its own, edging the new masculinity it inscribed into accepting the logic of its display in ways hardly envisaged by the state agencies that looked upon the body as a means of discipline—eugenics and nationalism. In particular, the dissolving of the distinction between spirit and the flesh that had characterized Nietzsche's celebration of the male body foregrounded desire and fabricated an image of the individual deeply invested in his libidinal economy. As such, the antibourgeois attack on reason perpetrated by Nietzschean vitalism widened in the fabric of bourgeois subjectivity and in the plenitude claimed by the superman and unmade the closely knit texture of productive and phallic masculinity. This tear became an open rift where the desires of mass commodity culture could circulate but also where these desires could be harnessed to the logic of (sexual) expenditure and deployed as a means to short-circuit purposeful, regulated consumption.

The antagonistic and potentially counterhegemonic value of the male bodies that I examine is signified by their spectacularity, their dramatized excessiveness and exhibited sexualization. All the bodies I consider are caught in the act of inviting the gaze. I propose that the disciplinary and disciplined male body organized through the image of the Nietzschean superman contains, without being able to fully manage it, its own excess; in turn, this excess may be read as the inscription of antiphallic masculinity, which both manifests itself through *and* contradicts the call to virility that the disciplined and self-possessed male body claims within the culture of modernity. In other words, the Nietzschean figuration of masculinity stands as an instance of gender trouble. By citing the abject sexuality of the homoerotic male body, the image of the athlete-soldier-strongman puts normative masculinity under erasure while impersonating and performing its very laws. Signs of this complex, antiphallic masculinity can be detected in the erotic display of the male body that early twentieth century European culture both allowed and tried to manage. Repeated spectacles of masculinity from Thomas Mann's Aschenbach to Edgar Rice Burroughs's Tarzan show a male body resexualized under the sign of abjection: The desire of these subjects that their bodies be seen enacts traces of a masochistic pleasure of showing off, of making an erotic sight of their suffering, degradation, and self-sacrificing discipline. As a mechanism for eroticizing lack, masochism therefore appears in this period as a chief means of phallic divestiture for the male subject.

回    回    回

The question of masochism has figured prominently in recent critiques of male sexuality, such as Kaja Silverman's investigation of perverse and marginal masculinities in film and modern literature, Paul Smith's study of the masochized and hysterical male hero in Clint Eastwood's films, Gilles Deleuze's analysis of Leopold von Sacher-Masoch's writing, or Gay Lynn Studlar's revision of Laura Mulvey's formulation of spectatorial pleasure in cinema through the hypothesis of a female-identified male spectator invested in pre-Oedipal *jouissance.*[6] Although these critics study masochism and its implicit renunciation of the paternal legacy from different perspectives—Freudian for Silverman and Smith, Deleuzian for Studlar—the effect is to show how masculinity is always "a product of the existing symbolic order and a reaction against it."[7] Silverman's critique, in particular, is an attempt to understand "deviant" masculinities as transgressing the phallic law and yet carrying Oedipal traces, albeit in a perverse fashion: "The male subject cannot avow his masochism without calling into question his identification with the masculine position, and aligning himself with femininity."[8] The desire to be loved by the father, and the erotic cathecting of the father by the son, which characterizes the condition of male masochism for Silverman, gives masochism an oppositional and radically transgressive value that turns its subject into an enemy of the symbolic order *tout court:*

> To begin with, he acts out in an insistent and exaggerated way the basic conditions of cultural subjectivity, conditions that are normally disavowed; he loudly proclaims that his meaning comes to him from the Other, prostrates himself before the Gaze even as he solicits it, exhibits his castration for all to see, and revels in the sacrificial basis of the social contract. The male masochist magnifies the losses and divisions upon which cultural identity is based, refusing to be sutured or recompensed. In short, he radiates a negativity inimical to the social order.[9]

The radical quality of male masochism that Silverman so decidedly affirms is put into question by Smith in his analysis of the masochized *and* redeemed masculinity of the protagonist of Clint Eastwood's films. Silverman finds proof and support for her thesis about the masochistic ruination of masculinity in Fassbinder's films; Smith argues that in texts of popular culture the images of male exhibitionism and masochism are encapsulated in and allowed by the narrative only to be contained and superseded. According to Smith, the masochistic suspension of sexual gratification is only a temporary disruption in the teleology of the sutured self and of "normal" sexuality, one that necessarily preludes the staging of the male subject's proper relation of identification with, and not desire for, the father. In his words, "The male masochist in important ways obeys and serves the phallic law. ... The masochist moment certainly promotes deferral and suspense, but a suspense that can work only if it is in the end undone. Male masochism is *at first* a way of not having to submit to the law, but equally important it turns out to be a way of not breaking (with) the law."[10] The masochistic scenarios depicted by Silverman and Smith are both enacted in the representations of the male body that I examine. In fact, the narrative of male masochism that this book traces is produced by two versions of these two scenarios: The early twentieth century state uses the discourse of masochistic self-sacrifice to interpellate young men into discipline and service to the nation so that the masochistic libidinality of suffering can be evoked and contained at the same time. On other occasions, masochism's logic of deferral has instead the effect of short-circuiting the call to self-sacrificial "functionality" and efficiency à la Weber, which defines a conventional version of bourgeois productive masculinity; this effect is brought about through a process of spectacular expenditure during which the body's libidinal capital is never prudently "reinvested" and kept under control but rather is squandered in order to postpone suture and suspend the narrative of the male self ad infinitum.

Both Silverman and Smith organize their discussion of masochism around the logic of transgression, arguing for and against the power of the male masochist to overthrow the Oedipal structure and its fixed system of parental identification. What these critics do not do is look at male masochism as a means of resignifying gender by formulating a notion of masculinity capable of exceeding (and not simply contradicting) the logic of the phallus as transcendental signifier. The distinction between the transgressive and resignificative power of masochism is important because it situates male masochism, and the masculinity it may fashion, in a strategic and liminal position where what is at stake is not precisely, or immediately, to "overthrow" the law but rather to work at its interstices, from its margins, by questioning its logic and resignifying its terms. The shortcomings of these current theories of perverse masculinity, centered on the notion of transgression and negation where male masochism remains a heteronormative process theorized within the logic of the phallus and its system of representation, have been pointed out by critics of gay and lesbian identities whose work aims at operating a resignification of existing gender categories.[11] What they reject in these theories is their collateral attempt to ultimately subject any form of "sexual dissidence" to the logic of the same so that difference is continually situated either outside the Oedipal universe or within it, only to be indissolubly tied to its law of compulsory heterosexuality. As Judith Butler points out in discussing the exclusionary logic through which the self achieves self-identity,

> Such a consideration of psychic identification would vitiate the possibility of any stable set of typologies that explain or describe something like gay or lesbian identities. And any effort to supply one—as evidenced in Kaja Silverman's recent inquiries into male homosexuality—suffers from simplification, and conforms, with alarming ease, to the regulatory requirements of diagnostic epistemic regimes. If incorporation in Freud's sense in 1914, is the effort to *preserve* a lost and loved object, and to refuse or postpone the recognition of loss and, hence, of grief, then to become *like* one's mother or father or sibling or other early "lovers" may be an act of love and/or a hate-

ful effort to replace or displace. How would we "typologize" the ambivalence at the heart of mimetic incorporations such as this?[12]

The ambivalence and instability, and therefore the impossibility of properly fitting an existing semiotic grid of gender lie at the core of the masculinities studied in this book, masculinities that are often situated in the sphere of homoeroticism. Thus although Silverman's insights on the representation of the masochized male body, and in particular her view of masochistic masculinity as "diversionary tactics," have great relevance for part of my own discussion, her argument about male masochism neither satisfactorily explains the proximity of normative masculinity to the abjection and homoeroticism that the Nietzschean body articulates nor fully speaks to the feminist political project of reformulating gender and sexual identities. Whether situating abject masculinity within or outside existing definitions of gender, contemporary critiques of male masochism do not succeed in putting into question and dislocating the central axiom of the logic of the phallus, compulsory heterosexuality—a logic that, from the point of view of the queer theorist, makes homosexual difference impossible to formulate and necessarily unrepresentable. Encoding normative masculinity while in fact defying its logic, the male bodies examined in this book invoke gender ambiguity and sexuality not only as transgressive of existing gender norms but as a way to revise and redefine their heteronormative logic.

In this book, therefore, I deploy Silverman's and Smith's theory of perverse masculinity and constantly revise it in the light of Butler's critique of gender trouble. My argument partakes of this critique by taking as its point of departure Butler's suspicion of identity categories as potential instruments of regulatory regimes and her valorization of semiotic indeterminacy. To embrace any specific identity, even the outlaw identity of "lesbian," means for Butler to mobilize the system of exclusions through which any hegemonic self constructs its illusionary ontology as well as the illusion of its stability. However, this system of exclusions and demarcations is extremely unstable, since its abjected others continually return to compromise its coherence. Thus the meaning of "man," "woman," or "lesbian" is never stabilized and never controlled by those who identify themselves through these terms. The impossibility of fully stabilizing meaning, and in particular the meaning of gender and sex categories, relying as they do on a set of unsteady and indeterminable elements ("If a sexuality is to be disclosed, what will be taken as the determinant of its meaning: its phantasy structure, the act, the orifice, the gender, the anatomy?"[13]), is welcomed by Butler as the troubling sign of abjection, whose presence decisively disrupts the coherence of the self.

In this theoretical perspective, the perverse masculinity inscribed onto the body of the Nietzschean superman can be understood as producing sexual and gender indeterminacy. This indeterminacy, by dislocating the representation of masculinity away from the binarism of the heterosexual gender divide, marks out a semiotically open territory between normative masculinity and its abjected others, for example, homosexuality and femininity, each time, as we will see, produced within a different array of practices and discourses. On this ground compulsory heterosexuality is constantly put under erasure so that new and not yet known figurations of gender can be imagined and emplotted. This semiotic space theorized by Butler is instrumental for my critique of modern masculinity: The nonphallic masculinity that the Nietzschean body reinscribes cannot be explained as "femininity" *tout court*. In fact, this male body opens onto the abjected realm of homosexuality, which is not, immediately or otherwise, the space of femininity (to say so would be to theorize the male gay body according to the equation gay = nonman = woman) but rather what is excluded by the symbolic economy of the phallus as the unthinkable. This same space of abjection, which for Butler is chiefly occupied by the gay body, continually edges onto and in fact, even though disavowed and unacknowledged, inhabits normative notions of masculinity and femininity to show that "compulsory heterosexual identities, those ontologically consolidated phantasms of 'man' and 'woman', are theatrically produced effects that posture as ground origins, the normative measure of the real."[14] The image of the abject other inhabiting the normative self is fully at work in what I have described as the double register of masculinity in early twentieth century representations of the Nietzschean body. This double register of masculinity, normative and perverse, invokes another crucial element of Butler's theory: "heterosexuality as an incessant and *panicked* imitation of its own naturalized idealization,"[15] its need to continually "repeat" its meaning for fear of becoming undone, "its compulsion to repeat which is at once the foreclosure of that which threatens its coherence." Heterosexuality's compulsion to repeat "its own phantasmatic idealization of itself" produces the image of gender as an absence and of masculinity as continually standing as a suspended narrative, never fully concluded, where the meaning of "man" is unceasingly constructed, contested, and unmade.

By looking at the position of the abject as a semiotically and ideologically productive space, I read early twentieth century Nietzschean male bodies as a form of interpellation into normative masculinity necessarily never fully answered by its addressee. At the same time I look at the modern hypermasculine corporeality of the athlete-soldier-strongman, to use Smith's phrase, as a hysterical body simultaneously disavowing and bearing the traces of abjection. Organized around principles of phallic plenitude, these Nietzschean bodies are always and at the same time "reversible" into a spectacle of male exhibitionism that functions as the index of a perverse masculinity. These spectacular and sexualized male bodies are the "foreign body" that, grafted onto and inhabiting the disciplined and functional hypermasculinity of versions of the superman, troubles the construction of normative masculinity and compromises its hegemonic value. The boy scout, the soldier-male, and the employee-athlete, whose representations I study, steel their muscles in the eugenicist spirit of sacrifice and identification with the state; at the same time, in the very process of reinforcing their self-contours, their displayed, exposed corporeality, calling attention to itself both through nakedness or such fetishized clothing as the uniform and the stage costume, becomes overtly sexualized and turns into a spectacle that can be deployed and enjoyed as an object of desire by both women and men. This happens, for example, with Peter Lobengula and the "savage" bodies of the South African actors on show at the London Imperial Exhibition of 1908, whose image I discuss in Chapter 5.

While considering the male body as a technology of gender, I also regard it as a locus of production of desire and of signification where power is affirmed and destabilized in an unresolved tension. In so doing, I foreground a crucial aspect of this body, that is, the fact that disciplinary and disciplined Nietzschean masculinity is also and at the same time the site of the production of pleasure. In this perspective the work of Klaus Theweleit assumes a particular poignancy for my argument. In *Male Fantasies* Theweleit reads the early twentieth century male fascist body as a hysterical body unable to contain its excess and continually caught in the unresolved and unresolvable dialectic of phallic self-containment, achieved through the strengthening of ego/body contours, and as an "explosion" of the self that Theweleit associates both with the violence and physical destruction of war and with "feminine" fluidity. By reconstructing what Smith calls "the somatics of the male imaginary," Theweleit reintroduces, in the wake of Deleuze and Guattari's anti-Oedipal theory of desire, what by definition is excluded from the representation of masculinity in a phallic symbolic economy, which he identifies as the pre-Oedipal register of masculine sexuality and the productive activity of the unconscious. Whereas Theweleit explains masculine sexuality and the hystericized male body within the cultural and historical space of German totalitarianism and of modern war, as he does in his analysis of the Freikorps soldiers, I discern analogous structures of fraught masculinity inscribed in other versions of the Nietzschean body at work in another sphere of modern culture, that of mass consumerism. Further, my work differs from Theweleit's in its theoretical emphasis: Whereas Theweleit's work is primarily psychoanalytical and secondarily cultural-materialist, here I attempt to integrate more closely both methods of analysis. Whereas masculine sexuality and the male unconscious seem to be for Theweleit transhistorical categories that find a "point of entry" into history through war and fascism, I look at perverse masculinity and its foregrounding of the unconscious as deeply imbricated in, and in fact taking shape through, the cultural conditions of a specific phase of modern capitalism and as overdetermined by their traffic with the modern culture of consumption. Attention to the material circumstances in which these images of the male body are encoded allows me to tentatively introduce the issue of the historical contexts to be inferred from my representations. By exploring in particular the attention to consumption in these texts, I bring out their situatedness in the cultural and social context of early modernist culture as it has been studied most recently by critics from Andreas Huyssen to Rachel Bowlby to Thomas Richards. In other words, I relate the formation of psychocultural constructs of masculinity to specific material conditions and consider their enactment of forces operating in a specific period more directly than has been attempted by other recent feminists theorizing male subjectivity. Thus the focus on a particular sociocultural formation helps me avoid deploying the notion of masochism as exclusively a psychoanalytical category and, consequently, helps me sidestep both the heterosexualizing paradigm of psychoanalysis and its almost ahistorical notion of the symbolic.

Focusing on the relation between the sexualized spectacle of the male body and the turn of the century culture of mass consumption, I consider the predominance of the commodity form as a structural condition of modernity and commodity fetishism as a productive, rather than repressive and "inauthentic," mechanism of desire. As such, my work also contributes to the ongoing theorization of the enabling pleasures of consumption, through which contemporary critics of consumer culture[16] counter the elitist orthodoxy first articulated by Adorno and Horkheimer and variously embraced by critics such as F. W. Haug and Jean Baudrillard. By relying on a view of consumer culture as an open "force field" (to perversely deploy a phrase of Adorno's) of different representations and as a terrain for forceful ideological dissemination and contestation where powers struggle for, rather than simply and automatically achieve, hegemony, I focus on how the affective structure of suspended pleasure established by commodity fetishism becomes the early twentieth century venue for an intermittently visible masochistic form of male desire. One purpose of the book is to examine to what degree and through what narrative structures antiphallic masculinities might be made visible and even enabled by forms of modern consumer culture. I demonstrate how, far from simply repressing or coopting desire—especially the desires of the body— the mechanisms of consumption, the staging of the commodity as phantasmagoria, and in particular the temporality of pleasure and fulfillment in the logic of consumption all serve to produce and enable the circulation of a transgressive, because visibly sexualized, image of the male body. This image, in turn, often gestured toward nonhegemonic forms of masculinity—masculinities that bourgeois patriarchy had made outlaw, unsymbolizable, and therefore abject.

This double register of masculinity, normative and perverse, which the modernist male body simultaneously inscribes and disavows, is also prompted by the very ambiguity of the image of the Nietzschean superman itself. This image is a spectacular creation that resounds on the one hand with the principle of bourgeois productivity and self-control (the will) and on the other with multiple possibilities for somatic excess (the instincts), the latter being in open opposition to the former. Structured as a spectacle and displayed as such, the Nietzschean male body of the early twentieth century becomes a vehicle both for the spectacle of male masochism as it is described in psychoanalytical discourse and for the spectacle of the commodity, discussed by critics of consumer culture since Debord. The modern spectacularization of masculinity and its masochistic structuration lead to a particular formation of masculine subjectivity and its politicization, its articulation within specific cultural and social scenarios. Each of the representations of the male body that I examine—even though they belong to a range of media and national high and popular cultures—focusing prominently on Britain with Germany, Italy, and France as ancillary examples, are organized according to this double register of masculine identity in which functionality, phallic plenitude, and unproductive sexual expenditure continually clash.

Here a particular aspect of male masochism as studied by critics such as Silverman, Smith, Theodor Reik, and Leo Bersani,[17] even with the caveats I have described, becomes instrumental for transcoding the subjective structures of identity and desire developed by psychoanalysis into the sociohistorical realm of modern consumer culture. However different these theorists of masochism might be in their theoretical assumptions, they all attach great relevance first, to the specific temporality of masochism as a formation of suspension and deferral of pleasure and second, to the male masochist's strategic exhibitionism and "demonstrativeness,"[18] a propensity to theatricality and impersonation.

For the masochist, pleasure is intensified by its suspension and deferral; he seeks out punishment-as-pleasure and at the same time he suspends its achievement to further prolong his excitation through preparatory rituals. These rituals function to expose the body or, as Silverman points out in her reading of Reik's theory, to mimic some prototype. The aim of this postponement and its theatrical strategies is both to prolong the tension, the pleasurable unpleasure of waiting for the coming of the libidinal gratification (the punishment/sexual act), and to attract punishment by doing "what is inexpedient." As Freud affirms, "In order to provoke punishment from [the superego], the masochist must do what is inexpedient, must act against his interests, must ruin the prospects which open out to him in the real world and must, perhaps, destroy his own real existence."[19] In particular, the postponement of pleasure functions as a form of rejection of closure, of suture, which, according to Bersani in his reading of Freud's "Three Essays on Sexuality," represents the stalling of a coherent (phallic) libidinal and subjective narrative.

The excitation built up in the masochistic game of postponement works to "shatter" the coherence of the self and in fact leads to the unmaking of identity itself. Bersani considers masochism as a process of designification, highly destructive of the coherence of the self and of meaning and forcefully subverting the phallic law. In *The Freudian Body* he extends the logic of masochism beyond questions of deviant identification with the paternal or maternal figure, to invest sexuality per se. He considers sexuality as "ontologically" grounded in masochism: "What would it mean to say that in sexuality pleasure is somehow distinct from satisfaction, perhaps even identical to a kind of pain?"[20] According to Bersani, the same structure of postponement of fulfillment, and the production of tension that characterizes infantile sexuality, persist in the adult and in fact characterize adult sexuality.

Commodity fetishism—when, for example, it is intensified by the spectacle of advertising—and male masochism are both affective systems that rely on the suspension of pleasure, on nonconsummation, and on an open-ended libidinal structure of the subject. My contention is that given this analogy, the libidinal structure of commodity culture, interpellating the male as well as the female subject as a consumer, might enable the circulation of and give a "visible" shape to the perverse masculine desire for nonproductive expenditure. Such nonproductive expenditure, as theorized by Georges Bataille in 1933, is the desire for loss, death, and destruction both of value and of "proper" masculinity, a desire that replicates the rejection of purpose and closure that male masochism enacts. Examples, by various degrees of approximation, of nonproductive expenditure include Dorian Gray's hoarding of collected objects, a materialization of his refusal of finalized "use," of consuming and reinvesting value, both economically and erotically; Aschenbach's ecstasy of "self-inflicted" death at the end of *Death in Venice;* and even more, Leiris's pleasure of abjection in recognizing himself both in and as the degraded female body in his autobiography, *Manhood.* The image of the male subject *actively* (rather than passively, as repressive theories of consumption claim) desiring through the desires of consumer culture and caught in the act of unmaking conventional versions of his masculine identity brings us back to the question of abjection and to the value that Butler attributes to this notion in her critique of gender. By reading the Nietzschean male bodies of the early twentieth century as abjected male bodies, that is, by attempting to figure what otherwise would remain invisible under the logic of the phallus, I intend to show how the open-ended desire of the male masochist in its interplay with the necessarily unsutured desired of consumption can become the potential venue for a type of nonproductive expenditure. The image of the male body "spending to death" (both a literal and a metaphoric death) points to the possibility of unmaking the naturalized structure of identity that defines gender under the heterosexual contract and posits abjection as the productive territory of semiotic indeterminacy where new meanings of sexual difference and gender might be elaborated.

I have developed my argument as a contribution to the exploration of gender formations and to debates about constructions and representations of masculinity. The critique of masculinity and of male sexuality is a recent development in feminist theory. Spurred by pioneering work in gay and lesbian studies and in queer theory, it is guided by an interest in examining and redefining what, under the heterosexual contract, has been naturalized as a norm and as such has for a long time escaped any theoretical scrutiny. This feminist endeavor is exemplified by the essays in the "Phallus" and "Male Subjectivity" issues of the journal *differences* and in the *Camera Obscura* "Male Trouble" issue, and in the works of such critics as Eve Kosofsky Sedgwick, Sharon Willis, Alan Sinfield, Jonathan Dollimore and Jeffrey Weeks, and Lynn Joyrich.[21] Feminist criticism has heretofore been chiefly concerned with female sexuality and the potential reconfiguration of the female subject as an agent in order to reclaim the representation of femininity from the logic of the phallus. Clearly, a corresponding project for male subjectivity is now needed, and clearly too, from a feminist point of view, the need to valorize alternative masculinities that undermine the phallic law is evident. Much of the work in this area has considered "marginal" masculinities: The outstanding example here is Kaja Silverman's *Male Subjectivity at the Margins.* My project, instead, is an examination of cultural constructions of masculinity that are often popular but very seldom marginal. My work adds to critiques such as Silverman's by showing how many of the categories and structures that she discerns in representations of marginal masculinity can also be traced in what I characterize as the almost uncannily vehement representations of hypermasculinity from the early years of this century, from Britain in particular.

Since the new feminist critique of masculinity has been developed mostly around film and television studies, my articulation of the problematic of the modern male body includes a transcoding of some of the issues of feminist film criticism into terms applicable to social texts generally. A central concern of feminist critique is to study how femininity and masculinity are produced, inscribed, and contested at the levels of both subjectivity and social formations. This study, in turn, is aimed at theorizing new formations of gender beyond those acknowledged as existing under the conditions of the present sex-gender system, formations that might be more enabling to those not identified as the norm. The complex aims of feminist analysis therefore demand a certain theoretical flexibility and a critical appropriation of existing analytical and theoretical systems, as the well-developed feminist revisions of psychoanalysis, Marxism, and poststructuralism show. My work embraces the theoretical hybridity that a feminist-materialist analysis of gender requires. The notion of the body as a technology of gender, deployed in this book, locates my inquiry within a feminist critique of ideology as theorized by Teresa de Lauretis in such texts as "The Technology of Gender."[22] The notion of Althusserian ideology that she deploys helps me to theorize gender as a form of ideological interpellation that functions to "subject" individuals and individual bodies into men and women, to facilitate their adaptation to the sociocultural conditions established within the existing mode of production (a task that, as the book makes clear, is never fully accomplished). In this mode I wish to explore how specific structures of gender subjectivity were articulated as crucial components of the political and symbolic economy of a specific phase of the current mode of production, that of emerging monopoly capitalism.

Thus the feminist-materialist analysis of masculinity proposed in the book relies primarily on a modified and psychoanalytically inflected Althusserian theory and at the same time turns to Foucault's theorization of the body as a contestatory terrain of power that both produces and never fully contains its excess. Some of the key concepts that I deploy—the body; technology of gender, as de Lauretis paraphrases Foucault's "technology of sex"; and the notion of heterotopia—remain Foucaultian. Certainly, any critic of the body needs to start with Foucault; and yet given the nonprominence of gender itself as a category of analysis in his work, feminist criticism of corporeality also needs to have a more forthright and specific sense of the powers in question, and of their oppressive nature. Thus whereas my definition of the body—a network where different institutional discourses and critical and daily life practices cohere, work to engender individual subjects, and are simultaneously contested—remains my (Foucaultian) point of departure, my perspective is rendered more circumstantial by the category of gender as a form of ideological interpellation, that is, an apparatus that partakes of the production and the maintenance of patriarchal hegemony.

回     回     回

My discussion of how a new model of modern western masculinity is articulated begins with the Wildean moment and continues to the advent of fascism. I begin, in Chapter 1, by exploring the encoding of transgressive, homoerotic masculinity in the body of the fin de siècle aesthete through an analysis of such symptomatic texts as Walter Pater's essay on Johann Winckelmann in *The Renaissance,* Oscar Wilde's *The Picture of Dorian Gray,* and Thomas Mann's *Death in Venice.* Each centers on the spectacle of the abject male body and its possibility of signaling homoerotic desire at the time when queer identity was yet in the making. By gauging the meaning of expenditure against the aesthete's pleasure in conspicuous consumption, I trace the construction and displacement of queer masculinity between Bataille's "general economy" and the culture of consumption of monopoly capitalism to show how the aesthete's effeminacy and ruinous pleasure of abjection functions to corrode bourgeois notions of both gender and value.

The ecstatic self-exposure of Aschenbach in Mann's *Death in Venice* is the image of the masochistically eroticized male body "spending" to death that the early twentieth century Nietzschean representation of masculinity tries to exclude from the field of social vision. However, this perverse male sexuality and its pleasures, flaunted by the body of the aesthete, reappear in the very icon of modern hypermasculinity, the body of the Nietzschean superman, thus making it a complex icon of gender instability. Chapter 2 attends to the disciplinary aspect of the Nietzschean body. The superman, as my reading of *Genealogy of Morals* and *Twilight of Idols* vis-à-vis Emile Zola's novel *The Human Beast* shows, is a modern remake of the body of the proletarian. As a classless symbol of "natural" virility, this image of the male body circulated in Edwardian England through the discourse of eugenics. Eugenics aimed at strengthening the body of the nation against racial and national physical decay by eliminating any degenerate "foreign" body: the unhealthy poor, the savage colonized, even the "weakling." I show how the new ideology of "natural masculinity" was useful to the state in the period preceding the First World War to interpellate the disaffected masses of petty bourgeois, and especially the class of the newly arrived modern clerkocracy, into figuring themselves as an integral part of the body of the nation. As such, they could become bodies "fit to fight" and sacrifice themselves to defend their country in the war. After explaining how the ideal of the Nietzschean body was "consumed" by the petty bourgeois employee—for instance, by Leonard Bast in E. M. Forster's *Howard's End* and by the "young man carbuncular" in T. S. Eliot's *The Waste Land*—I show how the health-conscious virility of the superman was successively encoded in the bodies of the new Boy Scouts and the members of the German Wandervogel as well as in the pure, self-sacrificial image of the First World War soldier, epitomized by the ephebic and upper class body of Rupert Brooke. The representation of Brooke in his own writing, in the state's discourse, and most famously in the photograph used as the frontispiece of his posthumously published sonnets invokes once again eroticism and the ambiguous disjunction between functionality and excess that characterizes the body of the superman. It is this ambiguity that made available, in the spectacular rituals of the gymnastic or military parade, the desexualized and unclothed male body "absorbed in the sportive gesture" as an object of desire both for the female and for the male gaze.

In Chapter 3 I examine how the masochistic spectacle of abject masculinity displayed through the body of the aesthete and kept under control by the state through the discourse of eugenics and nationalism reappears encoded in popular culture. The hugely popular icons of the Nietzschean superman on which I focus are the Edwardian strongman and music hall showman Eugen Sandow and the subsequent novelistic and cinematic versions of the same figure, Tarzan. Antonio Gramsci's definition of the superman as "primadonna" implicitly puts into question the naturalized virility of the Nietzschean body; I continue this work of deconstruction by pointing out how the chief characteristic of the superman, the instinctual animality that Nietzsche had ascribed to him, in fact acquired a new currency in this period through its commodified construction in the urban spaces of modernity, particularly in the zoo. Here "wildness" and nature are merely cited and artificially displaced into the heart of the modern metropolis. This work of citation and displacement—the distinctive elements of kitsch as a style—also defines the image of the superman when embodied as a popular culture icon. The citational quality of kitsch, which I explain through Adolf Loos's critique of ornament, foregrounds the artificiality rather than the "naturalness" of the Nietzschean body and, implicitly, of its masculinity. The chapter shows how this kitsch body functions as the space for the circulation of both erotic and consumerist desire and how the modern culture of the spectacle and of the spectacularized commodity may well be appropriated by the desirous male subject, both as spectator and as the subject of this spectacle, in order to signify forms of counterhegemonic identity and desire.

In Chapters 4 and 5 I examine how this spectacular male body is encoded in a series of modernist texts. In Chapter 4 the Nietzschean unresolved dialectic of masculinity is tested through one of the most macho discourses of high modernism, that of Futurism. The work of Filippo Tommaso Marinetti reinscribes the ambiguities of the modern superbody in the split between the puritanical, "functionalist" tone of his manifestos and his sensuous, decadent, and orientalist scenarios in his romances. In the romance *Mafarka* the male body is turned into an erotic spectacle through an intricate displacement of gender categories: Mafarka, the father, replaces the female body by "making" a son with whom he falls desperately in love, thus evoking also the aestheticist scenario exploited by Pater, Wilde, and Mann of an older man's passion for the younger male. The writing of the French avant-garde turn of the century artist Alfred Jarry brings to a sarcastic conclusion the negotiations between normativity and transgression, stable body and ego boundaries and their abject dissolution, that were being variously articulated by the images of the Nietzschean superman. The excessive sexuality of Jarry's hero in his novel *The Supermale,* described through an extraordinary series of adventures, has the effect of reducing the male body to the most extreme and contradictory symbolization of the steeled, regulated, and self-contained corporeality characteristic of both bourgeois and militaristic masculinity. At the end of the novel the contours of the supermale's body harden into the shape of a pearl-tear, the last vestige of his powerful and machine-like sexuality.

The image of masculinity as ornament, represented both by the pearl-tear and by the orientalist, theatrical costume of Jarry's supermale, is at the center of the final chapter. Here I examine the ideology and the practice of primitivism as a medium for the western male modernist to resexualize Nietzschean versions of bourgeois masculinity and to covertly deploy the male body once again as an object of homoerotic desire. However benevolent the high modernist's deployment of the image of the native might appear to be, it still participates in the discourse of colonialism: The native is invariably read as the "natural" other of the western subject, and his uncivilized and savage condition is valorized and recuperated but not disavowed. To expose how the colonialist subtext of primitivism read "native" bodies, the first part of the chapter examines the figure of Peter Lobengula, a black South African actor who came to England in the first years of this century as part of a troupe paid to impersonate native "savagery" at the Imperial Exhibitions in London. Lobengula married a white woman, created a huge scandal, and died claiming to be an African prince, an aristocrat. His transgression in terms of race and class is symptomatic of the crucial moment when the equation phallus/penis—and the alignment of terms that this equation sustained in late imperial Britain, masculinity, whiteness, authority, propriety—doesn't hold anymore and the phallus is revealed to be not a (male) body quality necessarily attached to an organ one possesses but rather a process, the process of occupying a position of power. By marrying a white woman and dressed as a gentleman, Lobengula threatened to obtain, in the eyes of his British contemporaries, the phallic investiture that, as a colonized and a black man, he was not allowed to possess.

By appropriating the unstable image of "savagery" signified by the body of the native through a complex play of clothing and unclothing male bodies, Michel Leiris and D. H. Lawrence, the two modernists whose work I study in the final chapter, try to renounce or at any rate jeopardize the phallus by displacing masculinity into the space of abjection and by resexualizing the body. This dangerous space of gender and sexual liminality is signified by the dialectic of clothes and body decoration, which figures prominently both in Leiris's autobiography, *Manhood*, and in D. H. Lawrence's novel *The Plumed Serpent*. By turning to J. C. Flugel's *The Psychology of Clothes* (1930), I interpret the masquerade at work in Leiris's and Lawrence's texts as an implicit contestatory attack on the rules of the "Great Masculine Renunciation," the historical moment when, after the French Revolution, the image of the sober, fully clothed, and self-restrained body of the black-coated male bourgeois became the norm of masculine appearance in Europe. At the same time, the ornamental, unclothed, and "primitive" male body described by Leiris and Lawrence seems to articulate a (metaphorically) cannibalistic and inclusive relationship with femininity, oscillating between a masochistic self-representation as the wounded female body and the attempt to reestablish and reconquer phallic wholeness and power through the very elements that had sanctioned its demise. The book closes on the undecidability of this gesture and of its choice.

# 1 THE ART OF CONSUMPTION: AESTHETICISM, DISPLAY, AND THE NEOCLASSICAL BODY IN THE FIN DE SIÈCLE

---

N.B.—Mr. Wilde will offer some observations on dress for both sexes, with special reference to his own personal attempts to influence American taste in favor of the adoption of a more graceful style than that which at present prevails.

—addendum to notice of lecture by Oscar Wilde,
Free Trade Hall, Manchester, October 8, 1883

IN THE FINAL CHAPTER of *The Renaissance* Walter Pater makes a curious slip of the tongue. The tale of Winckelmann's intellectual life and aesthetic choices is interrupted by a detail of a more private life. Pater tells us that on his way to Germany from Rome in 1786, the German critic stopped in Vienna, where "he was loaded with honors and presents."[1] After Vienna he suddenly changed his plans and decided to return to Rome, "and in Trieste a delay of a few days occurred." Here Winckelmann was strangled by "a fellow traveler, a man named Arcangeli," who wanted to steal from him some gold medals the critic had shown him. "As Winckelmann stooped to take them out of the chest, a chord was thrown around his neck. Sometimes afterwards, a child with whose companionship Winckelmann had beguiled his time in Trieste, knocked at the door, and receiving no answer gave the alarm." This figure of the child, presented as a meaningless detail and immediately glossed over, introduces and at once elides homosexuality and a concern with the critic's own body in Pater's writing. In disrupting Pater's tactful and calculated narrative balance between art and sexuality, the detail allows us to discern more than Pater had planned to disclose. For an instant we are granted a glimpse of Winckelmann's sexual desire, encoded in the figure of the child "with whom he had beguiled his time" in the port of Trieste. The detail establishes a nebulous connection between Winckelmann's intellectual and scholarly life and murder and robbery—and also between homosexuality and crime.

Why did Pater include in his writing a biographical element that so blatantly contradicted his carefully constructed narrative of Winckelmann as scholar-aesthete? Why did he not edit out of his text a detail that turns Winckelmann's intellectual and sensual contact with the youth into an *affaire* whose outcome would have hinted to his late Victorian readers, and even more to those in the decades following, of the existence of a scandal? Pater's unlikely slip of the tongue suggest two readings of the death of the German aesthete. The first portrays Winckelmann as the genius naive in the world's ways. A famous public man is killed away from home; since he is not "a man of the world" but an intellectual who does not value material things and crass pleasures, the Viennese awards and gold medals, he naively shows them to Arcangeli, who kills to steal. According to this sentimentalized reading, Winckelmann would have died *because* he was locked in his immaterial world of aesthetic beauty. At the same time, another reading is suggested: The famous man is involved in a pederastic liaison. This brings his intellectual sensuality, his profound appreciation of the human form sculpted in marble, back into the sphere of his own desiring and shameful body.

Nevertheless, without giving himself time for shame and embarrassment, Pater chooses to mention the child. Evidently this is a detail that cannot be eliminated, and since the author is not sure what value to attribute to it publicly (in fact, the dominant culture of Pater's own time offered little discursive means to explain Winckelmann's desire apart from medical and juridical knowledge), he passes it by in silence. Winckelmann's relationship to the body of the child is clearly different from his relationship to the beauty of the body in the Greek sculpture he studies and that Pater celebrates. Although the art critic's aesthetic sensibility is also expressed in his love of young male bodies, it can be represented by Pater as a passion that justifies "Winckelmann's native affinity to the Hellenic spirit" (Pater, 191); his being beguiled by the living boy, however, cannot be properly explained. Male homoeroticism, the detail implies, can be made visible when grafted onto the discourse of aestheticism, but when this discourse is absent and homoerotic desire is shown in life, it remains an event merely to be hinted at, then left unexplained. Surrounded by this silence, the episode of sexuality and crime that concluded Winckelmann's life becomes incongruous with the rest of the story, and cracks open the apparent seamlessness between art and life that characterizes the figure of Winckelmann for Pater. In the presence of the other, of the object of his desire, "the solitary man of genius" who had realized both in his scholarly practice and in his life "the wholeness, the unity of one's self, [the] intellectual integrity," that Pater's own times require is transformed into a divided subject, an image split between the public man of letters and his private body, the rigorous intellectual and his flesh.

Both Winckelmann's wounded body and the construction of his own nebulous corporeality in Pater's narrative are symptomatic of the process through which homoeroticism began to be made narratable and encoded in the male body in the fin de siècle. The image of Winckelmann's simultaneously degraded and victimized corporeality integrally partakes of the fin de siècle signification of homoeroticism insofar as it inscribes the very prohibition that it purports to disavow through the discourse of aestheticism and Hellenism. In other words, the desirous male body achieves its power to potentially contest bourgeois masculinity and heterosexual, reproductive sexuality only by liminally embodying the law that it claims to negate: the discourse of Christian prohibition that Pater's text apparently rejects. This body's transgression of an invisibly present law thus becomes the condition of its degradation. Because Pater refuses to see Winckelmann as a split subject and to place his defiled body under the sign of prohibition and because he remains unaware of how his own narrative is structured not only by the principles of Hellenism but also by those of Christianity, he is forced to pass silently over Winckelmann's homosexual, desirous body. Meanwhile, he is equally forced to declare two bodies identical: the god-like effigy of the Greek statue and Winckelmann's flesh, which, given that Pater's narrative ultimately partakes of the decorum of its period, are destined to remain irreconcilable.

This chapter focuses on the representation of the homoerotic body as a masochistic and sentimental spectacle of suffering and staged powerlessness in two symptomatic texts of fin de siècle aestheticism: Pater's essay "Winckelmann" in *The Renaissance* (1877) and Oscar Wilde's novel *The Picture of Dorian Gray* (1891). As an extraordinary example of the pervasive deployment of this trope in European high culture at large in the subsequent decades, as a coda to my critique of aestheticism and masculinity, the chapter closes with an analysis of Thomas Mann's novella *Death in Venice* (1912). The last two decades of the nineteenth century are regarded by gender theorists and historians of modern culture as the period in which a socially recognizable queer identity was being elaborated through an existing constellation of discursive fragments and cultural practices, from sexology to the juridical construction of the act of "sodomy," as well as through homosexual subcultures.[2] At the same time, homoeroticism was being made visible, albeit under cover, by an intense work of signification inscribed both in the texts and in the persona of the fin de siècle aesthete-dandy: The effeminacy attached to this figure allowed homoerotic desire to be spoken socially and pass at the same time. Recent critics of the turn of the century aesthete-dandy par excellence, Oscar Wilde, have comprehensively studied how bourgeois structures of masculinity and subjectivity are manipulated in his work to signify homoeroticism.[3] I want instead to bring to the fore how the homoerotic signification of the self in Wilde's work and life also produces a particular representation of the male body as a masochistic spectacle of its own degradation. My contention is that the self-willed abjection of the body of the fin de siècle aesthete is produced by a textual apparatus of prohibition, submission, and domination that complicates and disavows the Hellenic paradigm through which Pater constructed the male body as an object of sensuous enjoyment. In fact, the spectacle of the homoerotic male body, as well as the libidinal and semiotic economy of the aesthete, is structured by the self-sacrificial logic of expenditure, the "perverse" desire for loss and (self) destruction that Georges Bataille celebrates in his writing. In the text and in the persona of the aesthete, expenditure becomes conflated with his aristocratic and dissipating gesture of conspicuous consumption, in turn spurred by his unquenchable desire for new experiences that are pursued, as happens at the center of *The Picture of Dorian Gray*, through a fetishistic cathecting of the phantasmagoria of luxury commodities.

Each of the three texts through which I symptomatically trace this process of masochistic self-loss is centered on a dialectic of exposure and occlusion of the male body in ruin. This unresolved dialectic reaches a high complexity in Wilde, whose work and persona deeply interweave subjective structures of homoerotic masculinity both with a masochistic self-expenditure and with the desire to become an expendable commodity, as Wilde's magnificently self-marketed image shows.[4] Because of the crucial role Wilde played at this time in the production of a socially recognizable discourse of homoeroticism both in his texts and in the culture generally, my discussion of the homoerotic and masochistic male body as articulated at the turn of the century through the discourse of aestheticism is centered primarily on his work and self-fashioning and uses Pater's "Winckelmann" and Mann's *Death in Venice* as satellite texts. Pater's theory of aestheticism and Hellenism makes the male body available to his 1890s aesthete followers as an object of sensuous enjoyment through the neoclassical alibi. Wilde mobilizes the same scenario of neoclassical sexlessness to covertly signify homoerotic desire. However, he also recuperates the discourse of moral prohibition that Pater had excised from his text only to make it function perversely, as the law that needs to be transgressed in order for the aesthete to stage his masochistic theatrics—as a cultural variant, that is, of the punishing superego. The violation of the moral norm, as exemplified by Dorian's "sins," becomes the occasion for a self-inflicted punishment through which the aesthete's body turns into a spectacle of wounded masculinity simultaneously signifying power and powerlessness. To include *Death in Venice* in this critique of masculinity and aestheticism involves a spatial-temporal telescoping away from fin de siècle England into early twentieth century Germany, a time when Wilde's case had acquired resonance beyond England.[5] More significantly, Mann claimed to have no direct or personal investment in the discourse of homoeroticism. Nonetheless, *Death in Venice* is an apt conclusion to the narrative of the homoerotic body traced in this chapter, for it relates to both Pater's and Wilde's texts on two levels. First, it uncannily reevokes the story of Winckelmann dying in exotic Italy, and in so doing it defamiliarizes and "orientalizes" homoeroticism through the same geographical dislocation. Second, it brings to completion the aesthete's narrative of the body by fully displaying what neither Pater nor Wilde manage to or are willing to disclose: a male body whose grotesque degradation into illness and old age places it into a space of unredeemable and triumphant abjection, the impossible space of a body masochized to death, thus making the positions of subject and object indistinguishable.

## WINCKELMANN'S "UNSINGED HANDS"

In the eyes of the 1890s English middle class the aesthete—from Max Beerbohm to Oscar Wilde, from Aubrey Beardsley to James Whistler—was a decadent.[6] Clear signs of the aesthete's decadence were his refined and artistic uselessness and the self-absorption that, to a late Victorian public, signaled the effeminacy of literary and artistic culture as opposed to the productive, puritanical, and manly imperatives of bourgeois philistinism.[7] The figure of the aesthete signaled effeminacy but not homosexuality: Wilde's plan to go to America in 1882 to publicize Gilbert and Sullivan's operetta *Patience, or Bunthorne's Bride,* a satire of aestheticism, was even welcomed by Henry Labouchère, the author of the 1895 Criminal Law Amendment Act under which Wilde was later to be accused of homosexual acts, in the hope that "Wilde's hyperaestheticism would be an antidote to America's hypermaterialism."[8] With his words, gestures, and clothing Wilde contributed to popularize aestheticism as a pose. This pose was read by his culture, as both *Patience* and George Du Maurier's *Punch* cartoons show, as an extravagant and effeminate form of masculinity embodied in a narcissistic individual who was parasitically detached from reality in the attempt to make life into art.

Although aesthetes despised anything vulgar and plebeian, they did not exclude "materiality"; rather they advocated a perfect balance of spirit and matter, the mind and the senses, the intellectual and the physical, that found its model in the pre-Christian culture of Greece. Through Hellenism the aesthete's programmatic desire to aestheticize the natural and make art out of life was particularly directed to the body. This body had been represented as shameful both by the Judeo-Christian tradition of sexual prohibition and by the more recent history of western idealism and rationalism, which advocated the discipline of the body for productive ends. For the aesthete, who had learned to appreciate the beauty of the human form through the filter of modern Hellenism, there was nothing shameful—and nothing natural—about the body. Thus the interest in the classical world and in ancient art, which had reached its height, perhaps, with the arrival of the Elgin marbles in London almost a century earlier, became in the fin de siècle the vehicle of an altogether new language of corporeality. In this new perspective the body was no longer regarded as that which limits the work of the intellect; rather, the egalitarian articulation of the senses and the intellect advanced by the Greek ideal was considered to free the body of its original sin and shame, to recuperate it under the serene language of moral indifference.

By studying in the nineteenth century the culture of the Italian Renaissance, Pater aimed at reestablishing its lay and antimetaphysical values in his own epoch. In *The Renaissance* (the first edition was published in 1877, the third in 1888) Pater turned to the Italian fifteenth century as the moment in modern history when pagan antiquities came to be revalorized to counter the prohibitions of Christianity. Four centuries after the age of Botticelli, Christian morality—encoded in middle class ethics and propriety—had more than ever severed man's ties to nature and to his own sensuousness. It was necessary for modern man to reappropriate the life of the senses and in doing so to reconquer his oneness with the body. In the collection's final essay on Winckelmann, Pater's Hellenism read the sculpted male body of Greek statuary as the epitome of a seamless unity between the aesthetic object and human sensuousness.

The image of the body as unified intelligent sensuousness, and therefore the nonseparation of the senses from the intellect, was, Pater claimed in his essay, central to the Hellenic ideal and to ancient culture; this he celebrated Johann Winckelmann for rediscovering.[9] The two-part essay, the first on Winckelmann's own life and the second on the Greek ideal, is aimed at demonstrating the continuity between theory and practice; it aims to show how Winckelmann not only celebrated in his work but in fact "lived" the Greek ideal through his sensuous approach to art and, conversely, his intellectual approach to sexuality and to other male bodies. Yet when Pater tries to appropriate the characteristics of the Greek statue to Winckelmann's body, he fails. The meaning of this failure is not Pater's incapability to properly "hide" the German critic's homosexuality, nor is it a means for Pater to express his own homoerotic identity. As Richard Jenkyns suggests, what appears to the contemporary critic as clearly recognizable "signs" of homosexuality would possibly have been perceived differently by Pater's own audience, and by Pater himself.[10] Rather, what is significant in Pater's failed attempt to reconcile the qualities of the Greek statue with Winckelmann's body is the author's implicit disregard for how the discourse of prohibition shapes Winckelmann's desire and his own narrative. Even in Pater's own text, the two terms that structure neoclassical corporeality are not self-exclusive but rather, as Eve Kosofsky Sedgwick points out, interfacing.[11] In other words, the "case" of Winckelmann suggests that the sexless sensuousness of the Greek male body obtains its philosophical and erotic charge not from a reified notion of Hellenism, which can be directly and univocally invoked, but rather from the productive power of Christian (homo)phobic prohibition, which is in fact ingrained in Pater's notion of aestheticism.[12] Pater's blindness to the coexistence of classical and Christian discourse in his own text, although allowing him to boldly advance a radical project of cultural renovation, also prevents him from depicting Winckelmann himself in classical terms as the Greek statue. To underscore the terms of this inability, and to assess its enabling potential for the 1890s aesthete, I will now look closely at the representation of the male body in Pater's text.

"Winckelmann," first published anonymously in *The Westminster Review* in 1867, was a response to Matthew Arnold's discussion of Christianity and classical culture in his lecture "Pagan and Religious Sentiments" of 1864.[13] Pater works to envision a wholeness that, embodied in the work of art, can claim a higher ethical ground than the views of Newman or Arnold. Because of its sensuous content, the Greek ideal was best expressed in sculpture, and it is the image of the Greek statue that engages most of Pater's energies in the essay. The sensuous element that all art possesses as a medium for the ideal, he declares, becomes physically manifested in sculpture through the representation of the human body. Pater works to emphasize the simplicity and reserve of the sculpted bodies he describes; the characters of Greek sculpture are "*Heiterkeit,* blitheness or repose, and *Allgemeinheit,* generality of breadth" (Pater, 204). Inactive, expressionless, and impassive, the Greek statue, as well as the Greek ideal, "has nothing in common with the grotesque"; as such this dignified sensuousness is recuperated within a classical frame, and the notion of excess and grotesquerie as the inevitable realm of the enjoying body is jettisoned. The sculpted body's god-like ataraxia, its limited choice of poses, remind the implied connoisseur of the measured gesture of the aristocrat, and indeed Pater goes on to invoke its dignity in the language of class distinction. "To all but the aristocratic culture," he observes, "the reserved faces of the Gods will ever have something of insipidity." An elite of taste and class is suggested; Pater reads the Greek statue as an icon of aristocratic western beauty whose self-absorption and inactivity signifies not a refusal of productivity but rather a complete indifference to the accidental, to life.

Once he has established this difference as aristocratic, that is, as the key characteristic of the now fading class on which the rising British bourgeoisie wished to model its own styles, Pater goes on to register the sculpture's sensuousness as a kind of impassioned passionlessness. This youthful, desexualized image of the male body as "shameless and childlike" is the foundation of an idea of art meant to sensuously engage the audience. Christian asceticism, instead, discredited the senses and demonized artistic life as an immoral form of "intoxication" in contradiction with "the spiritual world." "From this intoxication," writes Pater, "Winckelmann is free: he fingers those pagan marbles with unsinged hands, with no sense of shame or loss. That is to deal with the sensuous side of art in the pagan manner" (Pater, 209). Here the statue's tactile quality is a register of its integrity just as the ideal critic's willingness to touch the marble, rather than merely look, is a sign of art appreciation as itself an unsullied and sensuous experience. However, when Pater tries to recast Winckelmann's biographical relation to young male bodies in the terms of his aesthetic relation to Greek sculpture, the two images never fully cohere but rather are separated by a semiotic chasm that jeopardizes the author's narrative effort.

More than once Winckelmann is posed by Pater as the actual embodiment of the Greek statue, reenacting one by one all its characteristics. For instance, aristocratic self-absorption is replayed, in the case of the German critic, in terms of his complete dedication to work. Above all, Winckelmann, in Pater's portrait, realizes the Greek ideal with his own life, particularly by constantly rekindling his taste for beauty through his contact with beautiful young men: "These friendships, bringing him into contact with the pride of the human form, and staining the thoughts with its bloom, perfected his reconciliation to the spirit of Greek sculpture" (Pater, 191). This is one of the rare moments in the essay when Pater's language uncannily points to the discourse of moral prohibition that his theory of aestheticism excludes: The sensuous appreciation of the male body has the function of balancing the excessively intellectual inclination of the artist, but the image of the "stain" that intrudes immediately evokes the discourse of guilt and immorality.

The equivalence between Winckelmann and the Hellenic ideal, as well as his identification with the statue that Pater continually affirms, is more than once contradicted by Winckelmann's own corporeality. For one, the description of the critic as a man of weak constitution, "Southern" in appearance, dark, small, restlessly swift, and sexualized, constructs his image as very different from the luminous, white, and sexless forms of the statue. Further, the statue's universality and aristocratic appearance stand in opposition to the nature of Winckelmann's desire. What Pater describes as the German critic's serene enjoyment of the human form is in fact a drama of sanguine passions whose erotic force is only partly dispelled by Pater's effort to show how Winckelmann's "physical excitement" becomes aesthetically productive: "These friendships, often the caprice of a moment, make Winckelmann's letters, with their troubled coloring, an instructive but bizarre addition to the *History of Art*" (Pater, 192). Homosexuality and homoerotic love are presented here as a bizarre detail: If Winckelmann can touch the marble with "unsinged hands," Pater cannot do as much in narrating the life of the German critic. The biographical element repeatedly tears apart the carefully woven fabric of Pater's narration, so that the tale of the new Greek innocence of the senses turns into a never fully acknowledged narrative of shame founded upon the elusive presence and absence of the connoisseur's sexual body.

There is always a gap between what the author discloses and what he actually says, between what he chooses to display and what the reader actually sees. Each level of the writing—structural, rhetorical, and discursive—reproduces this slippage between the art and the critic's life, which Pater's textual acrobatics continually try to mend. Structurally, Pater poses biography against art appreciation; rhetorically, he deploys gestures of understatement, as in the previous quote, and paradox; discursively, he deploys a language of sensuousness to bridge what he considers a false gap between the art appreciated and the life lived. The structure of the essay, with the first part dedicated to Winckelmann's biography and the second to a theoretical reflection on the Hellenic ideal, itself represents an initial obstacle to Pater's intentions. To draw a direct connection between Winckelmann and his ideal remains impossible, and Pater makes every effort to make the shadow of Winckelmann's tainted body disappear into the Greek statue and from the essay. It is strictly appropriate, therefore, that Winckelmann's death is both staged and then passed over in the text. The occlusion of the discourse of Christian sexual prohibition evoked by the circumstances of his death makes it impossible to coherently assimilate this episode to the rest of Pater's narrative. Thus Winckelmann's death in Trieste remains an excessive, nonfunctional element of the plot, implicitly disturbing its coherence: Pater seems to engage in an unending game of displacement of this embarrassing excess of Winckelmann's "corpse" in order to demonstrate that his text, as well as his body ideal, is without any taint of shame.

Without taking into account that a pure body is also a purged body, that is, by refusing to acknowledge that the unity of body and soul and the sexless beauty of the Greek statue are also produced under the aegis of Christian prohibition, Pater is compelled to depict the German critic as a healthy, beautiful, and masculine body (while he comes close to suggesting that in fact he is not), eternal and spiritual as the Greek statue. While interpreting Winckelmann's sexuality as an ideally sensuous medium, Pater tries to affirm the power and self-control of the male subject at all levels (spirit *and* body, reason *and* desire); but when he moves from spirit to biography the narration of Winckelmann's "death in Trieste" climaxes the text's subdued rhetoric of exposure. The accidental nature and grotesquerie of the episode seem to confirm—*despite* Pater—that the Greek ideal is not the body, that if the statue is a simulacrum of immortality, its fleshy replica, the child, can become the cause of death. The statue may be a figure of permanence, but the body kills.

At the end of the essay the identification between the desiring subject and the object (Winckelmann and the godlike statue) and of the subject with himself (the two images of Winckelmann as aesthete *ante litteram* and homosexual) does not take place. Although homoeroticism is implicitly invoked at every point, Winckelmann's desire remains unrepresented and unrepresentable in Pater's essay: In its place stands a gap opened by the narrative mechanism through which Winckelmann's image is constructed. In its "unrepresented" status, Winckelmann's death becomes a potentially lurid detail and uncannily comes to occupy a liminal space *between* innocence and guilt, aestheticism and prohibition, thus directly pointing to the interfacing of classical and Christian cultures that Pater's Hellenism implies. In this perspective we could say that in "Winckelmann" the homoerotic body is signified exactly by its unrepresentability and lack of signification. That is, it is rather "presented" and continually displaced under a semiotic code, that of a pure and purifying aestheticism, that fails to represent desire.

The discourse of sexual prohibition is nonetheless there, over and over again encoded into Winckelmann's corpse, as well as his body, but Pater does not see it, or he claims not to. By not acknowledging this prohibition, by implicitly suggesting a phobic denial of the body in his texts, Pater is able to imagine Winckelmann as a radiant, and paradoxically "moral," figure, shameless. In fact, by eliminating shame, Pater also denies abjection. Because Winckelmann is denied the pleasure of displaying his shame, which plays such an important role in Wilde's work, his body cannot be represented under the sign of masochism but rather becomes sentimentalized as the victim of inscrutable circumstances that Winckelmann is unable to control. Thus his shameless body will be finally restored to integrity, to a kitsch version—because reified and eternally fixed—of imagined perfection, as the essay's conclusion shows. The final words that reconvert Winckelmann's "deflowered flesh" into marble are Pater's, this time speaking through the voice of Goethe: "'He has' says Goethe, 'the advantage of figuring in the memory of posterity, as one eternally able and strong; for the image in which one leaves the world, is that in which one moves among the shadows'" (Pater, 156–157). The danger of having to admit to an excessive sensuousness has once again been defused, the rupture politely mended by the cadences of Goethe's oration. Winckelmann can touch the marble with "unsinged hands," without shame, because sexuality has been exchanged for art, shame for glory, embarrassed silence for eulogy. The sentimentalization of the male body, effected in the image of the beautiful and young dead figure, will return in Wilde's last image of Dorian Gray, but only through Wilde's attempt to strategically reintegrate the discourse of prohibition into his work, so that a camouflaged form of homoerotic desire as moral violation can become the occasion for an expiatory and ecstatic display of the male body.

## WILDE'S FOLDED GARMENTS

Both in his everyday self-fashioning and in his textual production, Wilde may be said to have worked toward a homoerotic representation of the self rather than a representation of the homoerotic self. The distinction is important: The image of a ready-made and fully recognizable homoerotic identity would be historically preposterous in a time when no socially recognized queer identity yet existed. Further, the notion of a "homoerotic self" evokes a depth-surface model of identity naturalized and essentialized by the bourgeois notion of expressive interiority, which Wilde subverts in both his writing and his self-fabricated appearance. At the same time Wilde never really allowed his general audience to establish any possible connection between his subversive signifying practices and homosexuality, which would have immediately been criminalized as "sodomy." He managed this by embodying, between the late 1870s and the 1890s, two different personae, respectively that of the aesthete and that of the dandy. Both figures, as their cultural encoding shows, were scorned and laughed at—and enjoyed—by the broad middle class because of what appeared as their parasitical and effeminate refinement. This very effeminacy could be used by Wilde to pass exactly because his contemporaries decoded it as a signifier of class rather than sexual dissidence.[14] I want now to investigate more closely both aestheticism and dandyism as cultural phenomena in the fin de siècle to examine how both intervened in Wilde's work of homoerotic signification; at the same time I want to show how he pitted one "pose" against the other in his work to articulate a transgressive representation of the male body in which homoeroticism is signaled through excessive expenditure and masochism.

In 1882, upon his return to England from the American tour, Wilde stopped wearing his "aesthetic dress"—a costume that he had agreed to wear by contract under the solicitation of the organizer of the tour, Richard D'Oyly Carte. This included the famous velvet breeches and short jacket, and the smoking jacket in which he was portrayed in languid and pensive pose by the New York photographer Napoleon Sarony in 1882. Back in England, Wilde discarded the flamboyant costumes of the aesthete for the more sober elegance of the dandy without renouncing some more subdued elements of extravagance, as, for example, the famous green carnation that he wore in his buttonhole. Historically dandyism had been a middle class phenomenon, specifically a manifestation of "middle class uppityism,"[15] as Richard Dellamora observes, signaling a desire of members of the middle class to appear aristocratic. The dandy's excessive concern with his looks and his interest in fashion and consumption marked his figure as "effeminate," yet such dandyism had no necessary connection in the eyes of Wilde's audience with homoeroticism, and rather signified aristocratic leisure. The change in Wilde's appearance pointed therefore to a change in his class status, or at least class identification; it also signaled, as I will explain, a new way of conceiving appearance and its relation to reality and the self. Crucially, this change of persona allowed Wilde to transcode the values of aestheticism into a more materially recognizable structure of expenditure via the consuming and consumerist practices of the dandy. Thus by relinquishing the romantic costume of the aesthete to impersonate the dandy, Wilde engineered a way to ground the aesthete's hedonistic excess, the desire to waste oneself in ever new pleasures, into the practices and the desires of the leisured and upper class's conspicuous consumption. Hence homoerotic desire, which could be implicitly circulated through the aestheticist invocation of sensuous expenditure, could also be reinscribed onto the male body in the form of the wasteful desires of commodity fetishism that late nineteenth century consumer culture demanded. In turn, the dandy's excessive squandering in the pursuit of pleasure stood as the alibi that could trigger the aesthete's need for punishment and expiation as a transgression of the moral law of Christian prohibition that coexisted with a valorization of classical amorality in the discourse of aestheticism itself.

To fully comprehend what is at stake in Wilde's change of personae, one needs to consider more closely the role of aestheticism and dandyism as integral aspects of fin de siècle culture. The aesthete's artistic "effeminacy," which at the level of personal appearance was signified by the gender impropriety of his dress code, relied on and implied the bourgeois construction of literary and artistic culture as effeminate. Since the time of the Romantics through Arnold's invocation of "the culture of sweetness and light," literature and poetry in particular had been represented in British culture as feminine, opposed to the productivity and materialism ingrained in the "manly" work ethic of the empire's bourgeoisie. The "refining" character of literary and artistic culture and its power to elevate the individual "above" the crass concerns of the middle class became the founding element of the antiutilitarian tone of aestheticism, as the famous invitation to live and experience that concludes *The Renaissance* shows: "To burn always with the hard gem-like flame, to maintain this ecstasy is success in life" (Pater, 218). Pater's definition of aestheticism as a modern hedonism, with its call to turn life into art, explicitly rejects the moral prohibition that structures bourgeois ideology. Paradoxically, however, by deploying the discourse of classicism to oppose the moral trappings of Christian culture, the aesthete may still concur with some of the puritanical assumptions of bourgeois morality: As we have seen in Pater's description of the Greek statue, by excluding sexuality from the sensuous-intellectual appreciation of the body, aestheticism marks its distance from middle class utilitarianism and at the same time, through this gesture of abstraction, colludes with the very asceticism that guarantees the preservation of the bourgeois self. Notwithstanding this collusion, the aesthete aims at "refashioning" the world against the principles and the values of bourgeois culture through his own aestheticized and hedonistic experiences: Like Wilde's hero Dorian Gray in his most visionary moment, he wishes to open his eyes one morning "upon a world that has been refashioned anew in the darkness for our own pleasure, a world in which things would have fresh shapes and colors, and be changed, or have other secrets."[16] In this instance, although the world that Dorian desires is fashioned in the darkness of the subject's unconscious rather than produced through an act of will, it is nonetheless devised and "projected" by the aesthete himself: Aestheticism, in other words, seems to invoke both the loss and the presence of the self.

The turn of the century dandy's effeminacy, in contrast to that of the aesthete, did not mobilize the notion of literary refinement but rather the image of idleness, vanity, immorality, and unmanly ineffectuality through which the middle class stigmatized the aristocracy and the leisured upper classes. Once again, as in the case of the aesthete, the dandy's effeminacy did not indicate same-sex desire. As Ellen Moers points out, the dandy was represented as a heterosexual philanderer; the dandiacal Lord Henry Wotton in *The Picture of Dorian Gray*, for example, betrays his wife with other women. It was his antisocial and unproductive self-absorption that made the dandy a transgressive and potentially dangerous figure in 1890s Europe. What appeared to critics of the period such as Max Nordau as the dandy's egotistic narcissism stood in open opposition to the chivalric virtues of self-sacrifice, courtesy, service, responsibility, and work, which for the late Victorian middle classes characterized an ideal masculine national type—the type of hero in the colonial adventure novels of R. M. Ballantyne and Rider

Haggard, for example. During the last decade of the century, when England, despite its empire, struck many commentators as being in danger of losing its economic preeminence on the world scene,[17] it was the dandy's ineffectuality, his effeminacy and narcissistic *otium,* more than any sign of homoeroticism that preoccupied and scandalized the middle class. Populist hostility against him could displace scattered anxieties about the coming decline of England's national power with fantasies of body invasion: The national body politic, as well as the individual, could be "invaded" and contaminated by the dandy's parasitical qualities, and turned into a subject "unfit for the labors of common life," as Nordau put it (Nordau, 301). In a period that bracketed its fears with horror tales of vampish male invaders from without (Bram Stoker's *Dracula*) or with vicious and secretive male attackers from within (R. L. Stevenson's *Dr. Jekyll and Mr. Hyde*), the dandy as aesthete could function as an easy scapegoat for such fears of "contamination."

The dandy's interest in fashion, appearance, and ephemeral triviality in the style of Beau Brummell, as well as his wasteful existence, showed the same insouciant disregard for bourgeois values as demonstrated by the aesthete. However, as a cynical pose of disbelief, his rebellious amorality was not aimed at "refashioning" the world. Rather, the fin de siècle dandy, as exemplified by Wilde's Lord Henry Wotton in *The Picture of Dorian Gray,* assumes a position of aristocratic detachment through which he can observe and, untouched, manipulate reality and others without ever leaving his fashionable and self-fashioned identity. The difference between the position of the aesthete and that of the dandy is encompassed by two exemplary statements, one by Pater and the other by Jules Barbey d'Aurevilly, the early nineteenth century French dandy and author of the essay *Of Dandyism and of George Brummell* (1844). Whereas the aesthete attempts to resemble the gods on whom the Greek statue is modeled, "those abstracted Gods," as Pater writes, "who can fold up their flesh as a garment and remain themselves" (Pater, 211), the dandy in d'Aurevilly's definition makes no attempt to self-preservation: "For dandies, like women, to seem is to be. These stoics of the boudoir drink their own blood under their mask and remain masked."[18] In the first instance the "artificial" clothing and the desiring body exchange places on the mere surface of appearances with a gesture of natural unnaturalness that still allows the aesthete to reclaim a self, an ephemeral identity of "flame-like" transformations that are aimed at "refashioning" reality. The dandy instead, narcissistically feeding off himself, seems to have severed his ties with reality, as d'Aurevilly implies in his mention of the secluded and private space of the boudoir; his self is nothing more than a mask, and he revels in this nonidentity.

Both aestheticism and dandyism offered Wilde the means to flaunt a homoerotic social identity in the making by providing a complex semiotic apparatus of transgression. Although the terms of this transgression, as I have shown, were played out in different spheres—artistic dissidence for the bohemian aesthete, upper class allegiance for the dandy—both aestheticism and dandyism seemed to represent a similar threat, that of an emasculating laxness that in middle class eyes signified decay. Max Nordau, one of the most influential fin de siècle critics of decadence, conflated aestheticism and dandyism in this way; decadence was for him characterized by a close proximity to weakness and degeneracy, two pseudomedical terms that in his lexicon suggested the spread of disfunction, exhaustion, and disease of the social body. The aesthete was demonized and scapegoated by Nordau and others because his antisocial drive, reflected in his appearance and writing, was seen as a disintegrating force in the uncertain social climate of the fin de siècle. In Book 3 of his polemic *Degeneration* (1893), "Decadents and Aesthetes," where Nordau retraces the origins of the contemporary aestheticist movement to French Symbolism and dandyism, he quotes the poet Paul Bourget as its most direct critic: "The word 'decadence' denotes a state of society which produces too great a number of individuals unfit for the labors of common life. … They cease to subordinate their energy to the total energy because they are ego-maniacs." Nordau wholly endorses this condemnation, adding that "decadence is synonymous with inaptitude for regular functions and subordination to social aims. … [Its] consequence…is anarchy and the ruin of the community" (Nordau, 301–302). The aesthete is castigated as an embodied subject who refuses to submit himself to the productivist laws of the bourgeois polity. Spending time, money, and energies in useless activities, he is a born consumer uninterested in the use or durability of material or ideological goods; rather he is attracted to their expendability. He is uninterested in what is "natural" or commonsense and, by extension, in realism as an epistemological and narrative mode: His aim is to recast life as art and beautify life's vulgarity. Nordau's hysterical critique (his text is dedicated to Cesare Lombroso, advocate of theories of degeneracy and author of *The Man of Genius* (1864, translated into English in 1894) flounders in its use of a pseudomedical model of a "healthy" society, but his fondness for metaphors of a productive corporeality may be seen as paralleling the focus on the body by the aesthetes he condemns.

Nordau's implicit collapsing of the figure of the aesthete into that of the dandy prefigures the way in which both modes of desire and styles of the self are inscribed in Wilde's own text and personae. His 1882 shift from the look of the aesthete to that of the dandy allowed him to appropriate art to consumption and to impart a material figuration to the hedonistic impulse of aestheticism. The association of art and consumption, both in Wilde's text and in his self-presentation, established a conflictual nexus of aristocratic classicism, wasteful pleasure, and self-dissipation, which in his work, as I will show, functions as a mechanism of transgression and expiation. In this scenario, expenditure represents both an innate disposition to waste, existing "for no reason other than the desire one may have for it," as Georges Bataille claims,[19] and the occasion for the aesthete-dandy to stage a form of self-punishment for his excesses, which situates his masochized body under the sign of abjection as shameful spectacularity.

Bataille's speculations on expenditure, introduced first in the essay "The Notion of Expenditure" (1933) and then explored more comprehensively in the first volume of *La part maudite* (The accursed share) (1949), even though formulated forty years after Wilde's moment, prove an enormously important instrument for fully understanding the implications of Wilde's subversive signifying practices. Bataille defines expenditure as a deviant form of consumption driven by a perverse desire for loss. His theory of general economy overthrows the principles of classical, capitalist economy by refusing the notion of a rational and productive reinvestment of surplus value (*la part maudite*, the accursed share) into more wealth. Rather, for Bataille this excess must be spectacularly squandered, as had happened in precapitalist, feudal times with the practice of medieval festivals, for instance, where the sumptuous spectacle of waste overwhelmed the audience with awe and fear. The notion of expenditure as spectacular destruction of wealth, which Bataille derived from Marcel Mauss's ethnographic studies of Native American cultures of the Pacific Northwest, finds its exemplary model in the ceremony of potlatch, or archaic gift-giving. This consisted in the sacrifice of enormous amounts of amassed goods, through which an individual member of a clan might crush a rival by his superior capability to dispose of precious objects: In this process, rank and honor were acquired through the sacrifice of wealth. Bataille identifies the desire for expenditure, with its distinctive features of violence, destruction, and (self) sacrifice, as a chief element of his notion of general economy, in open opposition to the bourgeois principles of calculated consumption, property, and self-preservation. The destructive force of expenditure as "absolutely contrary to the principle of balanced account" is recognized by Bataille in a series of events whose nonutilitarian excess confirms their transgressive quality:

> Luxury, mourning, war, cults, the construction of sumptuary monuments, games, spectacles, art, perverse sexual activities (i.e. deflected from genital finality); all these represent activities which, at least in primitive circumstances, have no end beyond themselves. ... Expenditure is different from] all modes of consumption that serve as a means to the end of production. The accent is posed on loss.[20]

The cluster of loss, luxury, art, and perverse sexual activities would be enough to trigger the idea of a connection between Bataillean expenditure and the activities of the aesthete-dandy I am examining. Indeed, fin de siècle aestheticism and Bataille's libidinal-economic theory share the same Nietzschean matrix: Although "clouded by practical reason and Christian morality,"[21] as Bataille claims, the need for expenditure is still visible in modern times in, for example, mysticism, eroticism, violence, and art. In these phenomena, as the critic Michèle Richman notices, "lies Bataille's version of the other—general—economy of surplus, which explains why people gamble, dissipate fortunes, and exhaust great resources of energy and goods while exhibiting equal disdain for the immediate preservation of the self and concern for the future."[22] By founding the notion of expenditure on the experience of potlatch, Bataille theorizes a form of power that affirms itself through the loss and waste not only of goods but also of the self (as happens in eroticism) and of meaning (in art, madness, and mysticism). The Bataillean notion of "sovereignty," which paradoxically manifests itself through sacrifice and *self*-sacrifice, the sacrifice and the loss of a coherent notion of the self, implies in fact an exquisitely masochistic logic. This same logic that intervenes in the representation of the implicit destructiveness and self-destruction through pleasure also characterizes the Wildean aesthete. Furthermore, by bringing together libidinal and political economy in the act of wasting and in the moment of loss, expenditure comes to function as a diacritical sign in Wilde's work of signification. It does so by allowing the transcoding of homoerotic excess, and of sexual pleasure, into the excesses of the aesthete's hedonistic consumption, so that Wilde's homoerotic somatics finds a conduit through and at the same time is shaped by a wasteful economy of expenditure, of which the ruinous pleasures and desires of aristocratic conspicuous consumption are signs.

As becomes evident in *The Picture of Dorian Gray*, the convergence of aestheticism and dandyism, as much as the nexus of art and consumption established by this convergence, invokes expenditure and its inextinguishable desire for loss. This loss takes the form of "inexpedient behavior," to use Freud's term, that is, a form of transgression that in Freud's definition of masochism calls for punishment. What is transgressed through the excesses of expenditure is the never fully relinquished logic of sexual prohibition that aestheticism carries with itself. By violating this prohibition through the pursuit of his dandiacal pleasures, the Wildean aesthetic subject, as figured by the character of Dorian Gray, engages in a project of self-punishment that ultimately turns his body into an icon of expiatory disfigurement. This masochistic management of excess is signaled by the collapse of self into other, which structures so much of Wilde's fiction. In short stories such as "The Portrait of W. H.," "The Model Millionaire," or in the essay "London Models," all written in 1889, and even more clearly in *Dorian Gray*, the homoerotic subject manages to make his desire visible by aesthetically encoding it onto the body of the other. Through such ex-corporation of desire, the painter of these short stories obliterates and displaces his self in a self-protective gesture that Sedgwick calls "the homophobic alibi," a form of camouflage that transforms desire for the other into narcissistic desire for the self, as summed up by the phrase "I do not love him; I am him."[23] If the dichotomy homo-hetero is converted into same-other, as Sedgwick suggests, homoeroticism can be refigured as narcissism, heterosexual love for the same. In this optic, the narcissism that is inevitably attributed to the Wildean aesthete by his contemporaries is in fact the effect of an act of masochistic self-erasure. By reading the figure of the aesthete as merely narcissistic, one misses the violence imbricated in his "feeding off himself" (Barbey d'Aurevilly's definition of the dandy allows perhaps a glimpse of this violence by evoking the image of vampiristic blood-drinking) as well as the game of power and domination through which the refined and apparently harmless "uselessness" of the aesthete-dandy is produced.

The process through which the Wildean subject of homoerotic desire "loses" his self to reinscribe it onto the object is recognized by such critics such as Eve Sedgwick, Moe Meyer, and Ed Cohen as one of the central features of Wilde's process of homoerotic signification, but it is never explicitly acknowledged as masochist. Meyer, for example, in reconstructing an archaeology of posing in Wilde's career and work, shows how Wilde revamped the pose of the dandy, fallen out of fashion for more than a century, by deploying a system of gesture and voice training for actors known as the Delsarte method.[24] In turn, the way in which the Delsartean "pose" defined the relation between exterior appearance—voice, gesture, pose—and the interiority of the actor implied a collapse of the distinction between self and other with which Wilde experimented in his writing. Wilde discovered the Delsartean method during his American tour, when he met one of Delsarte's disciples, Steele MacKay.[25] François Delsarte had founded a system of voice training that was popular in France among speakers and actors between 1839 and 1871. His method was extended to include physical movement, a technical schema of gestures and postures developed by MacKay, who became a famous acting teacher in New York in the 1870s and 1880s. By turning the rigid structure of cause and effect that structured the relation of interiority and exteriority in bourgeois discourse on its head, Delsarte demonstrated that an exterior system of signification could generate a certain image of interior states through a series of studied postures, gestures, and tones of voice so that an exterior surface would signify the artist's interiority. Conversely, by assuming a particular "pose" through a well-orchestrated manipulation of one's image, one could effect a collapse of the opposition between interior and exterior, encoding subject and encoded object, thus turning one's own self into a work of art.

The possibilities offered by Delsarte's method were fully deployed by Wilde in his public appearance as a dandy, through whose pose he worked to create a new image of himself and a new form of interiority. "Wilde's early experiments with dandyism," as Meyer affirms, "from 1883 to 1885, can be read then as an exploration of identity formulation through a signifying practice that was identifiably Delsartean."[26] However, through such Delsartean self-fabrication Wilde was able to signal only "non-masculinity" and not homoerotic desire. Thus he worked to elaborate strategies through which this desire, not taken into account by dominant culture, could be made "covertly" visible. Whereas the late nineteenth century notion of "sodomy" was conceived in social and juridical terms as a relational act between two partners and as structured on the model of a fixed subject-object hierarchy (between inserter and insertee, penetrator and penetrated), Wilde tried to signify homoerotic desire in a way that could subvert and confuse this very hierarchy of subject-object, active-passive. To do so he needed to make this same-sex desire visible by incorporating it onto the body of the other, albeit without allowing any sexual exchange, any "touch" between the two. For Meyer, the process through which self and other are collapsed into each other is an integral part of Wilde's "textual homoerotics,"[27] visible in his work from the 1880s short stories to *The Picture of Dorian Gray*.

By painting Dorian's portrait, Basil Hallward projects his desire for the model (a desire he redefines as his "self") onto the image of Dorian. Whereas the desiring subject appears to sacrifice his self by appropriating it to the body of the other, he also comes to "inhabit" the model that he cannot have by "becoming" him: This is the moment of the aesthetic transference that allows Basil to affirm, "Every portrait that is painted with feeling is a portrait of the artist, not of the sitter" (Wilde, 5). In this instance the model is conceived as a tabula rasa; his own self disappears absorbed by the painter's self-sacrificial and self-boosting displacement of desire. With a final act of magical transference, continues Meyer, the inscribed body of the other is recuperated: The portrait *becomes* Dorian, so that the artist's inscription of his desire on the body of the other no longer sanctions the disappearance of the model's own identity. Rather, self and other, inscriptor and inscriptee, seem to coexist, to merge into each other in a newly found balance. In this context Dorian's "apparent murder" of Basil "actually marks the conceptual birth of Wilde's homosexual social identity by freeing the artist from self-definitional dependence upon the posed model."[28]

Meyer's excellent and otherwise convincing discussion of the homoerotic production of the self in Wilde's text nevertheless does not take fully into account the violence inscribed in the prominent dialectic of submission and domination through which the homoerotic body is represented in *Dorian Gray*. The most relevant male corpse in the story, Basil's, is scientifically and discreetly removed from the scene—the image of the aesthete no longer burning "with a gem-like flame" but instead literally burned away by the scientist Alan Campbell's chemicals. No sign remains of Basil apart from Dorian's own self-corroding guilt. In fact, the collapse of the distinction between subject and object that would sanction "the birth of Wilde's homosocial identity" is less of a painless and unproblematic operation than Meyer suggests. For one, Basil's self-objectification, which can be read as a gesture of masochistic self-denial, also demands that the model relinquish his own self and become a blank surface for the artist. In this instance, then, the subject's strategic self-displacement is in fact an act of power. Indeed, by taking as his point of departure the relation between the artist and the model—an unequal, socially inscribed relation—Wilde engineers a strategy for signifying homoerotic desire that is imbricated in a sadomasochistic structure of submission and domination. I want now to show how this structure is articulated in *Dorian Gray* and to examine how it stages the disfigured male body as erotic spectacle.

The narrative of *Dorian Gray* is founded, at its opening, on two distinct relations of subjection. When Basil describes his interest in his model as "being under the influence" of Dorian, he implicitly admits to being dominated by him: His desire, in fact, is explained as an act of surrender. Having been, at the beginning of their friendship, the object of Dorian's gaze ("I suddenly became conscious that someone was looking at me. ... When our eyes met I felt that I was growing pale" [Wilde, 6]), Basil lives his desire for Dorian as a drama of self-abjection. Thus he sets himself up to be hurt by the youth: "I find a strange pleasure in saying things to him that I know I shall be sorry for having said. ... Now and then ... he is horribly thoughtless, and seems to take a real delight in giving me pain" (Wilde, 11–12). In turn, Dorian falls under the influence of Lord Henry and comes to occupy for him the position that Basil had initially occupied for Dorian himself, that of the object of the gaze, a gaze representing both scientific and detached scrutiny as well as erotic, albeit aestheticized, desire.

By desiring Dorian while at the same time sublimating his desire aesthetically, Basil manages to "inhabit" the youth's body; as he explains to Lord Henry when asked to exhibit the painting, "There's too much of me in that painting" (Wilde, 5). Through the same move, Wilde himself manages to represent homoerotic desire without actually bringing sexuality into the picture. Basil's "strange idolatry" regarding his model, which must not be disclosed to Dorian, is cast in Greek terms, implicitly excluding both sexuality and sexual prohibition: Erotic desire for the male body is allegedly sublimated into artistic appreciation. At the same time, the discourse of secrecy once again mobilizes the notion of prohibition, of shame, and of moral boundaries that cannot be transgressed. The sexual body and homoeroticism, obliquely signaled by Dorian's dandiacal expenditure, by his desire to waste his self, his body, and his wealth, are brought to the center of the narrative through Dorian's submission to Lord Henry. Wilde recuperates what Pater had (nominally) excluded from his theory of aestheticism, that is, Christian sexual prohibition as a productive element capable of mobilizing a mechanism of self-punishment. Through this mechanism the male body is ultimately eroticized in Wilde's book. By submitting to Lord Henry's influence, Dorian transgresses and exceeds the logic of innocence, purity, and unselfconsciousness that for Basil had defined his model. At the same time, even after Basil's death, his sublimated and purified desire for beauty and for Dorian as an object of beauty remains inscribed in Dorian in the form of the youth's sentimental moralizing (his remorse for having caused Sybil Vane's death, for instance) and, at the end of the novel, in his guilt for what he considers his wasteful, wicked, and hedonistic existence.

I want to underline once again that homosexuality as such is never mentioned or even indirectly suggested in the novel. Rather, same-sex desire is displaced and signified by the transgressive libidinal economy of the aesthete-dandy, whose narcissistic, unproductive conspicuous consumption always gestures, in bourgeois eyes, toward the dangers of expenditure. Once again, the aesthete's narcissistic pose reveals itself as a more complex operation than contemporary critics such as Nordau claimed: In fact, through Dorian's narcissism the novel attempts to manage desire. Left alone with his portrait, which he adores—"once, in a boyish mockery of Narcissus, he had kissed, or feigned to kiss, those painted lips. ... Morning after morning he sat in front of the portrait, wondering at its beauty, almost enamoured with it" (Wilde, 105)—Dorian wants only himself. Even at this moment, the narcissistic kiss is acknowledged as possibly a feigned act; the dissimulation that structures the dandified aesthete's self-representation finally prevents even self-love. In this moment Dorian's seemingly transgressive and decadent gesture reinscribes a crucial element of bourgeois ideology: Whereas he desires himself as image, itself a feigned version of himself, his self-absorption reiterates the "will to identification" that, from the mirror stage on, produces the identity of the Cartesian subject and with it the masculine subject's dream of autonomy and self-sufficiency.

⌸    ⌸    ⌸

At the same time, while preserving his image for his own love, the protagonist wants to "spend," to waste his life and his body in new sensations, thus reenacting Pater's invitation in the conclusion of *The Renaissance* to live and experience. Dorian's narcissism encompasses the opposite poles of a fantasy of nonconsumption, where self-preservation as a dream of self-sufficiency is achieved through a refusal to "use" the body (witness as part of this refusal his spectatorial position vis-à-vis the portrait as well as the absence of any sexuality as such in the novel) and through the desire to abuse it through an activity of full expenditure, a total spending of its energies. Although the fantasy of forgoing consumption testifies to the aesthete's (Wilde's own) desire to dominate and control the modalities of his self-fashioning, the imperative to spend and squander irrevocably subjects his dandified persona to laws that are not of his own making: the laws of the market. Rachel Bowlby effectively explains this subjection when she writes: "Lord Henry remakes Dorian as the advertiser markets his product. In representing his image to him as both the epitome of modern youth and beauty ... he gives him an advertisement for himself, in relation to which Dorian is both the consumer and what he buys. But his very uniqueness is entirely derivative."[29] In describing Dorian's fetishized and narcissistic image as "derivative," Bowlby implicitly evokes a repressive notion of consumer culture, where meaning is imposed on the commodity from above and maintained in this form throughout the process of circulation and consumption. Although it is true that it is Lord Henry who attributes a certain fetish value to Dorian ("Why it had been left for a stranger to reveal him to himself?" wonders Dorian [Wilde, 21]), this value becomes more and more complex semiotically once Dorian becomes the only consumer of his own image. In fact his narcissism, his pleasure in seeing himself as Henry had defined him—" the finest portrait of modern times"—points to a penchant for expenditure represented by Dorian's insatiable desire to live a life as beautiful as his portrait.

In turn, this desire for expenditure manifests itself through conspicuous consumption and its wasteful commodity fetishism. Through Dorian's pleasure in looking at objects and "possessing" them to the point of identifying with their imagined qualities, the circuit of commodity fetishism opens onto the logic of expenditure. Surrounded by all his bibelots, which he cannot stop himself from desiring and purchasing, Dorian himself is a figure of consumer out of control—his shopping far exceeds the range of his actual needs. The excessive spending that encompasses Dorian's libidinal economy was encoded, in a more limited form, in the culture of consumption of Wilde's own time. However, the extremity of Dorian's expenditure presupposes rather an economy of abundance where supply precedes demand and needs are indistinguishable from desires. This economic condition will become a full-fledged cultural phenomenon only in contemporary postindustrial societies, in which, as Jean-Joseph Goux points out, the blurring between necessary and superfluous "makes it so desperately difficult ... to find the opposition between the glorious, sacrificial, spectacular consumption of the accursed share ... and prosaically utilitarian consumption."[30] The representation of Dorian's excessively consuming body appeared so transgressive in Wilde's period because late nineteenth century capitalism was still shaped by notions of scarcity, productivity, and calculated consumption. Dorian's waste is therefore necessarily read as aristocratic, that is, attached to a class whose spendthrift modes, in the eyes of the Victorians, belonged to a prebourgeois past. As such, the protagonist's transgression could be read in social rather than in sexual terms and appeared potentially scandalous merely because of his excessive consumption.

In *The Picture of Dorian Gray* the discourses of scarcity and of abundance, which historically characterize two different phases of capitalist development, come to clash under the sign of Bataillean expenditure. What bourgeois culture presents as necessary, in Bataille's words "lodging, clothes, food and ..: a little harmless recreation,"[31] does not even slightly match the individual's interests in the "considerable loss" and "catastrophe" generated by nonproductive expenditure. In *Dorian Gray* the protagonist's penchant for waste and the squandering of wealth in useless objects that he consumes fetishistically appears as an enactment of Bataille's own protest against "[the] general atrophy of sumptuary processes" in bourgeois society.[32] This atrophy is more than once lamented in Wilde's novel, particularly when the hero denounces the narrow-mindedness of his elders in matters of consumption: "There was a rather heavy bill for a chased silver Louis Quinze toilet-set that he had not yet the courage to send on to his guardians, who were extremely old-fashioned people and did not realize that we live in an age when unnecessary things are our only necessities" (Wilde, 93). The slightest hint of shame regarding conspicuous consumption, discernible in quotes such as this, is, by the novel's ending, magnified into a Bataillean sense of "catastrophe" about the prolific consumption of the body itself.

For Bataille the principle of capitalist consumption is fully at odds with the logic of expenditure: Whereas the former advocates a calculated reinvestment of surplus, expenditure is a mechanism of loss. In *La part maudite* he concedes that when loss is turned into acquisition, the restricted exchange of capitalist consumption can reintegrate the accursed share as a thing: "The dilapidation of energy is always the opposite of a thing, but can only be considered once it has entered an order of things, transformed into a thing."[33] Yet the fetishistic logic of capitalist consumption distorts and obstructs the fluidity of expenditure. As Goux notes, expenditure is recognizable as transgressive only within the Weberian version of modern capitalism. When its impulse to loss is juxtaposed with and signified by the call to unproductive consumption trumpeted by contemporary consumer culture, for example, its transgressive power is lost: Productive consumption and unproductive squandering become indistinguishable. Notwithstanding Bataille's disavowal of "things"—commodities—as the appropriate channel for the wasteful dissipation of expenditure, in *Dorian Gray* the aristo-cratic conspicuous consumption of the protagonist is in fact a form of expendi-ture. In the novel to acquire means to waste, and accumulation of objects, plea-sures, new experiences, is perversely pitted against the bourgeois imperative to reinvest the surplus to produce more wealth. For instance, when Dorian buys the Louis Quinze "chased silver toilet-set" and doesn't dare to send the bill to his guardians, the possibility of bankruptcy is suggested by hints of moneylenders ("There were several very courteously worded communications ... offering to ad-vance any sum ... at the most reasonable rates of interest" [Wilde, 93]) willing to help Dorian plunge deeper in his ruinous economy.

The aesthete's desire for new sensations is granted through the conspicuous and fetishistic consumption of commodities. The expensive objects that Dorian collects allow his desire for the exotic and the new to circulate: Through his col-lections he assembles fantastic tableaux that he can inhabit and use to produce a newly fashioned self. The whole of the famous chapter 11 is dedicated to the al-most fastidiously accurate enumeration of the objects Dorian collects in his home museum:[34] The virtuoso, at the moment when the great public museums were being enlarged, becomes a subversive figure. In imitation of the unnamed protag-onist of the book Lord Henry had given him,[35] Dorian decorates a series of interi-ors, spectacles worthy of late-imperial exhibitions and glittering shop windows.[36] Through this spatialization of the phantasmagoria of the commodity, Dorian's identity changes and "multiplies" according, for instance, to the music to which he listens, the clothes he wears, or the location of the interior he inhabits. In "the sordid room of the little, ill-famed tavern near the Docks, which, under an as-sumed name and in disguise, it was his habit to frequent" (Wilde, 118), Dorian plays the role of the bohemian: The sordid aspect of the place "brings out" a con-sciousness of his abjection, in which he thrives. In the red and green music room, where "mad gypsies tore wild music from little zythers, or grave, yellow-shawled Tunisians plucked at the strained strings of monstrous lutes, while grinning ne-groes beat monotonously upon copper drums" (Wilde, 134), Dorian abandons himself to the pleasures of the "primitive." Or finally, when he takes up the study of jewels, he cross-dresses as an elegant woman "and appeared at a costume ball as Anne de Joyeuse, Admiral of France, in a dress covered with five-hundred and sixty pearls" (Wilde, 150).

With his life of imaginative debauchery Dorian fulfills Lord Henry's prophecy of the coming of "a new hedonism, that was to recreate life, and save it from that harsh, uncomely puritanism" of their times (Wilde, 130). But for the aesthete, as Dorian's tableaux show, to recreate the world means to repackage it as if it were a commodity on sale. The aesthete refuses the world's "use value," its prosaic puri-tanism, to refashion reality anew through his efforts to beautify his life. In this perspective aestheticism aims at transforming the phenomenal world in the same way that advertisement transforms the "meaning" of the commodity for the consumer by turning use value into pleasure-producing meaning. The desire to repackage reality and enjoy it fetishistically is written all over Wilde's novel; an exemplary moment is Dorian's rejection of Sybil Vane once her art vanishes, when he cries, "You have spoiled the romance of my life! ... Without art you are nothing. ... A third rate actress with a pretty face" (Wilde, 87). Along with her artifice disappears the fetish qualities that had attracted Dorian to her. The artificial and volatile character of Dorian's aestheticized reality, like the commodity fetish, promises a satisfaction that it will never give. Rather than melancholically lamenting this unkept promise, the novel deploys it to encode Dorian's transgressive expenditure in the circuit of suspended desire that sustains commodity fetishism.

In the universe of *Dorian Gray* a pleasure is such insofar as it denies satisfaction. A distilled image of the perverse libidinality that seals together consumption and expenditure is provided by one of Lord Henry's iconoclastic aphorisms: "A cigarette is the perfect type of perfect pleasure. It is exquisite and it leaves one unsatisfied. What more can one want?" (Wilde, 79). By apparently indulging in his debauches—from collecting precious and exotic artifacts to opium smoking to buying sprees—Dorian in fact suspends pleasure to let desire circulate indefinitely. This suspension is not an erasure. Satisfaction is not ruled out of the textual space of Wilde's text; rather, pleasure is encoded in the novel as a willed lack of satisfaction. This mode of suspension evokes the perverse libidinal temporality of masochism, and as such it becomes distinctive of Wilde's homoerotic signification. Both expenditure and masochism are subversive libidinal, diegetic, and economic tactics insofar as they disrupt a straight, linear articulation of desire. As such, this linear narrative structure relies on the orderly relation between production and limited consumption, and between desire and satisfaction, which characterizes both capitalist political economy and bourgeois signification. Because the aesthete relies on this masochistic suspension of pleasure, the very structure of his libidinality becomes outlaw. This is especially so when the aesthete's desire to "burn" his life away translates into the modes of the dandy's debauched expenditure: Then Dorian's excess becomes the occasion for a violation that must be punished and expiated. When the perfect balance between sensuousness and the intellect advocated by Pater seems to turn into the "vulgar profligacy" that, in Wilde's definition of aestheticism, is pitted against modern puritanism ("of the asceticism that deadens the senses, or of the vulgar profligacy that dulls them, it [aestheticism] knows nothing" [Wilde, 130]), the aesthete is subjected to punishment: Dorian's body, transferred onto the picture, begins to deteriorate and age grotesquely.

The portrait's changes are watched with a fascinated horror by Dorian, for whom the contemplation of the picture's disfigurement turns into a private spectacle of his own abjection. His expiatory self-degradation is, as Basil's "strange idolatry" had been, a secret: The masochistic pleasure in watching his bodily ruin is a solitary pleasure that Dorian experiences hidden in the secrecy of the attic. At the same time, particularly at the moment of Dorian's death, the disfigured body is presented to the reader as a sentimental spectacle of male suffering. The senti-mental tone punctuates the entire narrative of *Dorian Gray* through the recurring association of beauty, tragic suffering, and romanticized exceptionality: "My brains such as they are—my art, whatever it may be worth; Dorian Gray's good looks—we shall all suffer for what the gods have given us, suffer terribly" (Wilde, 31). This tone culminates in the novel's conclusion when the reader is reminded that although the dead Dorian is withered, in art—in the painting—he is beauti-ful and young. This sentimental finale, centered on the image of Dorian as victim, has the effect of erasing the memory of the process through which Dorian's body became degraded, a process of self-willed and self-imposed punishment. Dorian's liminal position between the sphere of masochism and that of sentimentality is prefigured by another masochized male body in the novel, that of the wounded and bejewelled body of Christ, whose camp image appears to be the focus of at-tention both for Dorian and for Wilde himself in chapter 11. From his collection of ecclesiastical vestments, Dorian had stored away in cedar chests "rare and beau-tiful specimens of what is really the raiment of the Bride of Christ, who must wear purple and jewels and fine linen that she may hide the pallid macerated body that is worn by the suffering that she seeks for, and wounded by self-inflicted pain" (Wilde, 139). The image of Christ "wearing" his wounded body underneath the church's flamboyantly decorative vestments suggests once again d'Aurevilly's view of the dandy drinking his own blood under his mask and remaining masked. At the same time, the "pallid, macerated body" of the male victim par excellence, Christ, is also a counterfigure of the wounded, degraded body of Wilde's hero, whose suddenly reconquered youth at the moment of his death allows his senti-mentalized image to reclaim his innocence and obtain sympathy from the reader.

After the trials, by subjecting his own body to the same sentimentalization, Wilde worked to displace his image as "the criminal" onto that of the victim. In *The Ballad of Reading Gaol* and in *De Profundis*, or even in his last persona as Sebastian Melmoth, Wilde tried to expose his by now publicly homosexual body as a martyred icon of innocence, the same icon of truncated youth that Dorian represented at the end of *Dorian Gray*. This identification with Dorian is more than a conjecture: In a famous statement, Wilde invited his public to read the novel's male characters as projections of his own aesthetic identity when he de-clared: "Basil Hallward is what I think I am; Lord Henry what the world thinks of me; and Dorian what I would like to be—in other ages, perhaps."[37] Wilde's desire to "be" Dorian had worked during his career as a means of both camouflage and exposure; it also implicitly affirmed a desire for social and national assimilation in a subject whom the British aristocracy and upper class, the class into which Wilde sought assimilation by posing as a dandy, reputed thrice improper: Irish, middle class, and gay. Dandyism had offered Wilde the means to produce a transgressive reinscription of bourgeois masculinity while at the same time revealing, if not flaunting, his homosexuality. It gave him the chance to "be Dorian" and yet be read by the public as an eccentric male subject *only* impersonating a series of roles (the professor of aesthetics, the editor of the women's magazine *Woman's World*, the brilliant socialite) whose gender ambiguity was always and promptly crashed against the bedrock of Wilde's identity as husband and father. By impersonating something that he really was (the subject/object of homoerotic desire) and forging anew something that he was not yet (the homosexual as a social subject), Wilde transformed himself into a masculine body in drag or, more precisely, in multiple drags: As a married man with a male lover, he was a gay man who "played himself" by masquerading as a (masculine) gentleman mimicking effeminacy. His eccentricity and gender-transgressive qualities, however, did not exclude Wilde from a highly visible public life, and from rigidly exclusive social circles. His appearance certainly played up the part of aspiring aristocrat that he had created for himself: His dandified persona, always tastefully attired, played the carnival without ever becoming grotesque.

Wilde's masquerades and multiple drags functioned to suggest and never fully show same-sex desire: Even in his "effeminate" elegance, the dandy's body aimed to be a classical body, androgynous, aristocratic, refined—once again, Dorian Gray's body. Wilde's desire to possess and to be the embodiment of the national idea of British masculine beauty was posed against what Sedgwick calls his own "alienizing physical heritage of unboundable bulk from his Irish nationalist mother, of a louche swarthiness from his celticizing father."[38] The anti-British witticisms that punctuate *Dorian Gray* and the rest of his work notwithstanding, Wilde's "body ideal" seems to signify a desire for assimilation into a national milieu within which he remained an outsider. Similarly, his dandiacal rejection of middle and lower class vulgarity in the name of aestheticism coincides with the bourgeois puritanical imperative of propriety in desexualizing the body. *Dorian Gray* is a novel centered on the gaze, and not on touch. Wilde uses the aestheticized beauty of the Greek statue, the cold sensuality of Greek (or British) perfection, to trick the eye of the middle class—that is, as a form of passing. At the same time, the abstraction that (despite Pater's denials) seems ingrained in Hellenism is advocated by Wilde to dismiss the mess of the body, the libidinal economy of the plebeian lower body, which, if made visible, would qualify him as an inadequate and uncouth outsider: Irish, a middle class parvenu, and a homosexual.[39]

By rejecting the materiality of sex in the name of art, Wilde repeats the gesture of one of the most famous dandies of the nineteenth century, Charles Baudelaire, who in *Mon coeur mis a nu* also divides the "cultivated" dandy from the uncouth masses: "Women cannot distinguish between soul and body ... whereas the dandy creates a more and more perceptible divorce between spirit and the brute. ... The more a man cultivates the arts, the less often he gets an erection. ... Only the brute gets really good erections, and fucking is the lyricism of the people."[40] Baudelaire opposes the brute, women, and the people with the spiritualized and aesthetic dandy. The same opposition, though not in the exact same terms, is reproposed in *Dorian Gray:*

> Good artists exist simply in what they make, and consequently are perfectly uninteresting in what they are. A great poet, a really great poet is the most unpoetical of all

creatures. But inferior poets are incredibly fascinating. The worse their rhymes are, the more picturesque they look. The mere fact of having published a book of second rate sonnets, makes a man quite irresistible. He lives the poetry that he cannot write. The others write the poetry that they cannot live. (Wilde, 56)

Yet the brute who gets really good erections and the bad poet who cannot write, and therefore makes of his life a work of art, are not quite the same figure. Art, even the dandy's art of living, while turning the body into a spectacle, also functions to conceal, displace, and erase its sexuality (in Baudelaire's words, "fucking"), to flatten it into a beautiful image, whether it be in Dorian's portrait or in a commercial advertisement.[41]

As long as art transfigures and redefines the vulgarity of life, the aesthete-dandy is fine. He can continue to weave his fictions and his selves and have good erections, too. Yet in 1895 art and life came to be at odds in Wilde's biography, at the time of the libel suit following Alfred Douglas's father's denunciation of Wilde as a "posing sodomite."[42] As in Pater's narration of Winckelmann's *Bildung,* touch, homoeroticism, and sexual transgression were violently reinscribed in the story of the aestheticized body as well as upon the persona of the dandy. While wearing his own body in drag through a sophisticated game of gender ambiguity, the refined aesthete had been having sex like the Baudelairean "people." In so doing, he had also transgressed the boundaries of his social class: His "fucking beneath" (with working class boys) or "fucking above" (with an aristocrat), when described in the courtroom, triggered in a time of relative social instability public anxieties about the solidity of the British social class structure. Fears about the permeability of the social body demanded a scapegoat; Wilde was decreed an outsider.

At the end of his career as an aesthete, Wilde had learned how "to fold his flesh as a garment," but he had not succeeded in remaining himself (after his textual and personal experimentations with subjectivity he knew, however, that there was no "self" under which to take shelter); nor had he managed to remain fully masked behind his mask. The complex and brilliant play of suspended signifiers of gender, sexuality, class, nationality, desire, and art itself through which Wilde had composed and dispersed his image was at the end used by the state's legal apparatus to freeze him in the mind of his public into the identity of the criminal. By refusing to leave England after the libel suit against Queensberry and before the beginning of the trials, he turned the state's condemnation into a gesture of self-immolation. Through his final self-impersonation as victim, Wilde evokes and encodes Dorian's body both as a wounded, pathetic image of male suffering and as a radiant, compensatory image of masculinity. Through this juxtaposition, that is, he attempted a reverse form of posing where his "criminal identity" could be redeemed through the sentimentality that his culture attached to the icon of the young, martyred male body. At the same time, desiring to be Dorian literally to death, he could be the first and most fascinated spectator of an exhibition of self-abjection finally made public—a spectacle he had been able to witness and to live only vicariously, in his writing, throughout his career.

# THE EPHEBE, THE SAINT,
# AND THE AESTHETE'S ILL BODY

The homoerotic male body, introduced and passed over without comment almost as soon as it was invoked by Pater in "Winckelmann" and subsequently made the object of dissimulative strategies of representation in *Dorian Gray*, is fully shown as an abject sight in Thomas Mann's *Death in Venice*, where it is displayed no longer through the filter of sentimentality but through the register of the grotesque. *Death in Venice* stands as a denouement of Wilde's narrative: By apparently renouncing the homophobic alibi—the conversion of the opposition homo-hetero into the dyad same-other, which produces the slippage between desire and identification we have seen in Wilde's work—Mann creates the image of an older male subject whose homoerotic desire is not displaced onto and appropriated to the younger body of the model as object. Rather, the protagonist's desire remains inscribed on the protagonist's own body and will, literally, contaminate him and make him ill. Mann's novella closes with the terrifying image of an infected, suffering male body joyously exposing his self-degradation, ecstatically disclosing his final and unredeemable abjection.

*Death in Venice* is the story of an upright and productive bourgeois, the writer Gustav von Aschenbach, who travels from Germany to Italy for a holiday, seeking to recover his health. Aschenbach travels from the North, coded as overtly rational and intellectual, *not* to be cured by a healthy South but to die a physical, real death in a miasmic Venice plagued by cholera. The place that should heal brings death; what should have been an ascent, a means of regaining his physical and intellectual powers, becomes a descent, a way to lose and expend them instead. Against this unstable background, Aschenbach's effort to reach beauty through the contemplation of the human form of the boy Tadzio becomes a story of self-abjection.[43] As in *Dorian Gray*, an older man's desire for a boy is at the center of the plot. But whereas Wilde excises this desire from the subject's body by projecting it onto that of the object, directing the reader's attention away from Hallward's desire onto the immaculate surface of Dorian's body and thus managing to safely lock away the artist's homoeroticism in the attic, *Death in Venice* foregrounds the story of the character that Wilde, as a form of self-protection, keeps out of sight. Notwithstanding his self-discipline, his resistance to and denial of same-sex desire—which pervades the novella—Aschenbach falls prey in the course of the story to the "abyss." In the book this abyss is defined first in terms of aesthetic theory as the Dionysian and erotic aspect of the artist's process of creation, then in geographical terms as "the South," and last in clinical terms as the epidemic that spreads in Venice and infects Aschenbach. The novella pervasively attempts to discipline the homoerotic body by placing it under the sign of disease. Mann turns the ill male body of the aging aesthete into the metaphorical image of the crisis of an entire class, the bourgeoisie at the outset of the twentieth century. With this metaphor, he implicitly seems to read homoerotic desire for the body of the ephebe under the sign of "degeneracy," which for Nordau and other conservative critics such as the eugenicists affected the social body of European culture in the fin de siècle.

However, while reimposing a phobic value upon the image of the sexualized male body, Mann uncannily creates the conditions for its full display as a spectacle to a degree that neither Pater nor Wilde had managed in the past. The spectacularization of masculinity in Mann's text, as in Germany in 1912, had not the same meaning as in 1890s England. Although in Germany homosexuality had been criminalized since the 1870s, this legal prohibition had had the effect of making the social identity of the homosexual visible with the formation of the first homosexual emancipatory movements,[44] so German homosexuals enjoyed a social visibility denied to their English counterparts. Furthermore, in contrast to Wilde, Mann had allegedly no personal interest in homosexuality, nor was he trying to articulate a representation of homoeroticism in the novella. In a 1920 letter to Carl Maria Weber he disavows the homoerotic intertext of *Death in Venice;* he admits to sharing Aschenbach's aesthetic concerns ("the altogether 'non-Greek,' but rather puritan, protestant ['bourgeois'] basic state of mind not only of the story protagonist, but also of myself"[45]), but he gives no relevance to the question of homoerotic desire. Rather homoeroticism seems to appear quite serendipitously in a fiction that he claims initially was supposed to tell the story of the aged Goethe's love for a girl in Marienbad: "Passion as confusion and a stripping of dignity, was really the subject of my tale. What I originally wanted to deal with was not anything homoerotic at all." Mann forecloses the question of his unqualified "slipping" into the representation of male homoerotic desire by defending homoeroticism against its contemporary detractors, who depicted it in terms of effeminacy and degeneracy (although, as I've pointed out, Mann himself situates same-sex desire under this rubric by enmeshing the theme of eroticism with that of disease); he affirms that neither Michelangelo, Frederick the Great, Winckelmann, nor Stefan George "were or are unmanly or feminine men."[46] He concludes his letter nonchalantly with a humanistic view of one version of homoerotic desire: "I see nothing unnatural, and a great deal of instructive significance, a good deal of high humanity, in the tenderness of mature masculinity for lovelier and frailer masculinity."[47] Notwithstanding Mann's claimed disengagement from the textualization of homoeroticism, it is significant that to tell a story of lost dignity and of bourgeois abjection, he deploys the structure of the "Greek" relationship between the artist and the model, the older man and the younger male figure, which had been integral to the fin de siècle discourse of aestheticism. The fact that the homoerotic male body is taken by a bourgeois novelist as the catalyst of aesthetic abjection, as the means, that is, to tell a story of demeaning fall and self-loss, points to what Sedgwick reads as one of the twentieth century underpinnings of the representation of homoeroticism, "a sentimental appropriation by the larger culture of male homosexuality as spectacle."[48] However, since the displacement of the older's subject's desire onto the body of the youth does not take place in *Death in Venice,* the sentimentalization of this desire cannot be completely accomplished. Aschenbach's corpse in the end inspires pity insofar as it is grotesque: Neither beauty nor youth, the qualities that he tries to reconquer by pursuing Tadzio, can redeem his complete abjection.

In turning Aschenbach into a body that "refuses" the protection and redemption provided by sentimentality, *Death in Venice* somehow reads the homophobic alibi backward, so that the slippage between desire and identification ("I do not love him; I am him") that we have seen at work both in Pater's and in Wilde's texts is reversed: Aschenbach pursues the boy Tadzio in order to "be" him rather than to love him. He needs to constantly watch the youth in the hope that his body will send back a refracted image of Aschenbach himself, and he ultimately follows Tadzio in order to occupy his place of young and exquisite victim. Whereas in *The Picture of Dorian Gray* the distinction between the subject and the object, the artist and the model, is collapsed to foreground a moment of oneness and of ecstatic fusion while at the same time allowing the older male figure to salvage his self, in the case of Aschenbach's pursuit of Tadzio, there is enacted a disincorporation between subject and object that leaves the older male figure contaminated by his own desire, inscriptor and inscriptee at the same time.

The image of Saint Sebastian is the key trope the novella provides to underscore Aschenbach's narcissistically desirous relationship to Tadzio. The choice of Saint Sebastian as the new "hero-type" on whom Aschenbach models himself is highlighted by one of the fictitious commentators on the writer's works quoted in the text: By borrowing the image of the saint, this commentator suggests, Aschenbach's puritan work ethic becomes tinged with an unexpected element of expenditure of which Aschenbach himself is not aware. Aschenbach's Saint Sebastian is "a youth that clenches his teeth in proud shame and stands calmly as swords and spears pass through his body," which he reads as "composure under the blows of fate, grace in the midst of torment—this is not only endurance; it is an active achievement, a positive triumph, ... the most perfect symbol ... of the kind of art here in question."[49] As the artist's very inspiration, the image of this pierced, wounded male body introduces an element of eroticism into the representation of Aschenbach himself, and it suggests that this eroticism is grounded in suffering. In this icon of youthful masculinity, where the Greek antiphobic enjoyment of the body and Christian sexual prohibition clash in a sexualized replica of the Greek statue, the marble of the ephebic form is replaced by a baroque triumph of the flesh, and physical pain is expressed as ecstasy. Aschenbach, as the "shrewd commentator" claims, embodies the elements of Saint Sebastian's image that point to the Hellenic ideal: "Elegant self-control ... the gracious pose and composure in the empty service of form." As such he appears not to see that the saint's self-restraint is not a form of detachment from the world, like the ataraxia of Pater's gods, or the asceticism required by the bourgeois work ethic, as with Aschenbach's own self-denying productivity, but rather a sign of masochism and of masochistic expenditure.

The saint's "proud shame" and the calm with which he clenches his teeth under the pain of the arrows do not fully foreground what made the image of the male martyr—in particular that of Saint Sebastian—so compelling to the turn of the century imaginary, especially, but not only, as a homoerotic fantasy. In its masochistic enjoyment of torture, the image of suffering becomes an expiatory occasion to flaunt the male body as a replica of the scandalous body of Christ.[50] The ambiguous juxtaposition of the sexual and the ascetic in the representation of the body of Saint Sebastian is foregrounded in a number of early twentieth century images of the saint, as well as in the portrayals of other masochized and saintly martyred male bodies. As an example, I will examine for a moment the photographs of the aesthete F. Holland Day.

Active in Boston at the turn of the century, Holland Day was affiliated with the British aesthetes, whose influence is recognizable in both the often homoerotic subjects and chiaroscuro technique of his art.[51] He was an innovative and experimental photographer as well as a publisher—the magazine the *Yellow Book,* unofficial journal of the aestheticist movement, appeared under the imprint of his firm, Copeland and Day. He met his idol Oscar Wilde during Wilde's 1882 tour of the United States and later became friends with William Butler Yeats and Aubrey Beardsley. Holland Day's series of photographs of youths impersonating Saint Sebastian embody the fin de siècle ideal of a Hellenic paganism stripped of any idealizing and classicizing abstraction and devoid of any religious alibi (Figure 1.1). In the photographs, sexualized male bodies seduce the viewer fetishistically, as do any representations of sadomasochism: Here Sebastian's "composure under the blows of fate" becomes pure sexual ecstasy, and the Greek statue's self-absorption is replayed as the self-absorption of a body experiencing an orgasm. In these images the pleasures of art of which Pater wrote in "Winckelmann," which demand "a higher sensibility than the beauty of nature, because the beauty of art like tears shed at a play, gives no pain … and must be awakened and repaired by nature" (Pater, 192), are juxtaposed with those of the homoerotic flesh under the same sign of artificiality. The painted wounds, the fiction of bondage shown in soft focus, reenact the algolagniac pleasure that played such an important role in the exquisitely perverse—or modernistically camp—homoerotic libido of the fin de siècle.[52] Both signifying the abjection of homoeroticism and the artist as suffering figure, Holland Day's Saint Sebastian represented an occasion for displaying masochized masculinity. The image of the wounded and seminaked male body recurs time and again in Beardsley's work, for instance; makes a cameo appearance in *Dorian Gray,* where Dorian owns a medallion with the saint's image; and was chosen by Wilde for his last impersonation, as Sebastian Melmoth, upon his release from Reading Gaol.

Aschenbach's narcissistic desire to "be" Tadzio, his using him as a mirror of his own self (albeit under the "aesthetic alibi," that is, by regarding him as the fleshy embodiment of the Hellenic ideal), becomes more and more obsessive and more and more shameful for the protagonist throughout the story. The way the austere writer and the boy exchange glances becomes an addictive, pleasurable, and shat-

*Figure 1.1 F. Holland Day,* Saint Sebastian. *From Estelle Jussim,* Slave to Beauty *(Boston: David Godine, 1981), p. 173.* Reprinted by permission of David R. Godine, Publisher, Inc. Copyright © 1981 by Estelle Jussim.

tering experience for Aschenbach, one that is continually sought at the expense of his own dignity and willpower. Ironically, as the narrator underlines, Aschenbach the ascetic producer and moral public figure is the author of *A Study of Abjection,* where he teaches that the human being can rehabilitate himself even when he has plumbed "the abyss of knowledge." Throughout Mann's novella "knowledge" stands for the "flame-like" sensations that Pater invites his readers to experience at the end of *The Renaissance* and for the very range of pleasures, passions, and expenditures that marked the homoerotic experience in *Dorian Gray.* While in Germany Aschenbach intentionally makes the decision to renounce "knowledge" ("in the recognition that knowledge can paralyze the will" [Mann, 294]); in the mind-numbing South he succumbs to his erotic-aesthetic desire for Tadzio as a means to again become in touch with his body and at the same time indulge in the fantasy that Tadzio's beauty will redeem both his "impure" desire for knowledge and his growing old.

Aschenbach's desire for and desire to "be" Tadzio is in fact frustrated by the incommensurable distance between the two bodies. His attempts to follow the youth, especially his indefatigable "chase" after Tadzio through the meandering *calle* of Venice and the impossibility of reaching him, make Aschenbach in the end pathetic, that is, worthy of the audience's sympathy. Indeed, Aschenbach situates himself in the sentimental position of the sacrificial victim when he heroically remains in Venice notwithstanding the explosion of the cholera epidemic. At this point the clientele of the elegant hotel where Aschenbach is spending his holiday are fleeing the city. Notwithstanding his desire to stay close to Tadzio, Aschenbach also goes, but because of a mishap he is forced to return to the hotel. The decision to stay in a city infected with cholera, thus exposing himself to the contagion that will be the cause of his death, is doubly self-sacrificial: On the one hand he sacrifices his life to be with Tadzio and on the other, by planning to go to the youth's mother and warn her to leave the city as the rationale for his staying, he transforms his return to the hotel into a fantasy of self-sacrificial expenditure, of complete self-dissipation through the waste of his own life. The act of self-denial through which Aschenbach achieves pleasure—the pleasure of his self-unmaking and, at the end, of his own shameful exposure, the horrible sight of his disfigured and suffering body—is intricately masochistic. Nonetheless, Aschenbach's "clenching his teeth in proud shame" once his health starts declining, and his more and more open pursuit of Tadzio, still cannot transform him into the sentimentalized image of "frailer masculinity" that the youth embodies. In fact, the way desire comes in the end to be grafted onto Aschenbach's body prevents the sentimentalizing maneuver that had redeemed, at the end of Pater's and Wilde's narratives, both Winckelmann and Dorian Gray.

The last scene of the novella is the moment when Aschenbach's abjection is theatrically displayed but not redeemed. Here, Mann accomplishes what neither Pater nor Wilde could do: He offers a full view of the desiring homoerotic subject at the moment of his self-devised abjection as a public exposure. This scene is dominated by the image of two bodies: While Tadzio is standing upright with his feet in the water, pointing for a moment to something high in the sky and following its trajectory with his arm, Aschenbach is lying in a deck chair, trying in vain to stretch his hand in the same direction. At the end of his quest, the writer has not become Tadzio: In fact, his effort to master his body into youth and shamelessness by beautifying it through makeup, new clothes, and died hair—all the dandy's ornaments—is what makes his death, within the ethical compass of the narrative, demeaning and the degradation of his body total. Before Aschenbach's final demise, his image comes to be inscribed with all the markers of abjection that Mann has disseminated throughout the novella: Disease, lower class impropriety (signaled by his clownish clothes), and the effeminacy of his makeup (which previously had signified the infectious dangers of some mandolin players who had entertained the guests at the hotel) reappear on Aschenbach's own body when, in the effort to appear younger and more attractive to Tadzio, he begins to wear loud clothes, jewelry, and scent. In his "broad-rimmed straw-hat, encircled with many-colored ribbons … the shape of his eyes lengthened, their brightness enhanced by a slight underlining of the lids" (Mann, 258–259), Aschenbach becomes a grotesque mask of the dandy, nothing less than the very image of d'Aurevilly's dandy who drinks his blood behind his mask and, this time in a game of total loss, remains masked too. The new dandified Aschenbach is a replica of the mandolin players, emanating his own odor of illness and death: His masquerade takes place when he has already contracted cholera, and rather than being a means of rejuvenation, it represents a tangible sign of the foreign body (of desire, homoeroticism, lower class vulgarity, sickness) that, the narrative implies, must be relinquished in order for the bourgeois subject to become healthy once again.

At the same time, this final scene is a triumph of masochistic ecstasy. The sight of Aschenbach's body—dying, dressed in an elegant suit, the brown of his hair dye leaking, the lipstick and the eyeliner smeared, his face reduced to a mask whose contours refuse to stay in place—is flaunted and comes to occupy center stage, replacing Tadzio as the reader's focus of attention. The presence of a camera on the beach—"On a tripod ... at the edge of the water, apparently abandoned, its black cloth snapped in the freshening wind" (Mann, 262)—reminds us that what contributes to Aschenbach's pleasure of abjection is his loss of control over the gaze: His voyeuristic pleasure in looking is finally transformed into the pleasure of being looked at, of attracting attention as a martyred body. While Tadzio's image fades in the background, Aschenbach is doubled up as the split subject of Freudian reflexive masochism who submits to his ego in order to obtain punishment, "beating" himself while at the same time watching himself being beaten or, in this case, witnessing the effect of having been beaten. By occupying two different positions at the same time, that of the gaze and that of the image, that of the subject and that of the object, Aschenbach dangerously threatens the structure of bourgeois masculine identity and of its exclusionary logic, and rather comes to literally occupy the place of the abject. Portrayed at the moment of his degrading death, Aschenbach is shown as becoming a corpse, taking up the space, as Julia Kristeva affirms,[53] where the subject ceases to be such.

However, the grotesquely devastated body of Aschenbach does not "magically" metamorphosize into the young, beautiful, and innocent body of Tadzio, as happens (if only to the painting) at the moment of Dorian Gray's death. Once this metamorphosis of the old and ugly into the young and beautiful corpse does not take place, Aschenbach can no longer be redeemed by becoming a sentimental icon of masculine suffering. In fact, his masochistic managing of this suffering signifies his resistance to being transformed into a sentimentally tragic victim of "fate" (as Saint Sebastian might be read): By desiring and orchestrating his own victimization, by reclaiming the power of staging this ecstatic squandering of the self, Aschenbach becomes an unmanageable corpse, an abject carcass that "doesn't go away" and cannot in any way be recuperated. Once Aschenbach is carried off the beach by two hotel servants, Tadzio comes to occupy once again the center of the reader's field of vision. This hysterical gesture of foreclosure through which the male homoerotic body is excised from sight at the end of *Death in Venice* is continually reiterated in early twentieth century culture and indeed comes to characterize the representation of masculinity in both high and popular culture at this time. The figuration of male eroticized abjection I have explored here returns to incite and even structure the radiant, healthy masculinity that in the new century mass culture is modeled on the image of a Tadzio-like ephebic and desexualized body.

# 2 THE HERO AND THE TYPIST: SUPERMEN, OFFICE CLERKS, AND THE PETTY BOURGEOIS BODY

A docile being, chiefly noticeable as the first hope of suburbia at any time. ...
If he has given the world any other impression ... it is the vague idea that he
has created the demand for five-a-penny cigarettes, the half-penny press, and
guinea mackintoshes.

—President, National Union of Clerks,
*Annual Report,* 1915

Obscure parson or distinguished judge, underpaid school-master or wealthy
merchant. ... Whatever the athlete's comparative failure or success in life, he
will rarely be found to have lost the self-respect that he acquired when he was
taught by those who trained him to respect and care for his body.

—Strongman Eugen Sandow,
*The Construction and Reconstruction
of the Human Body,* London, 1907

Dᴜʀɪɴɢ ᴛʜᴇ ꜰɪʀꜱᴛ two decades of the twentieth century a youthful
and natural body much like that of Tadzio became the symbol of a new concep-
tion of manliness, the outcome of a novel culture of rejuvenation organized
around ideals of purity, innocence, and rebellion. These tropes had a collective as
well as an individual dimension: Both the social body of the nation and European
culture itself as a sick body could be made stronger, polemics suggested, only
through the healing, cleansing, and training of the body of the individual. The
organizing trope of this new healthy and heroic masculine body was the corporeality of Nietzsche's superman, whose morally unfettered physical prowess and
self-affirming dynamism seemed to give form to the energies and protest of a gen-

eration, the famous "generation of 1914." The new apparently antibourgeois and certainly antidecadent culture of health and nature turned to Nietzscheanism and appropriated the Greek ideal that had been deployed by the aesthetes to tame it into a principle of disciplined, suffering, *and* instinctual masculinity—the agonistic masculinity of the superman turned athlete, boy scout, and, by 1914, soldier. This chapter is concerned with the transformation of the corporeal icon of the aestheticist 1890s—which in one strand of fin de siècle high culture had been the site upon which homoeroticism, expenditure, and dandified decadence could be at once celebrated and obscured—into an image of homophobic and authentic manliness acceptable to a newly arrived middle class.

The neoclassical body was now deployed to signify a masculine identity no longer founded on Victorian prohibitions; at the same time it was recast as a bulwark against the gender confusion produced by the aesthete's subversive signification. Wilde's textuality, and the effeminate dandyism through which he had passed both as a homosexual and as the member of the upper class, had implicitly denaturalized all gender categories by exposing the instability and inessentiality of masculinity. In the period following Wilde's trials, dominant culture deemed it necessary to firmly reestablish gender distinctions through an ideology of a "natural" masculinity that no masquerade could displace. Authentic virility appeared now to be inscribed on the body, solidly anchored to "nature" by virtue of its opposition to the feminine and artificial culture of consumption, that culture whose desires the fin de siècle aesthete had deployed to signify his transgressive excess.

This transformation of the idealized classical male body from ambiguous site of aestheticist masquerade to pillar of a new corporeality for an emerging middle class can be understood within the social context of the rise of a new urban petty bourgeoisie of clerks, shop assistants, typists, and "black-coated workers." In numerous European polemics of the years before and after the First World War fears of national and racial degeneration fed an antidecadent rhetoric that looked to nature as an agent of renovation. This renewed interest in "nature" was fueled by Nietzschean as well as by eugenicist discourses, both of which grew prominent in the prewar years. In turn, the new concept of the body that these discourses generated, and the idea of individual and national manliness attached to them, appealed strongly to the growing ranks of the petty bourgeoisie. In many cultural debates of the time this arriviste class was considered inferior and socially lacking in contrast to the established bourgeois ideal; figures such as Baden-Powell, writing after the Boer War, described this inferiority as a lack of virility. In the task of recuperating this virility, the classical body was refashioned as a middle class ideal.

Produced en masse by a vast expansion of the tertiary, clerical sector of the European economy, the black-coated petty bourgeois employee became a prominent figure in the cultural and social panorama of this period, from the comically obsequious clerks of *Punch* cartoons in Britain to the angst-ridden flaneur clerks of Kafka's Prague. With an ambiguous place in the rapidly realigning class structure, keen to repudiate his working-class or peasant origins but rejected by the established and now threatened upper middle class, the clerk could find a more fulfilling trope for his self-presentation in the apparently classless ideal of the natural body. The new image of instinctual manliness that was being manufactured through the discourses of eugenics and nationalism made available for the clerk a radical new image of masculine corporeality through which he could plot for himself a new identity, altogether different from the enfeebled and "feminine" subaltern role that bourgeois conservativism had attributed to him.

The particular technologies and spaces of the body that acquired such mass prominence during this period—sports, the gymnasium, the beach, and the countryside as the milieu of natural and *Volkisch* regeneration—fabricated images of athletic manliness for the male subject; at the same time they made his disciplined body available to the state, as well trained and responsive to its efforts toward bureaucratic efficiency, mass production, and military obedience. The employee, in turn, embraced the modern culture of the body both physically and ideologically in the attempt to fashion for himself a distinctive and positive social identity. Through the examination of the contrasting impulses at work in this cultural trajectory—Nietzschean libertarianism on the one hand and eugenicist puritanism on the other—I show how the clerk's self-representation and gendered sexual identity were invaded by the nation-state and used to interpellate him as a responsible citizen.

To illustrate how the image of the Greek statue is transformed into an icon of lower middle class national manliness, I analyze the economy of the body and its uses in the portrayal of two of the numerous literary representations of the petty bourgeois employee, beginning with the anonymous clerk in T. S. Eliot's *The Waste Land* (1922) and going on to explore how the clerk's masquerade is clothed in tropes of nature and natural struggle by Leonard Bast in E. M. Forster's novel *Howard's End* (1910). In each text, the authors' upper bourgeois gaze constructs these characters as inferior and inadequate. Eliot depicts the "young man carbuncular" as an emperor without clothes; Forster turns the clerk into a sentimentalized victim of the upper classes and of his own desire to "improve himself." Eliot's and Forster's condescending attitude betrays, I suggest, an intense anxiety about potential transgressions of class boundaries and the upsetting of social hierarchies: Their representation of the employee as an ersatz or shyly inferior figure has the curious effect of "feminizing" their characters' efforts to act and appear virile through their fabricated identity as, respectively, seducer and primeval man. Against the grain of this condescension, my analysis instead explains the "young man carbuncular"'s aggressiveness and Bast's desire to "return to the Earth" as these figures' particular appropriation of forms of early twentieth century Nietzscheanism then being made popular. By reading beyond each author's attempt to ridicule and victimize the employee, I focus on the specific strategies of self-representation through which these characters tried to overcome their sense of social inadequacy. I then go on in the second section of the chapter to show

how the discourse of eugenics colluded with and promoted this Nietzschean ideal of the strong male body and how this in turn was folded into the spreading ideology of nationalism: Nietzscheanism, eugenics, and rhetorics of nation all contributed, for example, to the image of Rupert Brooke, the icon of heroic and pure national masculinity at the time of the First World War. In the following section I turn to the figure upon which the employee's notion of manliness is structured, that of the Nietzschean superman, to investigate more thoroughly the reasons for its mass appeal for the petty bourgeoisie and for the younger generation in general. To do so I examine how Nietzscheanism was inscribed in social phenomena such as Baden-Powell's Boy Scout movement in England and the Wandervogel, the youth movement in Germany.

One reason for the superman's mass appeal lay in the classlessness of his body: His was a proletarian body strengthened by labor but now rendered as aristocratic. His aristocracy of the blood, rather than of birth or of money, made the superman equally distant from the established middle class and the lower class, and therefore placed him in the very position coming to be occupied by the petty bourgeoisie. The connection between the vitalistic "blond beast of prey," as Nietzsche defined the superman, and the body of the proletarian is foregrounded in such texts as Émile Zola's novel *La bête humaine* (The human beast) (1890), whose protagonist Jacques Lantier I analyze as a replica of the superman. Lantier's lack of moral conscience, which Zola attributes to heredity, would be demedicalized in the Nietzschean text and reworked into the joyous and classless animality of the superman. Subsequently, through the connected rhetorics of eugenics and patriotism, the Nietzschean ideal of rebellious and unbounded physical power was again disciplined into obedience and self-restraint. Thus it could be turned into the romanticized body of the young soldier who in 1914 would so eagerly volunteer for the trenches. The young Nietzschean, as well as the employee, at first saw the war as the climax and the realization of the heroism, aggression, and adventure that each had experienced only in his afterhours.

Although in the years preceding the First World War the unclothed modern male body modeled on the myth of the superman increasingly became a popular icon, it no longer signified pleasure and sexual expenditure but rather activity, finalized effort, and productivity. In fact, the image of the Nietzschean superman negotiates an unstable relationship between the aristocratic and self-contained neoclassical body and working class physical prowess signified by the immediate antecedent of Nietzsche's "blond beast of prey," the muscular body of the proletarian. Nietzschean corporeality is an attempt to suture this contradiction into a language of a "natural" aristocracy in which race and nation replace class in defining a new version of masculine power. The Nietzschean body as icon of modern virility remains riddled with irreconcilable contradictions: The asceticism and self-denial imposed on his body by the Nietzschean masculine subject through the use of his will invokes on the one hand the spirituality and self-restraint that bourgeois culture valorized and on the other the self-sacrificing quality of expenditure, the perverse logic of masochism whose shadow always haunts the healthy, sportive, and upright masculinity of the athlete, boy scout, and soldier. This merely hinted at, never fully invoked, masochistic pleasure of self-denial eroticizes the male body while apparently stripping it of its sexuality, and indirectly carries the memory of the wasting practices through which the fin de siècle aesthete had worked to unmake masculinity.

## MANAGING THE AFTERHOURS

The petty bourgeoisie that arrived on the European scene around the turn of the century was no longer the old lower middle class of "peasant farmers, artisans, shopkeepers, clerks, lower officials and elementary school teachers"[1] but rather a recognizable group whose origins can be traced to the aftermath of the Great Depression of 1875–1890. This depression ended the economic phase inaugurated by the British industrial revolution and marked the beginnings of a new monopoly capitalism based upon the decline of free markets, the rise of protectionism, and the rise of large trusts and cartels. The depression had resulted from a crisis of overproduction,[2] so attempts to end it gave an unprecedented impulse to national consumption and to new distribution businesses. As one social historian notes, "The 1,500 multiple stores of 1880 had grown to 11,645 by 1900 while the 217,000 people in commercial occupations in 1871 had expanded to 896,000 in 1911. There was a massive increase in consumer demand if only because of the expansion in population, which in a quarter of a century added ten million people to the number of consumers of clothes, foods and services."[3] The petty bourgeois employee occupied the newly important positions of salesman, account keeper, and organizer of distribution in the consumer culture of the fin de siècle (and the twentieth century), when the amalgamation of commercial firms, banks, and insurance companies created the need for ever more clerks, themselves all potential consumers in the new culture of leisure, mass advertising, and what Thorstein Veblen in 1900 labeled conspicuous consumption.

Already in the late nineteenth century the new petty bourgeoisie, spurred on by advertising, was striving to live up to the "lifestyle" (a term coined by Alfred Adler in this period)[4] of the middle class. One sign of middle class distinction, for example, was the possibility of taking holidays, and the employee became more and more visible at popular seaside resorts: "In 1888 William Miller found Scarborough 'a good deal frequented by clerks and others who got a week's holiday, or cared to spend as much as a week's holiday costs.'"[5] The article that launched H. G. Wells's career in journalism was a piece entitled "The Art of Staying at the Seaside," written in 1893.[6] For the employee, however, practicing the new consumerism was barely within his means: The yearly holiday or trip to the seaside, unless paid for by the firm, could not be taken easily. His wages were not much higher than those of the skilled working class, and his spending power was vastly less than that of the actual leisure classes, the middle and upper bourgeoisie. With the new century the expansion of clerical work in larger and larger offices massified and further lowered the employee's status. In England, the introduction of mass education in the 1870s increased the number of potential clerks by opening clerical careers to ambitious working class children.[7] With the introduction of the typewriter in the 1880s women entered the office en masse as typists, and by 1911 they constituted one-fourth of all clerical workers in England.[8] Since women clerks were paid less and granted a lower status than men, their presence contributed, in the eyes of their male counterparts, to lowering the clerk's status still further.

Earning usually between 25 and 300 pounds a year at the end of the century,[9] the clerk was rarely able to enjoy middle class living standards; yet the nonmanual character of his occupation gave him a degree of respectability that allowed him visibly to detach himself from the working class.[10] The clerk's bourgeois aspirations posed problems of definition and separation for the class above him, the group for whom an income of 1,000 pounds a year was considered adequate and from which most of the writers and intellectuals were drawn; its members, in turn, were attempting to shape their public lives on the model of the older elites' conspicuous leisure. Despite this spiral of consumer spectacles in which each class was urged by the new advertising to imitate that above it, signs of class demarcation in Edwardian Britain were, if anything, heightened rather than destabilized. Along with "the puritan ethic and the values of work and effort, accumulation through abstention, duty and moral earnestness," as well as "their ferocious energy,"[11] the petty bourgeois were keen to imitate the new impulse to leisure and consumption—the life that Ronald Firbank, Evelyn Waugh, Elizabeth Bowen, and others would satirize—that seemed to characterize the Edwardian middle class.

At the same time the lack of any class tradition and class consciousness made the employee a prey to any ideology that seemed to suture his sense of distance from the middle class and minimize his feelings of social impropriety. Whether produced through a process of social regression (as in the case of the "petty clerk" *morto di fame* ["starveling"] Antonio Gramsci describes in *The Prison Notebooks*[12])—or by social advancement, the petty bourgeois was haunted by an ambiguous social identity. No longer "popular" and not yet bourgeois either, he found himself outside his class of birth, always eager to demarcate himself from the working class, struggling to be included in the bourgeoisie. As Gramsci observed, its potentially subversive character made this class an important element in possible hegemonic alliances, either with the right or with the left, and a potential danger for the social order.[13] In reality, the new clerkocracy's stifled ressentiment of those above it and a guilty loathing of those beneath it, as well as the lack of a clear "place," made it highly receptive to the burgeoning ideology of nationalism. By identifying themselves emotionally with the nation, the petty bourgeois masses found an identity denied to them in class terms.[14]

The figure of the clerk refashioning himself as a virile hero appears again and again in literary works of the new century, as Gregor Samsa in Kafka's "The Metamorphosis," Leonard Bast in E. M. Forster's *Howard's End* (1910), George Emerson in *A Room with a View* (1908), Leopold Bloom in Joyce's *Ulysses* (1921), and the sensitive self-improver Paul Morel in the truss-factory office in D. H. Lawrence's *Sons and Lovers* (1913). It was in poetry, however, that the high bourgeois skepticism of the new class was expressed most vehemently, especially in the vision of the clerk in T. S. Eliot's *The Waste Land*. In "The Fire Sermon" the soothsayer Tiresias envisions the setting of a love scene:

> *At the violet hour, when the eyes and back*
> *Turn upward from the desk, …*
> *I Tiresias, though blind … can see …*
> *The typist home at teatime, … lights*
> *Her stove, and lays out food in tins.*
> *Out of the window, perilously spread*
> *Her dry combinations touched by the sun's last rays,*
> *On the divan are piled (at night her bed)*
> *Stockings, slippers, camisoles and stays.*[15]

In the schedule of the employee, the "violet hour" signals the moment when the freedom of the private sphere—in contrast to the uneventful and frustrating day-by-day working routine—can begin. A scene of seduction is about to start in this unusual version of the boudoir: The "young man carbuncular," another clerk, arrives, conquers, and leaves. Yet his self-assurance and boldness, through which he places himself in the role of the *homme fatal,* has extremely little impact on the typist. Although she dutifully yields to his caresses in an appropriately feminine way ("[he] Endeavors to engage her in caresses / Which still are unreproved, if undesired"), as soon as he leaves, she expresses her relief. She looks in the mirror to reclaim possession of her image, temporarily discomposed by the lovemaking:

> *Hardly aware of her departed lover;*
> *Her brain allows one half-formed thought to pass:*
> *"Well now that's done: and I am glad it's over."*
> *When lovely woman stoops to folly and*
> *Paces about her room again, alone,*
> *She smooths her hair with automatic hand,*
> *And puts the record on the gramophone.*

Eliot portrays the relationship of this petty bourgeois couple as the most sterile version of love, utterly filtered through the crass sensibility of massified modernity evacuated of value. What we see is indifference, instincts, "vile bodies" (Waugh's term about a higher class) enclosed in a claustrophobic space filled with commodities—the food tins, garments, sofa bed, gramophone—the consumer gadgets of a massified and throwaway culture. The poet's tone stresses his intense sense of the vulgarity of these figures and shows their actions—"love" in what he vilifies as an unromantic setting—as ennui-ridden and hopeless. As he makes clear in this condescending portrait of members of a class he abhorred, the clerk has neither *physique du rôle* to play the hero (he is a "young man carbuncular") nor social status: He belongs to a subaltern class, his everyday role that of a subordinate. Therefore, he has no right to the boldness and self-assurance he flaunts ("A small house agent's clerk, with one bold stare, / One of the low on whom assurance sits / As a silk hat on a Bradford millionaire"). However, Eliot's moralistic term "vanity" to indicate the clerk's will to live a banal situation as romance and his desire to "transfigure" reality is not quite adequate to register the pathos of the self-presentation that the clerk enacts. The encounter is told in a mock-heroic language, worthy of eighteenth century poetry, that naturalizes it while working as satire: "His vanity requires no response / And makes a welcome of indifference." Yet beyond Eliot's despising tone, this passage portrays more than a scene of petty bourgeois lovemaking rendered as triviality: On the one hand it symptomatically discloses the work of imaginary self-representation through which the petty bourgeois male and female subjects "figure" their relation to their real conditions of existence; on the other, it illustrates how the distinction between masculinity and femininity is enforced by situating the typist and the clerk on the two opposite sides of the "great divide" of mass culture. Eliot, despite his sarcasm, turns out to deftly side with the clerk in this tug of cultures; he presents the reader with an image of the "young man carbuncular" as a faded image of the self-creating genius, the character who transforms reality with his imagination and projects himself into the role of hero and conqueror.

At the same time, through the poet's spiteful irony, the scene suggests that the opposition between the two characters is less stable than their gestures and aspect claim: By virtue of their class status they both appear "feminized." Consider how the implied meanings of this scene of *The Waste Land* resonate with my discussion of the clerk's deployment of the Nietzschean body, and especially with the particular strategies by which both the clerk and the typist articulate their afterhours identities. What is interesting in the passage is neither the failure of the two characters to live a romance nor the result of this failure, the decline of an implied sacred character of love, but rather the *meaning* that is invested by the two figures in this effort. Why is the space and time of the afterhours so important for the roles with which these two characters supplement their everyday, public identities? Through which images are these characters emplotting themselves? How are these imaginary identities produced and made accessible to them during this period?

Notwithstanding this thoroughly traditional gender-coded division of romantic roles, with masculine activity matching feminine ennui, the distribution of power between the two is subtly ambiguous. When acting as a valiant body and as the hero of a romance, notwithstanding his class and his physical inadequacy, the "young man *carbuncular*" is already embodying the vigor and the virility that characterizes the Nietzschean superman. His manly self-representation in the guise of the conqueror enables the employee to separate himself from the "feminine" masses and the "mechanical" and tinned-food culture of which the typist is a symbol. In so doing, he tries to embody a self-possessed image of phallic plenitude, centered on the power of the instincts.

The clerk's performance of his masculinity is posed by the poet as the active role of self-creation, whereas femininity is presented as an effort to resemble, to look like, to appear. The "young man carbuncular" performs a version of gendered subjectivity, and Eliot allows his right to such a performance, however scathing he may be of it. The typist, instead, is not allowed to produce a magnified and larger-than-life version of herself. She is the image of woman in and as mass culture; she is enclosed in the claustrophobic sphere of feminine narcissism and artificiality. Turning herself into a "beautiful image"—the object of her own fetishistic desire—she is associated with the meaningless marginality of the everyday and of the commodity itself. This stark distinction between the clerk and the typist shows how the anxious effort by the middle class to stabilize gender definition worked in practice. The typist is posed by Eliot as an inscription of the devalued culture of the detail, which Naomi Schor sees as a crucial Other of idealistic aesthetics and humanistic discourse. In the early twentieth century, through a long-standing process of what Schor describes as "secularization, the disciplining of society, consumerism, the invention of the quotidian, the developing of means of mechanical reproduction and democratization,"[16] the particular, the nonoriginal, and kitsch as a secondhand aesthetics became the fulcrum of the culture of modernity. Yet its new visibility and diffusion at every social level merely worked further to devaluate the detail's status.[17] In the eyes of the conservative high bourgeois, as well as in those of such avant-garde modernists as Eliot himself, mass culture encoded as woman, as in the figure of the typist in her flat, remained an inferior medium of cultural expression. As such it was fully entwined with the male bourgeois subject's fear of the "feminine" masses and their engulfing power; in the words of Andreas Huyssen, "Male fears of an engulfing femininity are ... projected onto the metropolitan masses, who did indeed represent a threat to the rational bourgeois order. The haunting specter of a loss of power combines with fear of losing one's fortified and stable ego boundaries, which represents the sine qua non of male psychology and bourgeois order."[18] The projection of feminine qualities onto the masses and their culture was an apotropaic gesture through which the male bourgeois subject, whether established or arriviste, tried to compensate for his own anxieties about losing individual and social control; for example, the feminization of mass culture that took place at this time in aesthetic and political discourse expressed masculine anxieties about the lower-class and female invasion of the public sphere of the late liberal polity. The poet as spectator of the scene of seduction enters into an interclass pact with his "young man carbuncular" in which both have in common as males a distrust of the female as bearer of a kitschified consumer culture.

Whereas Eliot's typist needs to recompose in the mirror the idea of what a pretty view of herself should be, the clerk needs to discompose himself and un-make his frustrating everyday image. He cannot be a hero in the office: He needs a special time and space where he can play out his "real self" and his ressentiment in the role of Casanova. Ultimately, through his self-aggrandizing fantasies and his sexual expenditure, the clerk is himself a figure of the consumer trying to replicate, at the time of the afterhours and in the nobody's land of the typist's apartment, the image of glamorized and powerful masculinity that he might have seen in the cinema or in sports magazines.

The management of the time of what came to be called "leisure" and the manage-ment of leisure's potential excess was a major concern of modern workers' wel-fare, as evidenced by the program of building YMCA and YWCA gymnasia in British cities after 1880, the rise of Boys' Brigades before the Boy Scouts, and the new popularity of such mass spectator sports as football.[19] By these means, the production and government of the instincts was efficiently designated to particu-lar "sites dedicated to the body"—from sports stadia to "holiday camps"—where the employee's body could be celebrated, "liberated," and trained. These spaces may be seen in Foucault's terms as heterotopias,[20] which he defines as "counter-sites, effectively enacted utopias in which the 'real sites' that can be found within the culture, are simultaneously represented, contested and inverted." He cites gar-dens, brothels, cemeteries, and colonies as examples. The modern "other spaces" where the body could "be itself" include "nature"—the rambler's and cyclist's countryside, the beach, the newly invented holiday camp—and the gymnasium and football field, as well as the typist's apartment. During this period the after-hours and their heterotopic spaces, increasingly managed by industries of leisure and entertainment, expanded and progressively came to dominate the everyday experience of masses of people and of the black-coated clerks in particular.

Staged by the modern individual in such heterotopic spaces, the "representa-tion, contestation and inversion" of real social sites or of such real identities as the clerk's subalternity functioned for him as a dream of emancipation structured within subtle forms of subjection. Whereas the afterhours allowed the employee to fashion a more gratifying imagined identity that allowed him to escape at least temporarily his frustrating subalternity, the new spaces of leisure were organized in such ways that in them discipline was further introduced into his life. The spaces where the petty bourgeois compensated for his lack of social recognition through the effort to improve himself physically turned out to be dominated by the same principles of regimentation that organized his life in the office: As James Walvin points out, "The games were in keeping with that discipline, and in fact reinscribed regulated rhythms of work."[21] It must be underlined, however, that in the employee's new, powerful, and healthy corporeality, discipline was inscribed as a form of pleasure so that he could be transformed into a strong *and* docile body precisely at the moment when he was enjoying himself. Rationalization of the workplace was followed by rationalization on the playing field, especially in the turn of the century national organization of almost every popular sport: Wilde's accuser, Lord Queensberry, for example, was author of the rules governing boxing, and England's most popular sport, football, was given standard regulations by 1910. Its organization as a national game with specific rules, bureaucracy, and mass publications was staged at the time as a diffusion of upper class "British values"; the model invoked was the public school system, particularly the example provided by the "muscular Christianity" fostered by Dr. Arnold at Rugby.[22] These new rules inevitably encoded high bourgeois values into the employee's afterhours. Soon football, for example, changed from a pastime focused on violence and individual physical strength into ordered and well-orchestrated teamwork. Self-control, alertness, and discipline were prized by both the now professional team players and the increasingly important spectators.

This barely perceptible exchange of pleasure and discipline in the organization of leisure activities took place at a time when the older distinctions between private and public spheres were becoming tenuous. In a period concerned with the management of the masses ("efficiency" was one of the great slogans of the early twentieth century workplace) and rapidly moving toward an increasing regimentation of social life, the private sphere, a territory traditionally attached to domestic space, and the public one, most commonly signified by the arena of work, production, and subordination, became more permeable categories. The clerk's afterhours, the time away from the panopticist supervision of the office and from its ethos of duty, were no longer exclusively spent at home. Rather, the privacy and freedom that leisure seemed to provide were made available to him in the modern heterotopias as seaside trips, hikes in the countryside, organized sports, and paid holidays. The activities and the spaces through which the clerk contested his subalternity were more and more frequently managed publicly by his or her firm or by the state.[23] Often the individual entrepreneur's paternalistic care for the firm's employees provided the very comforts and relaxation that had been previously managed by the family or the individual himself.[24] At the same time, the home became more and more subjected to the very principles of efficiency, hygiene, and functionality that regulated the office and Edwardian society at large,[25] so that the heterotopia impinged more and more upon the everyday until the point was reached when they could be exchanged and confused. Just as the fin de siècle aesthete in his lavishly and extravagantly decorated interiors and through the fantasies inspired by his fetishistically collected bibelots had found a space where he could fashion new identities through an imaginary and compensatory fantasy of corporeality, so too the new middle class clerk found in the gymnasia, sports clubs, and rambles in the countryside heterotopias through which a novel culture of the body and a new form of normative masculinity might be fabricated.

## IMPROVING BODIES: FROM
## LEONARD BAST TO
## RUPERT BROOKE

The culture of the ambitious, uncertain petty bourgeois employee and the importance of the afterhours in his everyday experience are rendered ambivalently by E. M. Forster in *Howard's End*[26] (1910) in the figure of twenty-one-year-old Leonard Bast, who works as a clerk at the Porphyrion Fire Insurance Company. We first encounter him during his afterhours, at a classical music concert at Queen Anne's Hall. The concert, like his reading, expresses his claim to gentility and signals his effort to embourgeoisify himself through the education he never formally received. The pathos of Bast's efforts to improve himself and of his unequivocal sense of inferiority is accentuated by the implicitly socially superior narrator through a detailed description of the clerk's living quarters: His rented rooms, although furnished with an eye to status, with the piano and statuettes of Cupids on the mantelpiece, nevertheless, claims the narrator, strike "that shallow makeshift note that is so often heard in the modern dwelling place" (Forster, 48). Perusing this meager and massified existence, assuring the reader that it is not a slum but looking down on its tawdry vulgarity, the narrative voice undercuts the clerk's attempts at self-improvement with impunity. Bast plays the piano "bad and vulgarly," and his reading of Ruskin ("I care a good deal about improving myself by means of Literature and Art, and so I am getting a wider outlook. For instance, when you came in I was reading Ruskin's *The Stones of Venice*. I don't say this to boast, but to show you the kind of man I am" [Forster, 54]) is interrupted by a dinner that begins with "a soup square … just dissolved in some hot water." Notwithstanding its touches of cultivated gentility, Bast's apartment is reminiscent of the typist's "boudoir" in *The Waste Land* and is equally characterized by what both texts imply is the artificiality of mass culture, here grimly evoked by the "soup square."

Forster's novel is premised on an accidental encounter between Bast and a member of the higher bourgeoisie he imitates—an encounter that arises from his self-improving efforts. His only taste of upper class life, therefore, is obtained through a mishap. After the concert, Helen Schlegel, an upper bourgeois young woman of German descent who was also in the audience, takes his umbrella by mistake. The clerk follows her home, where he is given a card by Helen's sister, Margaret. Bast's next visit to the Schlegel women takes place after his Saturday walk in the countryside. Under the influence of his reading of Thoreau, Borrow, and Jeffreys and "talks of that at the office," Leonard has taken the subway to Wimbledon and from there gone "into the woods" (Forster, 118). By "getting back to the Earth," as he puts it, the clerk is trying to put into practice during his afterhours, and in a way he can afford, the knowledge he has acquired from his books. At the same time, he is attempting to redeem his stuffy and subordinate life by living an adventure and by impersonating the role of the primeval man in nature.

(His is the ethos that was giving rise to the spreading residential suburbs and "garden cities" of the period.) What is most important for him, however, is the fact that he can tell the Schlegels about his adventure: Returning to nature and rising socially are intertwined in his mind while the ironies of this conjunction are played out in the text.

The Schlegels' interest in his night walk makes it appear as transgressive and heroic and, at the same time, makes him feel as if he is their peer. However, the different meaning that the sisters and the clerk attribute to his hike reveals Forster's own ambiguously deprecatory *and* sympathetic view of the lower middle class and its members' use of their bodies. For Bast his return to the Earth is enacted as a drama from the pages of high culture, a literary pilgrimage through hiking: "Have you ever read *The Ordeal of Richard Feverel?*" Margaret nodded. "It's a beautiful book. I wanted to get back to the Earth, don't you see, like Richard does at the end. Or have you ever read Stevenson's *Prince Otto?*" (Forster, 117). In a scene of farcical contrasts, the Schlegels, instead, are stirred by the sublimity of what they perceive as a merely natural and physical experience and are not in the least interested in Bast's middlebrow literary knowledge. Margaret and Helen project onto Bast's night excursion their own desire for adventure and nature; the Surrey countryside through which the employee roamed appears to them as a romanticized heterotopia, and as such signifies the "wildness" and freedom they are denied because of their gender and class. As an upper bourgeois woman, Margaret knows only a domesticated version of the "Earth," the English countryside at Howard's End, the cottage that in the end she will inherit from the Wilcoxes. In this context, Margaret's nationality is represented as a key element of her character: Whereas socially she is an insider of British high society, her Germanic background constructs her as an outsider, sharing similar desires and fantasies as those of the arriviste employee.

Although Margaret romanticizes Bast's "return to the Earth," she never stops regarding him as an inferior, just as, for the clerk himself, his Thoreau-and-Stevenson-inspired dreams of his own postromantic communion with the natural does not manage to erase the awareness of class. For Margaret, his only redeeming, and at the same time degrading, quality is his peasant origins, which she reads as the outcome of a tragic modernity: "One guessed him as a third generation, grandson to the shepherd or the plough-boy whom civilization had sucked into the town; ... one of the thousands who had lost the life of the body and failed to reach the life of the spirit ... and Margaret wondered ... whether it paid to give up the glory of the animal for a tailcoat and a couple of ideas" (Forster, 113). Notwithstanding Bast's symbolic return to the primeval life of the woods, the "glory of the animal" in this case is certainly not that of the superman. In fact, the "lost life of the body," which Bast has given up after two generations (his grandparents were "nothing at all ... agricultural labourers" [Forster, 237]), is simply the life of the peasant, an already archaic figure in England at the turn of the century, whose associations were most starkly enunciated by Marx in his infamous phrase "rural idiocy." As a cultural icon, the peasant belonged to a disappearing natural order that was at any rate, as Hardy's fiction made clear, always already inscribed by social power—that of the landed class that often owned the land the peasant worked. Through her further romanticization of the clerk as a peasant manqué, her counterposing of Bast's reading of Thoreau with her own of Hardy and Yeats, Margaret depicts him as a figure valorized and degraded at the same time.[27]

It is fitting, therefore, that Bast gazes at peasants for the first and last time in his life when he travels to Hilton by train on his way to Howard's End: "That they were men of the finest type only the sentimentalist can declare. But they kept to the life of daylight. They were England's hope. Clumsily they carried forward the touch of the sun, until such time as the nation sees fit to take it up" (Forster, 323). Here Bast anticipates the sun as image of vitalism that D. H. Lawrence would employ in his later stories; Lawrence also examined his own relation to agrarianism in his first novel, *The White Peacock,* published in 1911. The narrator's view of the peasants as a pure, higher race of "yeomen" whose earnest qualities, despite their appearance, distinguish them from the destructive but energetic "imperial" figure ventriloquizes Forster's own national sentimentalism, a modernist version of the agrarian romanticism that had nurtured national identities at least since Michelet's *The People* of 1838. Against this vision of the "yeomanry," Leonard Bast will always be found wanting. With appropriate irony, Bast's vision of the peasants comes before he is (unintentionally) ruined by his benefactresses; at Howard's End he is killed by the very means through which he had tried to improve himself, nature and books. This employee dies away from the city, once again immersed in nature, and at the hands of one of the Wilcox sons. Helen Schlegel is expecting a child from Bast and Charles Wilcox, with the intent of avenging Helen's honor, wounds him with a sword: The clerk loses his balance and hits a bookshelf, which collapses upon him. Thus he dies literally suffocated by books.

This ironic conclusion to the novel and Margaret's shifting attitude toward the clerk point to the author's ambivalent feelings about lower middle class ambitions and the nexus of sentimentalized corporeality and socially pretentious high culture in which he had placed them. Forster projects onto both Margaret and Bast his own discontent with the ossified conventions of bourgeois life, but at the same time he distances himself from this antibourgeois protest by representing the clerk as an inferior and insignificant individual, whose social inadequacy is a fit object of ridicule. At times, Bast is derided by the narrator quite gratuitously, and many of these jokes, beginning with that of the mistaken umbrella, focus on the clerk's clothing, his appearance, his body. Thus, for example, when Leonard, bare-headed in Regent Street, imagines that he's attracting the hostile attention of the crowd, "He put his hat on. It was too big; his head disappeared like a pudding into a basin, the ears bending outwards at the touch of the curly brim. ... Thus equipped he escaped criticism. No one felt uneasy as he titupped along the pavements, the heart of a man ticking fast in his chest" (Forster, 125). This Chaplinesque image of the human machine, of the employee as a modern automaton with feelings, for a moment seems to humanize Bast, but his portrayal by Forster is as condescending as Eliot's description of the "young man carbuncular." *Howard's End* represents the lower class clerk as a subaltern, inferior (to the author and, he expects, to other members of his class) both culturally and physically. Bast's "return to the Earth" does not turn him into a superman but rather reveals how grossly unfit he is to play such a role. Instead of being even an enjoyable experience, his walk exhausted him: "Lord, I did feel bad! Looking back, it wasn't what you may call enjoyment. It was more a case of sticking to it. I did stick. I—I was determined" (Forster, 120). Bast's unathletic body, along with the clerk's determination, is made the butt of Forster's joke to further degrade his character to the status of the supposedly "narrow-chested" yet dangerous poor.

Leonard Bast, moreover, does not show any sign of petty bourgeois ressentiment. Rather, in Forster's representation, he appears to have thoroughly and obsequiously internalized the condescending gaze of the middle class. Eliot's "young man carbuncular's" rambunctious pretenses as Don Juan, on the contrary, let the reader guess this resentment. Eliot's employee is not trying to imitate the manners and the culture of the bourgeoisie; rather his desire to aggressively and actively overcome the badge of social inferiority given him by the class above finds its medium not in the master's tools (literature and art) but in what is forbidden by upper class morality and propriety: sexual pleasure and physical prowess. The role model for Eliot's clerk is not Richard Feverel, the hero of a novel, but the modern popular culture icons of the sports star, embodying strength and physical power, and the film star, representing the same values in a more sexualized form. Between 1910, when *Howard's End* appeared, and 1922, the year of *The Wasteland*, George Meredith's self-conscious, literary kind of male hero had, for the new class of clerks, been replaced by the stars of the football leagues and the reinstituted Olympic Games and by new film stars such as Rudolph Valentino.

From the point of view of the hegemonic class, the petty bourgeois clerk as an individual who lives according to a fabricated image of himself, modeled like Leonard Bast on the image of the proper bourgeois or, like Eliot's antihero, on that of the popular star, is always an impoverished copy of an original that remains inaccessible to him. His own identity is constructed by a double gaze: Although he sees himself as a master through his self-reflection in the champion, the star sportsman who performs before a crowd, his self-representation is also shaped by the gaze of the class to which he aspires to belong—a class that, on the contrary, sees him as mass, crowd, mob. The effect of this double gaze is visible in Eliot's clerk: This figure's act of mastery, his affirmation of power over the typist, is realized as an act of self-abandonment, expenditure, and irrationality. In this instance, the moment when the clerk affirms his individual identity is also, paradoxically, the moment when he loses it by losing his self-control.

〇   〇   〇

This double aspect of the clerk's personality, at once self-assertive and self-conscious of his "commonness," made him vulnerable to the image of the massified individual studied by such consciously antidemocratic polemicists as Gustave Le Bon in his *Psychology of the Crowd* of 1895.[28] The possibility of being confused with what Le Bon saw as the herd-like modern masses was dreaded by the employee, because the feminine irrationality and lack of self-restraint attributed to the crowd were the very features that the middle class in its polemics, and as we have seen in its literature, had used to characterize the petty bourgeois character. For Le Bon, the stable boundaries of identity were dissolved when the individual became part of the hysterical mob: "By the mere fact that he forms part of an organized crowd, a man descends several rungs in the ladder of civilization. Isolated, he may be a cultivated individual; in a crowd he is a barbarian—that is, a creature acting by instinct."[29] The crowd, he explained, has the power to make the individual not only act differently but also "feel" and perceive himself differently: "The transformation is so profound as to change ... the honest man into a criminal, and the coward into a hero." Le Bon attacked mass psychology as having the power to unchain the worst qualities of the individual, making him regress to a primitive state: "impulsivity, irritability, incapacity to reason, ... which are almost always observed in beings belonging to inferior forms of evolution—in women, savages and children, for instance."[30] The reference to "women and savages" as nonhuman here exemplifies the way in which, in Le Bon's schema, masculinity is the qualifying element of individual identity. The individual, to be recognized as such, must be able to show at all times a manly character. What Le Bon warns his readers against is the danger of regressing to a bodily existence—to instincts unchecked by reason, morality, responsibility—and, therefore, of becoming "like a woman." By following the spirit of these ideas, the clerk could have salvaged the effective subjectivity that high bourgeois suspicion had denied him, but only by embracing a version of virile and "independent" masculinity.

Le Bon's argument was part of a widespread turn of the century discourse, often couched in metaphors of a degraded and diseased body, through which conservatives and Fabian reformers alike trumpeted the ruin of western civilization. These metaphors acquired an immediate and lasting resonance in the first decades of the new century; in Oswald Spengler's *The Decline of The West* (1926), for example, this downfall was described in clinical terms as the physical decay of the body politic: The West was compared to an ill organism, weakened, exhausted, ultimately lacking vitality. Following the logic of the metaphor, it was felt that if civilization was an ill organism, the medico-cultural problem of its decay must be resolved on the terrain of real bodies: The ill must be singled out, cured, and separated from the healthy. The element that could guarantee this discrimination, it was realized, was no longer, strictly speaking, property, money, education, manners, and social status, which were by now not only coveted but were also being made accessible in various degrees to the petty bourgeois arrivistes.[31] Given the instability of the old boundaries of class, the new criteria of social demarcation and exclusion were not so much based (in these polemics at least) on education or "worth" as on the body itself, regarded as a biological entity in which "blood," race, and gender are naturally inscribed as strains of a potential nobility. As such, the spectacle of the body became crucial as the site where various polemics could adduce supporting evidence—where the biological sciences and the nascent strands of sociology could make common cause, above all in the discourse of eugenics.

The new prominence of the individual body as itself a symptomatic, evidence-bearing site where the social body would show up its physical realities was grounded in and reinforced by a discourse of public health deeply steeped in eugenicist theory. Eugenics was driven by a dream of the medicalization of public policy; in 1904 one of its leading propagandists in England, Francis Galton, declared eugenics to be "the study of agencies under social control that may improve or impair the racial qualities of the future generations either physically or mentally."[32] For the eugenicists, medical and biological knowledge was to be applied to the practical aim of improving the level of fitness of the human species. This interest in improving the species, and in particular the white race, appeared particularly urgent at the beginning of the twentieth century, when the fear of national degeneration, specifically imagined through the decay of the national physique, became a prominent subject of polemics in England. The tenor of the times is suggested by the titles of active committees: The Committee on Physical Deterioration, for example, was convened in 1903; the National Council for Public Morals, which included such figures as Rider Haggard, published *Youth and the Race* in 1922.[33] This fear of decay dated back to the last two decades of the nineteenth century, a response to the acceleration of urbanization and industrialization. The period witnessed a renewed concern for slum conditions: G.F.C. Masterman's *The Heart of Empire* of 1901, for example, speaks of the young men of the East End of London as "stunted, narrow-chested, easily wearied, yet voluble, excitable, with little ballast, stamina or endurance."[34]

By the turn of the century, such texts as Charles Booth's *Life and Labor of the People of London,* which was published in volumes between 1989 and 1903 and which described a "Class A" of "loafers" and a "Class B" of laborers, and Seebohm Rowntree's 1901 work, *Poverty: A Study of Town Life,* had provided the social research and statistics in urban squalor and destitution that the eugenicists cited as proof of the "general decay" of the British population. In the newly popular penny press, as in the reporting on the work of the Committee on Physical Deterioration of 1903, statistical evidence was used in sensational fashion to support the eugenicist theory of racial deterioration. This theory acquired the patriotic resonance that had always underlined it when, at the time of the Boer War, reports of the Inspector General of Recruiting revealed that in Manchester three out of five men who wanted to enlist in 1899 had to be rejected because they were physically unfit.[35] In the face of such evidence of "national physical decay," figures such as Baden-Powell and Rider Haggard called for measures to improve the vigor of "the British race." For the eugenicists, such improvements could be accomplished only by reestablishing a perfect balance between the healthy groups of the population, represented by the professional middle classes (or, as Sidney Webb called them, "the servant keeping class"[36]), and the unhealthy ones, the poor and the colonized. It was the eugenicists' contention that this balance had been deeply upset: A major public concern, shared by Fabians such as Webb, was the declining birth rate in England and, in particular, its uneven decline across the population. Francis Galton's disciple, the geneticist Karl Pearson, pointed out that "twenty five percent of the population are producing fifty percent of the next generation. The racial mixture of the British people ... is undergoing a rapid transformation, and since the 'worst' stock in the community are increasing, while the 'best' stock are drying out, the process signifies nothing less than national degeneration."[37] For Pearson selection by parentage was the answer to this problem; less extreme eugenicists saw a possible solution to the question of decay in national campaigns of hygiene and exercise. These campaigns, aimed at the poor, were inevitably most successful at interpellating the new middle class, who were taught to find respectability in the pursuit of "nature" and above all in the disciplining of the physical body.

The patriotic and nationalist tenor of the eugenics movement became most apparent in the years before the First World War; at this point, the Edwardian dream of efficiency was united to that of racial superiority in the notion of the nation's, as well as the body's, fitness. Galton wrote about fostering "a more virile sentiment, based on the desire of promoting the natural gifts and the National Efficiency of future generations."[38] A prominent eugenicist couple, W.C.D. and C. D. Whetham, specified that only patriotism, the love for one's nation, and the desire for racial purity could motivate individuals to improve the national physique: "The social instinct, readiness for self-sacrifice to the common good, love of home, country and race ... all are needed to bring to birth ... a nation fit to hold its own in the fiery trial of war, and in the slow, grinding stress of economic competition."[39] In such passages, the image of the healthy, powerful male body, which Nietzscheanism had spread as a model of antiliberal and antisocial rebellion, was harnessed by the rhetoric of the nation and shown as a fit sacrifice to the common good. The Whethams' phrase "social instinct" handily mediates between the shameless, individualistic corporeality of the nationalistic superman and the bourgeois imperative of selfless service to the community.

Nationalism and eugenics in tandem signaled the reassuring message to the new lower middle class that they could, by individual effort, differentiate themselves from those beneath them and feel themselves, in Webb's approving term, among "those sections of the population that gave proofs of thrift and foresight."[40] Eugenicists considered the symptoms of decay they saw in modern England as problems of national physiology; eugenics suggested a biological, medical solution to problems that were social. At the same time, eugenics as a discourse of nationalism blurred questions of class difference through the rhetoric of the national body, of which each British subject, without distinction, was part. Further, it provided new reasons, with the legitimizing trappings of scientific proof, to brand and eliminate undesirable strains in the population: the poor with their tuberculosis and bad habits, the "anomalous" and restless colonized, unpopular foreigners. The healthy insiders were identified with what was believed to be the physical and moral traits of the Nordic race: blue eyes, blond hair, and the "masculine" capability of mastering and self-mastering. Those who would not conform to this stereotype—women, homosexuals, Jews, "savages," and strangers—could be branded, with scientific backing, as outsiders. The clerk's fit body, then, would be a guarantee of his superiority to the feared "submerged tenth."

If British eugenicist polemics used a creed of bodily improvement to interpellate the expanding middle classes to national fellow feeling, in mainland Europe the principles of eugenics represented the scientific foundation of an even more blatant Aryanism, the racial theory that proclaimed the superiority of a particular type of body—male, white, blond, and blue-eyed. In Germany in particular this racist discourse, focusing on the body, underpinned the arguments of right-wing nationalism. Arthur Moeller van den Bruck, the major theorist of the *Volkisch* ideology around the time of the First World War, affirmed that the *Volk*, the nation, was defined by a common culture centered upon the correspondence of *Blut und Boden*, blood and soil, race and the land. Moeller defined nationalism in terms of the relation of the body to a landscape: *Das Volkstum*, the essential quality of the nation, was founded upon this inner identification between the individual, the group, and "the land," the national landscape. The rootedness of the nation in its land he interpreted as a transcendental, and transcendence-granting, relationship capable of generating power and renewal. Such rootedness was deemed historical: The ancient Teutons, he wrote, brought to others the culture they learned from the land. In *Die italienische Schönheit* (The Italian beauty) (1913), he explains how the destruction that the Langobards brought in the Middle Ages was proof of their "worldview" (*Weltbild*), "acquired in the woods and marshes of their native home, under the dawn of Nordic light ... [and brought] for the first time into the daylight of world history."[41] Whereas the British eugenicist polemics had often thematized class rather than race and were often tempered by a liberal concern for the actual conditions of poverty, from both the eugenicist and *Volkisch* perspectives, the most important characteristic of the nation was its physical efficiency and its "purity." Only by sharing the same blood, the same country, and the same language, both discourses suggested, could the national body be healthy and pure.

回      回      回

In Britain, in the early stages of the First World War, the body of Rupert Brooke was made to perfectly represent these very national virtues. If stardom, an invention of popular entertainment in this period, is the inscription of glamour for a mass audience upon the body of an "ordinary" figure, then Brooke was the first star of a new twentieth century mass nationalism. The image of his refined, "aristocratic," and "Aryan" beauty, reproduced on the frontispiece of his posthumously published collection of sonnets and publicized as widely as the images of music hall and screen stars of the same period, made available a body type representing innocent and manly heroism for much of his generation of young Englishmen.[42] Transformed into a patriotic monument after his death (he died from blood poisoning on his way to Gallipoli in 1915), Brooke had lived a life of mild bohemian rebellion against the bourgeois values of the intellectual elite to which he belonged by birth.[43] In Cambridge he had, as one of the Pagans, practiced an upper class version of a more free and natural mode of living and reveled in spontaneous activities centered on the body: walking in the countryside, swimming naked, and sunbathing. In a 1918 memorial article on Brooke, Virginia Woolf even praises this version of heartiness in assuring her audience that his "return to nature" was not a pose but a deeply felt impulse: "He was the type of English young manhood at its heartiest and most vigorous. ... Under his influence the country near Cambridge was full of young men and women walking barefoot, sharing his passion for bathing and fish diet, disdaining book learning and proclaiming that there was something deep and wonderful in the man who brought the milk and the woman who watched the cows."[44]

Woolf's eulogy represents Brooke as a figure in whom the return to nature and to the body mixes a romanticization of the life in the countryside with the imperatives of hygienic self-restraint (the diet of fish, the walking, the swimming) preached by eugenics as the means to restore national health. The image of Brooke offered to the arriviste class of clerks like Leonard Bast was a new model of contact between the subject and nature, one that suggested intensity but was in most aspects suburban. Just as the house of the same name in the novel *Howard's End* offered the book's newly bourgeois readers an ur-version of the half-timbered Tudor suburban villa, so Rupert Brooke presented would-be suburban dwellers with a vision of corporeality in touch with nature that appeared rebellious but was firmly focused on restraint.

For the purposes of wartime propaganda, moreover, these complex signals of naturalness and class had to be further abstracted (and almost, but not quite, disembodied) into a sacrificial ideal of manliness. By foregrounding the disciplined aspect of Brooke's identity, Winston Churchill, First Lord of the Admiralty in 1915, turned the young upper class poet who had imitated R. L. Stevenson in his colonial tourism to the South Seas[45] (whereas Leonard Bast could merely read Stevenson's works) into a disembodied and sacrificial figure: "Joyous, fearless, ver-

*Figure 2.1 Rupert Brooke in 1913 in a retouched photograph by Sherill Schell, frontispiece of* Sonnets, *1915 (Cambridge, Mass.: Harvard University Press, 1979).*

satile, with classical symmetry of mind and body, he was all that one would wish England's noble sons would be in days when no sacrifice but the most precious is acceptable, and the most precious is that which is finely proffered."[46] After Brooke's death in April 1915, his war sonnets were published and immediately became a cult text for British young men of his generation. The frontispiece of the volume was a heavily retouched photograph Sherill Schell had taken of an ethereal Brooke in profile with his shoulders bare (Figure 2.1). This stylized photograph, even more than the poems themselves, turned him into an ephebic and spiritualized figure whose elegiac gloss covered over the vigor, rebellion, and earthiness that, according to Woolf, his body had signified for himself and his friends.[47] Brooke's upper class, athletic body was Hellenized by the state to advertise the pure and strong manliness that could save England from degeneration and from its enemies as well. In fact, Schell's photograph as an image of the beautiful boy dying young exposes Brooke's body as a sentimentalized *and* sexualized icon of masculinity and makes it available for consumption not only to bourgeois pietism but also to a desirous gaze. Yet in the eyes of the state Brooke's ephebic and wounded masculinity—a trace of what in the fin de siècle had been a chief vehicle of homoerotic signification—functioned now merely as advertisement for the nation. Brooke's image validated the choice of the 1.5 million volunteers who had signed up for the war by the end of 1914 alone—half of this number was recruited at football stadia in speeches after the games. These idealistic Tommies, like Leonard Bast during his night hike, would soon become hungry during their march, and after encountering not the gamesmanship and the adventure that war propaganda advertised but the death and desolation of the trenches, they would discover, like Forster's employee, that they did not enjoy the walk.

Brooke's was the perfect representation of the new modern male body, in which the Nietzschean impulse to nature and vitalism was rationalized by the state through eugenicist discipline and patriotic sentimentality and immediately fetishized into the sacred figure of the pure young man who offers this body for his country. Hence, Brooke's innocent naturalism marks the culmination of the process through which the Greek body, which in Tadzio remained marked by vestiges of homoerotic desire, is progressively desexualized and finally turned into a national, purged, and functional version of the animal masculinity of Nietzsche's superman.

"Come and die. It'll be great fun. And there's great health in the preparation," Brooke had written with ironic bravado to his friend John Drinkwater in January 1915. The fictional death of Leonard Bast in 1910 and the real death, popularized for mass consumption, of Rupert Brooke in 1915 bracket a historical moment of an interclass exchange of ideas and motifs in which the body of the new type of male employee was addressed as natural in order that it might be controlled by the ruling class. Bast's death—after it turns out that his body, despite its peasant ancestors, does not measure up to any Thoreauean or Nietzschean ideal of the natural—reassures the upper bourgeois reader that the threat the ambitious clerk with his thrusting body seems to signify is in fact a mirage. Bast is exposed, implicitly, as a pathetically incomplete figure and as a weakling—a word that had gained common currency among moralists in those years. Brooke, in contrast, was a member of the high bourgeoisie: A graduate of Cambridge, he had an income of 150 pounds a year, which was not much more than an ambitious clerk could aspire to in midcareer except that Brooke did not have to work to earn it. With the popularization of his sonnets after his death, however, these specifics of his class position were elided; even the famous portrait of him revealing naked shoulders not only cast him as a classical ephebe but also removed the collar and coat that would have marked him as belonging to a certain class. Transformed, through his representation as the same Greek statue that we have already seen valorized by the aesthete, into an English everyman, his purpose as icon was to appeal to the (presumably callow) Leonard Basts and invite them to imitate him by going off to fight and die in the Great War. In other words, the presumed wildness or dangerous "uncouthness" of the clerk, a potential for disorder that might be discerned on his body, was by 1915 being successfully interpellated by the ruling powers on their own terms; rendered as a model of Aryan and classical heroism upon the body of one of their own class, it could be given back to the clerks and shop assistants as an embodiment of British character to which they might aspire. This successful fitting of a "refined" neoclassical body upon the "uncouth" and potentially disruptive body of the clerk meant that what was now offered to the employee, whose corporeality had been derided, was nothing less than the body of the superman. The superimposition of the neoclassical body upon the body of the clerk was accomplished through recourse to a popularized Nietzscheanism, the diffusion and effects of which I will examine now.

## NIETZSCHEANISM AND THE NOVELTY OF THE SUPERMAN

The most outstanding trope of this modern culture of the body as the site of spontaneous naturalness and authenticity for the individual was the image of the Nietzschean superman. Nietzsche's ideas had become extremely popular among young educated Europeans from the 1890s onward, when his critique of German Wilhelmine society and of Judeo-Christian morality gave impetus to and fused with a wide range of political positions from anarchism, sexual libertarianism, and feminism to right-wing nationalism and socialism.[48] (By 1918 Thomas Mann could write that one did not merely read Nietzsche, "one experienced him.") Nietzsche's work was itself the product of a late nineteenth century shift in intellectual and cultural attitudes; it was influenced by, even as it influenced, the fin de siècle disaffection with liberal pieties and the kind of polemics that read the social body through tropes of the strength of the physical body. As such, Nietzscheanism contributed to a series of antirationalist movements of social and cultural protest of the time. These included the generational rebellion of groups (like that around Rupert Brooke) that helped fuel a new "youth culture" and the anticapitalist and neoromantic desire to return to the land, which in turn informed both the *Volkisch* ideology of the Ramblers in Germany and the versions of vitalism described by modernists such as Forster and D. H. Lawrence.

Nietzsche's superman, the *Übermensch*, provided the petty bourgeois with a larger-than-life identity on which to model his own self. Yet as Forster's own ultimately romanticized view of the peasants in *Howard's End* shows, the animality of the superman was already encoded in the body of the lower class laborer, either the peasant or the proletarian. Before turning to the early twentieth century readings of Nietzsche and to the Nietzschean text itself, one needs to remember that the immediate precedent for the superman's physical power and instinctuality was the body of the proletarian. Given these antecedents, to claim that the new class of clerks found in the image of the superman a version of ideal corporeality raises a set of questions regarding class confidence and the representation of the body. How could the employee class, aspiring to become bourgeois, invoke as the model of its own subjectivity a corporeality that throughout the previous century had been associated with the brute force of the laboring classes? How can the petty bourgeois himself appropriate this body without becoming engulfed in the class and gender it had traditionally signified and rather see it as signifying an elitist "aristocracy of blood"? What I will suggest is that once a large part of the working male population was no longer engaged in manual labor or even on the new assembly lines of the factories but rather employed as clerks and "white collar" workers, there was no practical need for a physically strong body. The body of the clerk was newly made available as a site of an alternative constellation of signs symbolizing forces from personal integrity to national power. His newly superfluous body, having ceased to become necessary to the actual work of production, had become the scene instead of ideological contestation. In this spectacle, the return to a valorization of a physically strong body, which had formerly been the body of the laborer, represented a strategic deployment of an archaism. It represented at once a muted tribute to the clerk's origins, a betrayal of his fear of the power of the class he had left behind, an attempt to outdo that class at its own self-display, an acknowledgment of the unconscious appeal of the worker's sexuality, and above all an attempt to inscribe new idioms of personal hegemony upon an older spectacle of the physically strong body. Uniting this array of signs inscribed upon the clerk's exercised body, the Nietzschean notion of the superman allowed the clerk to transform what could be read as traces of the laborer's body, and hence of the clerk's own origins, into a spectacle of a new kind of aristocracy based on individual will. The clerk's unnecessarily muscled body could connote his new aspirations along with traces of the origins he rejected: It was these two messages that the Nietzschean narrative could absorb.

The particular quality of the superman's lingering monstrosity, the anxiety about classes left behind that would continue to be implicit in the image of the strong male body, had already been made evident in the way Émile Zola had articulated the abnormal in his novel *La bête humaine* (The human beast) of 1890.[49] Part of Zola's Rougon-Macquart cycle, the novel is a net of interwoven stories about fin de siècle French railroad life. As a social document, a story of love and adultery and a thriller *noir*, *La bête humaine* was initially conceived by its author as an investigation into the figure of the murderer as a type of abnormal personality. The "human beast" is Jacques Lantier, a young train driver implicated in two murders, once as a witness and once as the perpetrator. As the offspring of a family "contaminated" by alcoholism, he is "doomed" by heredity to be a criminal with uncontrollable homicidal tendencies: Jacques cannot make love to a woman without desiring to hurt and destroy her body. Thus he kills his lover, Severine, driven by an inexplicable impulse, incomprehensible to her and to himself.

Zola's construction of the beast relies on a view of sexuality as the channel where irrepressible drives as well as the "poison" tainting Jacques's blood flow together. In this way, while the weakness of his flesh is presented as evil, it is at the same time pathologized, and—if not made acceptable—at least justified in biological terms that the eugenicists would have found familiar, that is, as "hereditary taint." Jacques's homicidal impulses are specifically aimed at women. Depicted as an ancestral vengeance, his violence is defined as male; as such, it reinscribes a patriarchal paradigm of female submission. Notwithstanding its atrocity, the idea of a primordial "voice of the blood" is almost glamorized: "Did it come from the remote past, some malady with which women had infected his race, the resentment passed down from male to male since the first betrayal in the depth of some cave?" (Zola, 67). The image of "the blond beast of prey" employed at about the same time by Nietzsche is anticipated in the moment when the word "male" slips into the place of "beast." "He realized that the male in him ... would push open that door and strangle that girl, lashed on by the instinct of rape and the urge to avenge the age-old outrage" (Zola, 69). But this is only a moment: "Animality," monstrosity, and murder are posed as hereditary and pathological and given a precise class character. Jacques is a proletarian, the product of disadvantaged social conditions: Through this particular explanation of his "instinct," Zola unravels his social agenda, transforming the reader's condemnation into possible empathy. Conversely, the sexual perversion of Grandmorin, the president of the railway company, and his own compulsive instinct to rape is foregrounded but never analyzed by Zola.

By focusing on Lantier, the author ultimately works to medicalize and discursify the proletarian body and to declass its unruly sexuality while winning the reader to the cause of the protagonist. Jacques never ceases to be the figure of a "good giant," and the conclusion of the novel enforces this image by bringing together, at the core of a powerful, beast-like image of masculinity, a masochistic gesture of self-sacrifice among the sentimental figures of a troop of dying young soldiers. In what might be considered a final expiatory (and protofuturist) gesture, Jacques launches his train in a suicidal race while transporting a convoy of young soldiers to the German frontier. In this final scene, the "human beast" atones for his criminal tendencies with his own violent death, and his image seems to be redeemed by the proximity of the young soldiers, the custodians of peace and of France's national security. Yet Lantier never acquires a sense of guilt or morality: Even his act of final expiation is another crime. As the Nietzschean "blond beast of prey," he never repents of his misdeeds.

This symptomatology of "the beast within" is provided by Zola through his study of the abnormal male body of the dangerous proletarian—a member of the class of mechanics that was growing up alongside that of the clerks. It is foregrounded also in Nietzsche's texts, but here cleansed of the class anxiety that marks Zola's writing. In his rage, violence, and destructiveness, Lantier might be considered a protosuperman: His most Nietzschean quality is the *masculinity* of his violence. For Nietzsche too the beast is male: Both in *Twilight of Idols* (1888) and in *On the Genealogy of Morals* (1887),[50] the German philosopher stages a breathtaking reversal of traditional tropes of gender, so that instinct is no longer coded as feminine and reason is not valorized as a male trait. In both texts, instinct, animality, and the body are now represented as masculine, whereas reason, morality, and the intellect are put under erasure and associated with feminized figures: priests, women, slaves, the herd, and the rabble. Yet comparing *la bête humaine* of Zola and "the blond beast" of European philosophy, one discerns elements that unequivocally distance these two conceptions of the body: First, Nietzsche abandons Zola's social discourse; therefore, the blond beast is *not* the body of the proletarian. Further, Nietzsche elides class as an explicit social category; his hero belongs to a racial elite. Second, the superman's criminality is devoid of any immediate sexual overtones; his desire to kill is not centered primarily on women but rather is represented as a form of unchanneled and unspent energy. Nietzsche's view of criminality unequivocally reverses Zola's paradigm: What makes man criminally abnormal is not the wildness of the body and the distance from civilization, denounced by Zola in the living conditions of the worker, but rather man's *being in* civilization itself. The Nietzschean monstrosity cannot be explained by physical degeneration or heredity: The sick body of man, instead, has been produced through centuries of discipline, that of Judeo-Christian morality:

> The criminal type is the type of the strong human being under unfavorable circumstances: a strong human being made sick. He lacks the wildness, a somehow freer and more dangerous environment and form of existence. ... It is society, our tame, mediocre, emasculated society, in which a natural human being ... necessarily degenerates into a criminal.[51]

Deprived of a space where his wildness can be appropriately expressed, tied down by Christianity, this man has been reduced to one of the herd, and his body has grown ill.

In Nietzsche's schema, the superman's criminality and illness are *produced:* They are the material effects of an ideological activity, Christian morality, that has been at work in social and religious practices for centuries. Yet when Nietzsche moves to the *pars construens* of his theory—how to recuperate that which the priest has atrophied by discursifying it negatively, the body—he reverts to a language of origins, thus falling into what could be called an essentialist trap. The body as the place of instincts and nature is posed as an authentic and transhistorical category, always already present in the "noble races" of the past and the present—"the Roman, Arabian, Germanic, Japanese nobility, the Homeric heroes, the Scandinavian Vikings," as Nietzsche lists them in *The Genealogy of Morals.*[52] The "blond beast" is dormant in man, but it can be "awakened" at special moments and in special spaces:

> Once they go outside, where the strange, the stranger is found, they are not much better than uncaged beasts of prey. There they savor a freedom from all social con-

straints. ... They go back to the innocent conscience of the beast of prey, as triumphant monsters who perhaps emerge from a disgusting procession of murder, arson, rape and torture exhilarated and undisturbed of spirit. ... The hidden core has to erupt from time to time, the animal has to get out again and go back to the wilderness.[53]

The space "outside" of civilization, where man can become superman and recover all his feral and joyous freedom, here again functions as the employee's heterotopia, his afterhours, the place where he thinks he can finally take off his encumbering social mask and become himself.

Just as Nietzsche represents the "animal" in each man as a bedrock of authenticity, so he falls into the same form of essentialism when writing specifically about the body in *Thus Spoke Zarathustra* (1892). On the one hand, the body is presented as "performing" subjectivity: "Your intelligence, my brother, which you call 'spirit' is also an instrument of your body. ... You say 'I' and you are proud of this word. But greater than this ... is your body and its great intelligence, which does not say 'I' but performs 'I.' "[54] On the other hand, the body is presented as the *source* of identity, authenticity, and truth, as no longer subverting but replacing reason and its function: "Body I am and soul—thus speaks the child. ... But the awakened and knowing says: body I am entirely, and nothing else; and soul is only another word for something about the body."[55] The Cartesian deletion and submission of the flesh is reversed into an almost Blakean triumph of the body over the soul. This central reversal became instrumental for the generational protest against the culture of the "elders" and their authority, which made Nietzscheanism such a pervasive cultural force and animated German youth culture in particular in the early twentieth century. The image of the prophet Zarathustra, alone in nature, speaking his wisdom from a wild mountain landscape, inspired and reinforced the modern cult of *Bergeimsamkeit,* the "solitude in the mountains," the desire to flee the city to "find oneself" in the heterotopic space of nature or, subsequently, in the romanticized and heroically dangerous "elsewhere" of the battlefield. At the outbreak of the war, *Thus Spoke Zarathustra* was the most popular book among literate German soldiers; copies were given free to the troops and commentators noted that it was even more popular in the trenches than the Bible.[56]

Nonetheless, the Nietzschean body is not lawless, nor does Nietzsche wish to do away with the subject: In the new subjectivity of the superman the body and its instincts are no longer held in check by reason but by will. Kant's question of the "self-imposed tutelage" upon the individual self and of action through the individual's exercise of his own discernment—two elements through which the autonomy and free will of the bourgeois self had been historically predicated—is recast in terms of the individual's power over the body through the exercise of his will. As the locus of a "material spirituality" no longer governed by the priests, the body is not allowed to dissipate itself in expenditure but rather becomes the testing ground for the subject's willpower. The most important evidence of this corporeal spirituality is "not to react at once to a stimulus, but to gain control of all the inhibiting excluding instincts. ... [This] is what is called a strong will; the essential feature is precisely *not* to will, to be able to suspend desire. All unspirituality, all vulgar commonness depends on the inability to resist a stimulus."[57] Notwithstanding the parallels in this concept with the masochistic logic of suspension of pleasure, here the Nietzschean superman's will to power has very little to do with the aesthete's "disciplinary" self-indulgence. Whereas for Wilde, as a character in *The Picture of Dorian Gray* suggests, "the only way to get rid of a temptation is to yield to it" (Wilde, 18), the superman considers the inability to resist a stimulus a sign of vulgarity and a lack of virility.

In employing the language of taste ("vulgar commonness") to define the aristocratic qualities of the superman, Nietzsche appears to share Gustave Le Bon's concern about the emotional crowd. The Nietzschean blond beast as another version of Le Bon's masculine individualist flaunts desire only in order to be able to display his mastery of it. What distinguishes the superman from the herd is his capability to control his flesh and its natural violence. Paradoxically, the blond beast's excessive body is constructed as an excess without desire and without any superfluousness. The superman is, as Nietzsche affirms in *Thus Spoke Zarathustra,* a "necessary man" whose nonmundane qualities of self-mastery and frugality reinscribe his body in the economy of asceticism and, despite his independence, make him compatible with the bourgeois imperatives of order, restraint, functionality, and respectability.[58]

In order to become the prototype of the Aryan national figure, the blond beast and his violence had to be adapted to the moral principles of the middle class, chief upholders of the ideology of nationalism. The *embourgeoisement* of the superman and of his excessive body works on two levels: It serves the exclusive and xenophobic interest of the middle class and also represents a myth of identification for the petty bourgeois who wants to be part of that class. Through the image of the blond beast a discourse of elitist separation is spoken in a subtly interclassist language. In the end, the muscled body is taken from the manual laborer and the proletarian and given to the bourgeois male, who will care for it within the precepts of the Nietzschean protest, revised for popular application. Through a suitable domestication of Nietzschean ideas, so that the superman's grandiosity could also be a model for what Webb had termed "those sections of the population that give proof of thrift and foresight," the petty bourgeois inherits this body with the charge that he care for it in the name of race and nation.

## POPULARIZING MANLINESS

In the decade before the First World War this antidecadent Nietzschean discourse of the body, which paradoxically championed the same neoclassical physique that the decadents had praised, was diffused in a range of activities that flourished with the increasing regimentation and militarization of European society. Besides fostering more and more mass sports activities from lawn tennis to cycling and athletics, the maintenance of the healthy body made for fashions and fashionable crusades with dieting, vegetarianism, exercise, nudism, and abstention from alcohol and smoking all finding fierce advocates. Although these movements often did not immediately appear connected to each other, they all spoke a vitalistic and eugenicist jargon of renewal that functioned as an ideological Esperanto for masses of self-improvers. Most widespread was the mass organization of sport. With the rise of sports as an industry akin to tourism by the turn of the century, athletics, gymnastics, football, and cycling became enormously popular.[59] In 1896 the first modern Olympic Games were held in Athens; their French organizer, Baron Pierre de Coubertin, spoke of sport as a means of national elevation, a spectacle that refines and improves both the character and the body of the nation. His model was the relation, noted again and again in this period, between the physical and moral education of British public schools and the power of the British Empire.[60] Although the new ethos of mass sports liked to trace its origins to the public schools, such places were not the major terrain where the politicized sphere of sport now proliferated. In France gymnastics clubs emerged in conspicuous numbers after the defeat that Germany inflicted on France in 1870, and their membership was dominated by the petty bourgeoisie and the working class. In Germany gymnastics had from the first a patriotic character: Gymnasts practiced both in the exclusive sphere of the university Bruderschaft,[61] where the tone was strictly militaristic, and in the nationally organized local sports unions, so that the Deutsche Turnschaft counted 627,000 members in 1898.[62] In Germany in particular, the connection between athleticism, virility, and national renewal came to be particularly influential; the conditions were put in place in these years for the subsequent fascist colonization of corporeality: "The body," as the Nazi sport theorist Alfred Baumler would declare in 1937, "is a political concept/space" ("*Das Leib ist ein Politikum*").[63] The qualities of endurance, discipline, and strength suggested by the toned muscles of the national athlete anticipated and provided an image for the agonistic-sportive totalitarian state of thirty years later, in which ideological muscularity would be deliberately trumpeted against liberalism and its "disembodied," weak politics.

The same concern with fitness, physical and cultural regeneration, coupled with a distrust of liberal institutions—in this case the family and the school—characterized the German Youth Movement, an early "countercultural" phenomenon that spread nationally after its founding in a Berlin suburb in 1901. The slogan of the movement, "youth for itself alone," pointed to its members' claim to independence from their elders and their values. The Wandervogel (the Ramblers), a movement of urban middle class boys who desired freedom from the tutelage of parents and teachers to create their own mode of life,[64] did not, however, invoke social change; rather, it constituted an unspecified rebellion against bourgeois values in the name of spontaneity and the Nietzschean ideal of self-creation.

Camping, hiking in the countryside, and especially the interest in mountain climbing were celebrated by Wandervogel culture for their purifying and ascetic value modeled on the myth of Zarathustra. As with the Nietzschean superman, the movement's intent to challenge values through the power and spontaneity of the body did not imply expenditure, pleasure, or waste but rather produced a corporeality disciplined through the will. Nietzsche's influence on the ethos of the Wandervogel was never fully acknowledged by the movement itself: Some of the leaders rejected Nietzsche's influence; others, such as Paul de Lagarde, openly embraced Nietzscheanism and used it to give a *Volkisch* tone to the group's activities.[65] Besides strengthening the body, the walks in the countryside were praised for establishing a more immediate contact between the boys and the fatherland. A favorite activity of the Wandervogel was to collect and perform traditional folk songs, considered an integral part of the group's German cultural heritage. The growing presence of nationalistic sentiments in the movement can be seen in the three successive introductions to the *Zupfgeigenhansl,* their famous songbook: In the 1909 version the editor Hans Breuer wishs the members "a happy rambling"; in the preface to the fourth edition (1911) he describes rambling as the real German way of life, deeply rooted in the native soil; in the war edition of the songbook he writes: "We should become even more German. Rambling is the most German of all innate instincts, it is our basic existence, the mirror of our national character."[66]

In uniting its fascination with elemental nature, youth, and an ideal of physical well-being to nationalist sentiments, the Wandervogel is symptomatic of the specific course taken in the early twentieth century rediscovery of the male body in European culture. The free and pure bodiliness for which these youths searched simultaneously challenged and reinforced bourgeois respectability: Whereas the group's emphasis on spontaneity and instinct taught that there was no shame in the body and in its activities, it also proposed a chivalric ideal of manliness through the image of a steeled, "bronzed," and drilled body in which purity and self-mastery had deleted any trace of sexuality. This noble and natural body, in the words of Carl Boesch, the editor of the movement's publication *Der Vortrupp,* was defined in opposition to "the ugly human being of modernity, the physically underdeveloped urban type, disfigured by debauchery, a hypocritical way of life and the spiritual paltriness of the employee."[67] In Boesch's harangue, the language that the late Victorian commissions had used to describe the effects of slum living on proletarians is employed against modernity in general, with an added admonishment to the employee as the bearer of such modernity. What distinguished this paltry urban type from the "real man" was the latter's capability to endure, to stick to physical discipline *and* enjoy it. In England these qualities of manly agonism had earlier been inculcated in the upper classes through the ethos and the athleticism (of "prefects" and Kiplingesque gamesmanship) learned in the public schools. This ideal of manliness, both powerful and self-sacrificial, was popularized among boys of the "lower classes" through the most popular youth movement of all, the Boy Scouts of Robert Baden-Powell, founded in 1908.

From the beginning, the British Boy Scout movement mixed Nietzschean ideals of individualism, will, and physical power with the patriotic concerns of eugenics. Baden-Powell was deeply concerned with the "boys' problem," which he saw as the waste of youthful energies in the dissipated life of the city. His writing, as well as the summer camps, weekly meetings, and regime of exercise in nature that his movement instituted, aimed at producing a new type of young man, whose health and physical prowess could counteract the implicitly degenerative tendencies of modern England. "God made men to be men," wrote Baden-Powell. "We badly need some training for our lads, if we are to keep up manliness in our race instead of lapsing into a nation of soft, sloppy, cigarette suckers."[68] In a sketch that appeared in the first edition of *Scouting for Boys* (1908), Baden-Powell translated in visual terms the opposition between the "real man" and the paltry urban creature: An upstanding, healthy-looking, self-possessed young man is contrasted with the "streetcorner loafer" who, with his apathetic look and curved shoulders, wastes himself away in smoking and in idling as a spectator of football matches (Figure 2.2). Baden-Powell's degenerate smoker is also wearing glasses: This detail signals the author's disdain, shared by much German *Wandervogel* writing, for formal education and "mental work." Occasionally in his writing, Baden-Powell attacks intellectualism as a form of snobbery opposed to the vigor and the dynamism inscribed in the boy scout's body.

The ideal of a spartan life in the woods and the importance of a healthy physique and "character" over social and intellectual skills was shared by both the German Youth Movement and the British Boy Scouts. Yet both had evolved from different impulses: Whereas the Wandervogel began as a generational protest to become more openly enmeshed in the rhetoric and the aims of nationalism at the time of the First World War, Baden-Powell's ideals were from the first explicitly militaristic, and only after the Great War did the Boy Scout movement relinquish its full patriotic trappings. The idea of military training for boys occurred to Baden-Powell at the time of the Boer War and was modeled on Lord Cecil's Boys Troop formed in Mafeking during the siege of 1899–1890.[69] The training of boys in boxing, wrestling, stalking wild animals, and, above all, marksmanship in time of peace was conceived as a preparation for war: "Everybody has to learn how to shoot and to obey orders, else he is no more good when the war breaks out, than an old woman."[70] The goal was to produce the best, most efficient, and disciplined male body for the nation—a body whose virtues of endurance, obedience, and physical prowess could function interchangeably in society and on the battlefield. Through scouting, therefore, the Nietzschean representation of the male body came to be fully integrated into the emergent ideology of conservative nationalism. In *Scouting for Boys* the Zarathustrian principles of health, purity, and vitalism do not produce the potentially criminal and monstrous body of the superman but the disciplined and even ascetic corporeality of the boy scout—good citizen and soldier. Baden-Powell assimilated the Nietzschean concern regarding decadence and the eugenicist fear of degeneration without taking into account that for Nietzsche the source of degeneration was civilization and the bourgeois

*Figure 2.2 Baden-Powell's own drawing of the "loafer" and the Boy Scout, 1911.*

subject itself; at the same time, eugenics proposed a program of social and individual improvement to strengthen the very class that Nietzsche loathed.

The "real man" that Baden-Powell wanted to create was modeled on the image of the colonial frontiersman, the pioneer imperialist whose qualities of courage and sportsmanship were for him the essential virtues of the virile nation. In *Scouting for Boys* he distinguished between virile imperialist nations capable of dominating themselves and others, such as England, Germany, and America, and "effeminate" imperial powers such as France and Belgium. The French and the Belgians, in the view of Baden-Powell and other boosters of British imperialism, "were too epicurean, enjoying food and wine too much, and preferring the joys of the harem to the ascetic manliness of hunting."[71] In this instance, virility is achieved through a strict regime of ascetic denial and of purification of the body that recalls both Rupert Brooke's "diet of fish" during his time at Cambridge and the hygienic intent of the many Life Reform movements such as vegetarianism, dieting, and abstention from smoking, which flourished both in Germany and in Britain at this time.[72] In Baden-Powell's schema hunting, the pastime that the aristocrats at home shared with the "big game" hunters in the colonies, represented a form of sexual sublimation, a way of channeling the energy of the body away from sexuality; to become a "real man" meant to invigorate the body toward a purpose other than pleasure or expenditure.

The emphasis on self-improvement that animated the scout movement echoed the petty bourgeois employee's effort to elevate himself to the level of the established bourgeoisie by acquiring education and taste, or even to overcome bourgeois manners altogether through a return to nature and the building of a strong body. In Forster's *Howard's End,* which was begun in 1908, the same year the Boy Scout movement was founded, Leonard Bast soon finds out that his literary pilgrimage to the woods of Surrey makes him tired and that his adventure is not at all enjoyable. The boy scout who also went hiking to improve himself, however, did not notice the difference between enjoyment and discipline: For him "sticking to it," to use Bast's phrase, had become a form of pleasure or at least a necessary, and as such pleasurable, self-sacrifice.

In Baden-Powell's eugenicist discourse of national improvement, in the Youth Movement's romantic return to nature, and even in the spectacularized athleticism of sports, Nietzschean vitalism was transformed into a sentimentalized and heroical ethos of purposeful male endurance and even suffering. In fact, the young manliness of the athlete, boy scout, and soldier of this period was an icon of masculinity whose disciplinary character also included a transgressive and sexual edge. The way the body of the Nietzschean superman was "marketed" and circulated in early twentieth century European culture as the natural foundation of a new form of normative masculinity was mostly the index of this culture's anxiety vis-à-vis the social and gender instabilities of the period. Because of its structural ambivalence, of its capability to speak both to bourgeois asceticism and self-control (the will) and to the desire to subvert these very bourgeois values through a language of somatic excess (the instincts), the Nietzschean hyperbody constituted an ambiguous form of interpellation. While urging the New Man to master his own excess in a gesture of superior spirituality, as was visible both in the self-imposed discipline of the athlete and in the sacrificial self-expenditure of the patriotic soldier, the early twentieth century Nietzschean production of masculine corporeality also displayed the male body as an object of consumption. The unclothed body exposed to the gaze—either at a sporting event or during the rambler's hike, on the beach or in the context of such sentimentally homoerotic scenes as those of soldiers bathing from the First World War—became sexualized and upset bourgeois norms of visibility and propriety. In these figurations the male body was sexualized by its staging in public and through the very practices that were supposed to produce a socially healing and safer image of masculinity. The state's insistence that male suffering and self-discipline be purposeful, directed to improving the racialized body of the nation, for example, or to "saving" one's own country, as nationalist and eugenicist rhetoric claimed, can be read as an attempt to guard against the excess of a masculine corporeality that appeared to dangerously border on expenditure and masochistic self-loss.

Thus the body of the superman, for Nietzsche a declassed icon of manliness that combined proletarian muscles and aristocratic will to power, came to be reorganized for mass consumption through the norms of visibility and propriety that had belonged to bourgeois representation. The new-style corporeality that the Boy Scouts' language of puritanism and renunciation produced was paradoxical: Although the body was always foregrounded, even shown naked or seminaked, sexuality had been wiped off its image. In this arena, the type of instinctuality Zola displayed through Jacques Lantier—but also the "young man carbuncular"'s playful expenditure—was banned altogether. The sexuality of the foregrounded body would be considered directly only in treatises of abnormal sexuality, such as Cesare Lombroso's *The Delinquent Woman* and Havelock Ellis's *Studies in the Psychology of Sex* (vol. 1, 1900), or hidden beneath the quasi-mystical vitalism that can be traced from the utopias of Samuel Butler to D. H. Lawrence or dissimulated under the sign of "the force of life" in vitalist texts such as G. B. Shaw's *Man and Superman.* This renewed splitting of the revealed body into an image akin to that of the Greek statue on the one hand and into outlaw wildness on the other was enforced by the two spheres where each fragment was confined and discursified. The healthy body became more and more the object of photographic inquiry, but in its images as they appeared in publications of the Youth Movement, such as Herman Popert's *Der Vortrupp,* or in the official journal of Baden-Powell's Boy Scouts, *The Headquarters Gazette,* particular visual strategies assured that nakedness was not pornography: The young male body, almost always portrayed in movement against a natural background, was shown as disciplining itself and consuming its excess in the sportive gesture. This seminaked, sportive male body, precursor to the famous visual displays of the athlete's body in, for example, Leni Riefenstahl's 1936 film *Olympiad,* was made visible as nature to be contemplated. At the same time, the other body was medicalized in the inquiry of psychoanalysis and sexology by Havelock Ellis, Krafft-Ebing, Freud, and Hirschfeld or transformed into a tourist attraction, as happened in occasional texts such as *Berlin drittes Geschlecht* (Berlin's third sex) (1904), a sort of Baedeker of the city's homosexual culture, listing all the major clubs, restaurants, cafés, and bathhouses where homosexuals could be found and joined but also watched as a curiosity.[73]

The split between visible and invisible bodiliness was articulated in terms of gender by such figures as the German cultural critic and racialist Otto Weininger. Weininger's *Sex and Character* of 1907, probably the most influential racial tract of the early twentieth century,[74] depicted the desexualized body as the perfect master of its instincts and as such "spiritual" and male. Thanks to this mastery, the male subject was cast as the creator, the founder of civilization. Women, in Weininger's scheme, preoccupied with their narcissistic sexuality, never matured socially: Their biological emotionality relegated them to the private, infantile sphere of the home. True men, insisted Weininger, did not yield to their senses: Their manliness, in a very Nietzschean way, resided exactly in their capability to practice self-restraint. As Lord Baden-Powell wrote in a sentence that might be considered a corollary to Weininger's theory, "The energy that the primitive animal puts almost solely into sex, in the human is turned into all sorts of other activities, such as science. ... "[75] Women were excluded from such activities, and so were the "inferior races," which, lacking a substantial portion of masculinity, were biologically constituted according to the feminine incapability of controlling their sexuality and emotions.

This view of sexuality as an unrestrainable and feminine quality helped Weininger to reaffirm, on a new ground, the patriarchal claims of a natural division of labor. If the opposition of man as breadwinner to woman as homemaker was less stable by the turn of the century, when women, such as Eliot's typist, entered the European job market en masse, a new gendered distribution of public and private roles was now made possible through Weininger's argument: Because of his physical qualities and spiritual characteristics man could conquer a new public space, further away from the newly feminized sphere of the office, by going to war. Women, whose bodies signified passivity and weakness, did not fight and remained caught in the private space of the city apartment and of civilian life.

The First World War indeed represented the ultimate goal of almost two decades dedicated to the ideals of male corporeal renewal and the cult of youth. When the war became more than a remote possibility, the conflict was presented to an extraordinary degree by nationalists in every European country, such as Gabriele D'Annunzio in Italy, Maurice Barrés in France, Walter Flex in Germany[76]—and soon, as we have seen, by Rupert Brooke's sonnets in England—as an apocalyptic event. Among the numerous intellectuals who—whether through rhetorical effort or idealistic faith—produced the image of the war and of the trenches as a heterotopic space of adventure, risk, and heroism, the Italian futurist Filippo Tommaso Marinetti gave an alternative formulation, less senti-mentalized and more forthright, of this masculine heroism: "Only war knows how to rejuvenate, accelerate and sharpen human intelligence, to make more joy-ful and air the nerves, to liberate man from the weight of daily burdens, to give flavor to life and talent to imbeciles."[77] This declaration has the ring of an adver-tisement, and Marinetti sounds like a salesman praising the virtues of his prod-uct. Marinetti's view of the hero as "acting out" a role rather than naturally em-bodying an essence seems to oppose and debunk the claim to authenticity that the instinctual corporeality of the superman invokes. War possesses a series of spe-cific properties: It enhances life, lifting the spirit from the boredom of everyday routine, and provides the space where the common man can become a hero. War, for Marinetti, implies that one is not *born* a hero but can *become* one. This is the message that the petty bourgeois clerk, body culturist, spectator sportsman, and eager claimant of full bourgeois status was presumed to want to hear. "Talent" is only a matter of bodily appearance, something that can be acquired, given, and taken away: Its volatility dangerously shortens the distance between the hero and the imbecile. The doubt will always remain whether any winning "noble beast of prey" is not, after all, a talented imbecile. Marinetti's sarcastic boosterism throws the shadow of a doubt upon the Nietzschean representation of the male body. The masculine subjectivity solidly anchored to the body of the superman reveals itself, at the moment of crisis, to be an unstable entity.

Although in Marinetti's words there is no specific mention of social classes, it can be inferred that the mediocre man metamorphosed into a hero is the petty bourgeois. The image of the afterhours and of the double identity of Eliot's post-war "young man carbuncular" comes to mind. The imbecile shows his talent by subscribing to the ideology of action, adventure, and renewal that fueled nation-alism. Bored with his own everyday routine (or if he is more politicized, with the routine of the liberal state) and literate enough to access the channels of circula-tion of Nietzschean ideology—through night school, working men's education, newspapers, and mass printings of literature like the Everyman series in England—the petty bourgeois subject is interpellated exactly through his desire for an outside to the everyday, where his "real" other self—his otherwise misrec-ognized talent—can be fully revealed.

In Marinetti's argument the war is aestheticized to promote its marketability: His rhetoric of promises ("knows how to rejuvenate") borrows from the new grammar of mass advertising and commodity aesthetics. Presented as an "out-side" to the quotidian, the war is produced as another heterotopia, as analogous to the typist's shabby apartment, to the Surrey countryside roamed by Leonard Bast, to the novel space of the urban movie theater, or to the image of a holiday camp in an advertisement. The petty bourgeois who is aware of the Nietzschean inter-text of the call to patriotism is still an avant-garde. A whole mass of "untalented imbeciles," the vast unpolitical and often barely literate lower class majority, were less eager for the call of the cultural loudspeakers of nationalism; they remained relatively excluded from its call until conscription was introduced. How were these masses who did not have the clerk's anxious need to self-improve and who did not read Nietzsche or even Baden-Powell reached and addressed by the same ideology? How were the images employed by this ideology changed by a different range of media that propagated them? After examining the creation of the vitalistic, steeled body of the male hero that fed into discourses of militant nationalism, I want now to turn to the different images through which the superman's animality and the natural qualities it signified were reproduced in popular culture.

# 3 THE ZOO, THE JUNGLE, AND THE AFTERHOURS: MASS SUPERMAN

The idolizing of the vital phenomenon, from the "blond beast of prey" to the South Sea Islanders, inevitably leads to the "sarong film" and the advertising posters for vitamins and pills which stand for the immanent aim of publicity: the new, grand, beautiful and noble type of man—the Führer and his storm troopers.

—T. Adorno and M. Horkheimer, *Dialectic of Enlightenment*

There are many theatrical, outward elements in the popular character of the "superman," with more of the "primadonna" than the superman about them; a great deal of "subjective and objective" formalism and childish ambition to be "the top of the class," but especially to be considered and proclaimed as such.

—Antonio Gramsci, *Selections from Cultural Writings*

THE SUPERMAN as chastely powerful body was deployed by official culture as a form of interpellation into national identity, but it was by functioning as an icon of popular culture that the Nietzschean representation of masculinity was made available to masses of people of every class. The blond beast of prey was turned into a very successful popular icon and became marketable; his qualities of strength and manliness, and above all a strategically displayed and contained wildness, became part of the imaginary of masses of people by circulating in advertisements and in popular performances such as that of the gymnast and the strongman in the music hall, in the circus, and soon, in the cinema.

The image of the blond beast that Nietzsche celebrated was always doubly embedded culturally as both nationalist icon and a consumable commodity. Nationalism and its ideals of race, which used discourses of eugenics and genetics

93

to imagine society as a healthy body, took root at the moment when capitalism was learning, through mass advertisement and new sales techniques, to successfully interpellate the masses as consumers. Notwithstanding the elitist and aristocratic qualities attached to the image of the perfected Aryan male body in the Nietzschean text, the image of the athlete-warrior was reproduced in popular culture through the parodic embodiment of the strongman's physique, in which the puritan and ascetic "will" of the superman was replaced by the self-sacrificial discipline of the bodybuilder, who pumps iron to become a perfect spectacle, idolized and coveted by the audience.

The modern consumer, at whom the commodity, in Marx's words, casts "amorous glances," is an individual whose desire is aroused not so much by the use value of the commodity but by its phantasmagoria, the semiotic and libidinal excess that the commodity as staged image encodes. In the early twentieth century the body of the superman became part of this phantasmagoria. The "theatrical, outward elements" that for Gramsci characterized the popular image of the superman redefined the unique, perfectly masculine Nietzschean body in terms of artifice, decoration, and self-display. "Being Nietzschean in a folk sense," as Gramsci noted, "is more a matter of imitating Alexander Dumas' hero the Count of Montecristo, than Nietzsche's Zarathustra."[1] That is, the popular reproduction of the superman took as its model not the classless, spiritual nobility of the philosophical hero but rather the more gratifying aristocracy of the hero of the serial novel: The genre of high life and gossip took precedence over that of philosophical truth. Moreover, the ambition to be "the top of the class, but especially to be considered and proclaimed as such," which Gramsci recognized as a chief characteristic of the superman, made him an eminently theatrical figure whose value and power actually relied on the gaze of the audience.

This character of the Nietzschean "blond beast" as actor and body on show is fully captured by the two popular representations of the superman's wildness I examine here, the publicity generated by Edwardian bodybuilder Eugen Sandow and the body of Tarzan in the first Edgar Rice Burroughs novel, *Tarzan of the Apes* (1912), which, like the film that followed in 1917, was immensely popular in Europe. Both the historical and the fictional hero are spectacular masculine physiques, in which the wildness of the Nietzschean "beast of prey," with its attributes of manliness and self-control, becomes irrevocably juxtaposed with the gratuitous and aestheticized exhibition of a perfect body. In both cases, the brute strength of the superman is equally domesticated and denaturalized: What is exhibited in the strongman's stunts—Sandow lifting a horse, for example, or Tarzan fighting a lion—is in fact obtained through a meticulous regime of self-discipline. This kitsch juxtaposition of functionality and ornament, which for Adolf Loos brands the early twentieth century petty bourgeoisie's predilection for Victorian clutter as bad taste, also characterizes the popular culture displays of the heroic male body. In turn, the useless beauty of this body recalls the similarly embellished image of the commodity in advertisements: Just as the commodity's use value, its function, is displaced by its phantasmagorical image, so the excessive and decorative prowess of these male bodies disavows the phallic plenitude claimed by the image of masculine physical perfection. In fact, the phallic plenitude of the superman's body is predicated on an absence. The solid ideological boundaries that define his corporeality by sanctioning his separation from the crowd, women, the weak, and the racially other are actually under siege during this period, so the virile ideal of the superman comes into being, it may be claimed, as an attempt to disavow a crisis of masculine prestige. Thus a rift in the social conditions that produced phallic versions of masculinity is redressed at the level of cultural representation: The image of masculine prowess that via Nietzscheanism invaded the popular imaginary in the early twentieth century was presented to the consumer as a coherent visual signifier, a supposedly gratifying image of powerful masculinity substituting an always already inexistent referent.

In its popular culture versions the Nietzschean blond beast, as I will show, becomes a polysemous object, a vehicle upon which multiple and competing ideologies of gender and class are displayed and come into conflict with one another. For a start, its excessiveness makes visible the fictional quality of the discourse of nature on which the new model of masculinity was founded. Like the wild animal caged in the zoo, one of the images whose politics of display I analyze here, the popular version of the Nietzschean male body was an image of fetishized nature. This body's physical strength, apparently replacing the male subject's jeopardized cultural authority, was now increasingly anachronistic whether in the office, in modern mechanized warfare, or in the factory that used Taylorist work principles. Thus the powerful, muscular, and unclothed male body, the blond beast on display, existed mainly to be consumed as a spectacle, an image that masses of people could pursue as an ideal, imitate, or simply watch in their free time. The image of Eugen Sandow, flexing his muscles on the stage of the music hall, or Tarzan's broad-chested body, performing the extraordinary antics of the strongman on the cinema screen (the first Tarzan film, starring Elmo Lincoln, was made by Scott Sidney in 1917; see Figure 3.1) or in the pages of Burroughs's highly successful adventure novel, show that this powerful male physique was functional mainly as an image capable of mobilizing desire.

In its capacity as a spectacle, the body of the superman is an ornament in which the element of embellishment—the libidinality and the instinctuality signified by its brute strength as well as its beauty—supersedes its purpose. As a popularized replica of the efficient, streamlined body of the athlete-warrior examined in the previous chapter, the hyperbody of the strongman flaunts signs of excess that contradict its phallic quality. The ornamentality, the stunt performed for the audience as a suffered effort, the aestheticized and often sentimentalized beauty of his naked physique, inscribes the body of the strongman with a form of masochistic excess that also characterized the male homoerotic body in the discourse of aestheticism. The version of manliness as physique displayed on stage in the Edwardian period, therefore, was eroticized both as a fetishistic replica of the

*Figure 3.1     Elmo Lincoln as the first screen Tarzan, 1917.*

superman, whose power the male spectator might try to emulate, and as a languid image of beauty: Arranged in the poses of classical sculptures, flexing its muscles in the image of ancient heroes, this body enjoyed its spectacularity as the object of the gaze, and as such incorporated for its audience a kitsch version of the pleasures of expenditure. By consciously posing to sell—Sandow's photographic cards were included in packets of cigarettes and used in beer advertisements, for example—the body of the superman as popular hero simultaneously mobilized and was mobilized by the desire of commodity fetishism; his body was eroticized not only as a sexualized display of male nudity but also as an object that promoted sales.

In this chapter, after examining how kitsch as theorized by Loos, Adorno, and Umberto Eco informs both the staging of the commodity for consumption and the way "nature" is similarly staged as a spectacle, I analyze two prewar versions of the male body as kitsch object, bodies that, in Gramsci's terms, reveal the popular origin of the superman as primadonna, Sandow and Tarzan. Both are emblematic of representations of naked and complexly eroticized masculinity in the popular culture of the period, from the circus strongman and the *tableaux vivants* of the music hall to the physiques of "adventurers" and early sports stars. At the same time, to understand what the image of the beautiful and suffering male body, already encountered both in the figure of the aesthete and of the nationalist male idol Rupert Brooke, signified in the context of popular culture and what the potential outlaw and erotic effect of this excess may be, I also study the image of the bodybuilder as part of an iconographic tradition that had staged and justified the display of the naked male body since the nineteenth century: Late Victorian photographic "artistic studies" and their popularization in *cartes de visite* paved the way for the international popularity of Sandow and Tarzan in the early twentieth century. The focus on the physique of the male bodybuilder in Edwardian entertainment allows me to discern how kitsch spectacles of eroticized masculinity work as an incitement to forms of consumption, and at the same time as a spectacle through which the wildness of the superman can be read against the grain.

## THE BEAST AS KITSCH

In the section of *Prison Notebooks* entitled "Popular Origins of the Superman," Gramsci outlined a study of the image of the superman in popular literature in order to consider its influence on the masses. Its larger-than-life qualities interested him because, he suggested, they had the magic power to invest the everyday, mediocre existence of "the petty bourgeois and the petty intellectual" with a new value that turns them into something other than what they are. "From this," he writes, "comes the popularity of certain sayings like 'It is better to live one day as a lion than a hundred years as a sheep,' particularly successful among those who are really and irremediably sheep."[2] This saying was a fascist motto; the sheep Gramsci critiques are Mussolini's followers, the masses who refashion themselves into the leonine and superhuman image of the leader. However, the motto applies also to an earlier period when fascism was not yet a historical reality; the "black-coated armies" of male employees and workers of the pre–First World War period, more and more regimented in Taylorized offices and assembly-line workplaces and deprived of the traditional prestige accorded to them qua men, were offered a new image of powerful masculinity in the popular replicas of the Nietzschean superman. Yet this body, far from being a stable signifier of masculinity, turned out to be crisscrossed by multiple and unstable meanings that extended well beyond any simple notion of phallic authority.

When reproduced in mass culture the Nietzschean body no longer functions as an apparently transparent medium of authentic virility and rather becomes, like the commodity fetish in Marx's words, a "social hieroglyph," a semiotically opaque object that can be libidinally invested by the desiring subject. The blond beast in the age and space of mechanical reproduction sheds the aura of the "natural" with which the state and its eugenicist and militaristic supporters had wished to endow it and becomes engulfed instead in the logic of semblance and pleasure. In this carnival, efforts to master the body according to an ascetic regime of productivity, so that its excess is consumed and reduced to a pure functionality that leaves no residue, is short-circuited. Husbanding this excess, the mass culture image of the body as a signifier of nature and wildness is produced according to the logic that prepares the image of the commodity for consumption. In becoming part of the imaginary of the masses that buy it and watch it, this staged image turns into a medium for capturing, producing, and circulating desire. The Nietzschean body as spectacle of mass consumer culture becomes a site, as I will show, where the body's excess is foregrounded as kitsch. In the kitsch object, the fetish character that the "natural" body shares with the commodity is made visible. A brief excursus into the role of kitsch as a strategic medium for the inauguration of early twentieth century European mass consumer culture shows how the kitsch "taste" and sensibility of consumers opened an appropriate commercial space where the Aryan, male body of the blond beast could be refashioned as a more ambiguous spectacle.

Kitsch has been read by its critics—from the fin de siècle Austrian architect and advocate of modernist minimalism Adolf Loos to Theodor Adorno and, more recently, Umberto Eco—as an attack on authenticity and on what Walter Benjamin termed the aura of the original. As a derivative "bad copy," kitsch merely imitates, but it imitates in excess. Its raison d'être is decoration rather than function, and its excess of signification, its decorative quality, is the same that produces the semiotic opacity of the commodity fetish. The notion of kitsch as ersatz, as pseudo-art, is a recent concept that became widespread only in the early years of this century to account for the effect of mass production on "taste," particularly in relation to the identity of the rising new petty bourgeois class.[3] Openly celebrating its nonelitist character, kitsch as a category of representation addresses an audience whose education, taste, and financial means allow cultural pretensions that can be satisfied by copies: either the cheaply reproduced object, such as the factory-carved ornate furniture favored by the nouveau riche that Adolf Loos found so despicable in fin de siècle Vienna, or the "secondhand" experience of an act or reality, perhaps best epitomized by magazines such as *Reader's Digest,* a part of the "self-improving" that both Adorno and Eco critique. According to both critics, kitsch as a second-degree art belongs avowedly to the sphere of consumption and partakes of the commodity's keenness to comfort the consumer: It is not meant to unsettle an already established set of values but rather to confirm and consolidate them.[4] This "digestible" art does not, they claim, demand critical alertness; thus, the operation of decoding and constructing meaning is unnecessary. With kitsch, in their view, one is asked only to enjoy the effects of an aesthetic operation performed in advance; the major danger of this pseudo-art therefore becomes the audience's supposed acquiescent and uncritical identification. Adorno unflinchingly rejects any potential value in the kitsch artifact: "Because the masses are denied real enjoyment they, out of resentment, enjoy the substitutes that come their way. The claim that low art and entertainment are socially legitimate is no more than an ideology testifying to the ubiquity of repression."[5] This uncompromising perspective, however, which wishes to speak for "the masses" while keeping a distance from their taste in "low art," can itself be critiqued as partaking in an elitist anxiety that had pervaded theorizations of kitsch since the first use of the term by Munich art dealers in the 1860s.

Adorno's repressive hypothesis does not take into account that the "objectively reproduced state of debasement" is constructed as pleasurable and that this pleasure need not function simply as a bait for the audience, useful to dupe the spectator, but can in fact be, as a structural condition of consumer capitalism, the means of a multidirectional circulation of desire as well as the space of a transgressive signification. In order to see mass culture artifacts and images as traversed—producing and not only produced—by power, one needs to repudiate Adorno's elitist view of the culture industry; as many critics since have suggested, the "culture industry" does fulfill public functions, and represents in fact a crucial ideological terrain where social contradictions are articulated and not merely homogenized.[6] To take popular culture seriously as a field of articulation of ideological and social contradictions means that one is alert to the fact that the most extreme and decorative elements of popular representations of the Nietzschean body are not simply a means of a regressive interpellation of a presumed and passive spectator but rather a space where different ideologies of masculinity are made available and contested in the culture. In this space the male or female spectator's desires can actively refunction and appropriate the spectacles of masculinity he or she consumes. Only a detailed analysis of the signifying strategies that create this "smooth surface" of the commodity-spectacle can explain how social and gender contradictions are structured in "the mesh of repression and wish-fulfillment, of the gratification and displacement and production of desire."[7] The debate over kitsch and the hegemonic possibilities of forms of popular culture have an extra resonance when the discussion focuses on the body, for it is there that the issues of individual autonomy and consumer behavior intersect; the male consumer, offered a spectacle of the male body, is offered an ambiguous version of himself, simultaneously enacting an exaggerated image of phallic masculinity and a deviation from this norm. From this perspective, the kitschified body of the superman in mass culture functions not merely as a conduit for class resentment repressed into secondhand pleasure, as Adorno would have it, but as a stage where the contradictions of the social control over the citizen's own body may clash, and where the circuits of consumption might be interrupted and other desires put into play.

The value of kitsch as the arena where dissonant values and competing ideologies converge is visible in the very structural organization of the kitsch object. In "The Structure of Bad Taste" Eco proposes a structural reading of kitsch as a semiotic mechanism of apparent coherence that in fact dissimulates the juxtaposition of two different elements—one literally out of context yet contributing to an allegedly homogeneous meaning. "The kitsch object," writes Eco, "is the winged figure on the radiator of the Rolls Royce, a Grecian, classical element introduced only as a flaunted sign of prestige upon an object which should conform, instead, to the most honest criteria of utility."[8] The winged figure (a neoclassical body as kitsch) works by quoting something that is not there and captures desire by projecting the shadow of something that is lacking but hinted at. This logic of citation from one object to another—classical sculpture into modern technology in Eco's example—destabilizes the notion of authenticity and contradicts the idea that the object is "itself" or in itself, or that in itself it possesses any innate and essential quality. This destabilization is what, at the turn of the century, alarmed Adolf Loos: Among the many tasteless modern artifacts that he examines in the essays of *Spoken into the Void*,[9] the *Lusterweibchen*, a chandelier in the shape of a wood-carved female figure holding candles with a deer antler, exemplifies how the mechanism Eco describes is once again worked out on an image of a female body. With Loos the irony of the structuralist is replaced by the anxiety of the conservative cultural critic writing at the historical moment of the rise of the new bourgeoisie and its members' search for prestige in copies of great art.[10] He reads kitsch as an attack not only on authenticity but even more on the class (the late nineteenth century established, now threatened, bourgeoisie) that at this time needed the concept of authenticity as a criterion of self-legitimation. Hence kitsch appears to Loos an an "outlaw" style, signifying epistemological and social instability. His denunciation of the inappropriateness of decorated objects implies a critique of the social inappropriateness of their users. Kitsch corresponds to the taste of the parvenu, that figure of upward social mobility who shows artistic pretensions without having the money—and by implication the taste—to afford the original. The semiotic ambiguity of the kitsch object, in turn, with its blurring of established boundaries between use and ornament, function and show, the necessary and the superfluous—signifies the desire of an inferior class to climb, invade, and take over a forbidden social territory. When the transgressive element of impropriety crosses over from the sphere of class to that of male sexuality, as happens with the popular icon of the Nietzschean superman, the male body turns into a contradictory image: The split between use and embellishment, duty and pleasure, is deeply unsettling for the hypermasculinity that the superman claims to be carrying written across his muscles.

Loos's attack on kitsch implicitly signals the inception of a modernist sensibility founded on principles of efficiency, linearity, and functionality. It's the streamlined aesthetics of modernism and its ascetic strain that decree the anachronism of Victorian ornamentality and sentimentality: In Loos's view decoration is passé and as such it becomes associated with the lower classes and hence with the notion of social decay. Kitsch pretenses might have been used by the clerk and the typist to "pass" as real middle class members; the connoisseur as cultural critic reacted by learning to brand such taste as lower and subaltern. Loos defensively responds to this style of social subversion by criminalizing decoration and by ridiculing kitsch and its users.[11] He is overreacting. Yet his cry that all is for show, nothing is for use, signals that the real and the authentic are losing their value as steady and fully recognizable cultural categories and that a new economy of excess, no longer disciplined by the logic of necessity, is being elaborated as he writes.

The way function and embellishment are articulated in the flood of kitsch objects from the early stages of mass consumerism foreshadowed a new way of producing and circulating excess in the "countersites" where the body was displayed and exercised, and ultimately in the male body itself as it became the site for the dislocation and refocusing of desire. The unfinalized wildness of male corporeality could be appropriated as a colonizable space by the logic of consumption: No longer a heterotopic outside, the space of excess is turned into excess *as* space. In turn this unfinalized excess could be deployed by the male subject to "waste" his libidinal capital or, as happens with Sandow, to turn himself into a fetishistic spectacle of phallic totality that promises, and forever postpones, fulfillment to the spectator. Thus, the audience's desire for suture, assuaged by its identification with the body of the superman, comes to be juxtaposed with the promise of fulfillment made by the commodity. Ultimately the early twentieth century fashion for the display of male prowess produced a masculine subject no longer invested primarily in production and self-restraint but rather in vitalism and consumption. The mass superman, watching with pleasure the novel spectacles of the commodity, participated in its phantasmagoria in two ways: as the consumer of the scene and as the "carrier" of the desire consumed by commodity fetishism itself.

When the image of the superman is reproduced in the sphere of mass culture early in this century, its wildness and natural character reveals itself as ersatz. The logic of kitsch that organizes the body of the male hero in popular culture not only exposes his inauthenticity but also implies the obsolescence of the discourse of nature that structures his body, and discloses the fictitious character of the manliness that this discourse supports. Paradoxically, in an age of heroism there is no room for the superman himself: Machines are supplanting his strength and energies on a larger and larger scale. Even many of the "heroic" achievements celebrated in the popular culture of these years, which carried the trope of the lone colonist explorer-adventurer into the twentieth century, turn out to have been rather the result of a symbiosis between man and machine, as in the case of Lindbergh's first flight across the Atlantic. Factories demanded fewer craftspeople and more technicians to operate their increasingly sophisticated machines. When the use value of the physical body faded, the moment had come for its relaunching by consumer culture as wholly an object of desire in which, as with Loos's extravagant chandelier, use would be superseded by glamorous display. The blond beast, exhibited as a spectacle to a mass audience, was intrinsically a kitsch body, citing something (nature, the organic) quite out of context in the mechanized environment in which this body operated. It is appropriate that the image concluding Zola's *La bête humaine* is of a Victorian technology that now overpowers man: Both Jacques Lantier and the French soldiers die victims of the locomotive and its unarrestable and fatal run.

A body that, like the body of the blond beast in the age of the machine, has lost most of its functionality can be consumed only as excess. This contradiction explains the particular practices and spaces where the discourse of the free-natural-animal body was formulated: war, which could be romanticized as the site of heroism, and the gymnasium, the beach, the music hall, fashion magazines, cinema, cabarets, pulp fiction, romances, and adventure stories, which were all arenas where the body was displayed as an object of leisure and desire. In these spaces the body was made into an object of scopophilic pleasure that appealed to the imaginary of the viewer. The management of these heterotopic spaces showing "animal" strength employed precisely the specular model by which the wildness of animals is safely displayed in the zoo itself, one of the characteristic places where nature was rationalized in urban modernity.

As social spaces, modern public zoos were created in the mid-nineteenth century in European cities by the culture of colonialism: The animals, captured and sent to the homeland, were an immediate and tangible symbol for the masses on a Sunday outing of the conquest of exotic lands.[12] The further development of the zoo as another kind of museum, a museum of nature, testifies to the cultural marginalization of animals for the human population that had left the countryside. This marginalization, as John Berger argues, was produced by nothing less than a changed relationship between animal and man: "Public zoos came into existence at the beginning of a period which was to see the disappearance of animals from public life. The zoo to which people go to meet animals, to observe them, to see them is, in fact, a monument to the impossibility of such an encounter."[13] Zoos were monuments to a loss of contact with "wildness" produced by the rationalization of urban space and by the modern culture of consumerism: In a more and more mechanized economy, animals had lost their usefulness and, superseded by the machine, had been transformed into pets or into a spectacle—in the zoo, in the circus, and in the newly popular genre of books for children. The ancient, traditional dependence of man upon animals for "food, work, transport and clothing" that in Berger's words made "the peasant [be] fond of his pig *and* … glad to salt its pork" had been fading away as a functional relationship and reversed into pleasurable contemplation.[14] This is also the moment, however, when with the Taylorization and the increasing mechanization of the workplace, now focused on efficiency rather than craftsmanship, the worker's body as motor was being usurped by the machine. Thus a relationship with one's body and its physical labor as the source of one's sustenance was being lost for the new middle class, and spaces where the now "excessive" body might be confronted and even monumentalized and memorialized, such as the zoo, needed to be invented.

When the animals in the zoo turn into a spectacle, their wildness becomes fetishized and commodified. On the one hand the site is constructed nostalgically as lost nature, a memento of what-was-there-before-the-loss; on the other, the act of paying for a ticket to enter the zoo or the circus turns "nature" into a commodity itself. Yet a distinction should be drawn between these examples of commodified and spectacularized animality, the animal in the zoo and in the circus. Their reified representation is produced by different strategies: Whereas the dancing bear in the circus or in the sideshow is anthropomorphized, considered comic to the extent that it mimics the human body and is required to perform acts completely alien to its nature *outside* its cage, it is demanded of the animal in the zoo that it maintain its wildness inside a cage, that it be "itself," real in a fake natural background that *resembles* its natural habitat only in the eyes of the human spectator. In this way, its wildness is deceptively maintained *and* tamed while being brought closer to the viewer. As such, the scene of the "wild" animal in the zoo is a kitsch spectacle par excellence: The doubling of utility and embellishment that structures the kitsch object is cast here within the poignant frame of freedom and entrapment. Zoo animals are displayed to simulate "nature" for popular consumption; as such, they stand as an appropriate allegory for the spectacle of the mass-consumed male body in the early twentieth century.

It is upon the question of distance between viewer and spectacle that the Nietzschean blond beast and its popular culture image show their difference. Nietzsche animalizes man in order to separate him from "the rabble"; instead, while apparently echoing Nietzsche, late imperial European discourses of nationalism reexoticize what is close—these very masses—and glamorizes the crowd as *Volk* by distancing its members as individuals from the banality of the urban everyday. In the image of the caged lion, the Nietzschean logic of the beast as noble is reversed: Wildness is brought closer, tamed, and made banal again. The manipulation of spectacular space is crucial in this reversal: The reproduction of the jungle or of the tropical island in the zoo creates an ambiguous out-of-placedness *and* in-placedness of the animal that occupies this space. Its image is constructed by quoting a faraway land and by placing this quote in the everyday through a series of embedded heterotopias: Through its presence in the cage ("Africa"), the lion is put in the center of London, Zurich, Berlin. In this moment of displacement, the necessary and the superfluous, the banal and the exceptional, merge: The taming of the beast has the effect of bringing the heterotopic space it signifies closer to the audience, ultimately to the point of invading the everyday. The image of the wild animal caged and displayed in the zoo is another symptom of the intense social production of "nature" and wildness—precisely the elements and their management that characterize the new masculine corporeality of the early twentieth century. The spatial dislocation between the faraway and the here and now, the exotic land and the familiar space of the everyday that the zoo establishes at the level of the imaginary, structures itself upon the logic of kitsch; like the animal in the fake locale, the authenticity and natural spontaneity of the male body displayed in after-hours spaces flaunts its role as spectacular performance.

## WEARING THE BODY: SANDOW AS SANDWICHMAN

Both the strongman Eugen Sandow, who became famous throughout Europe and in the United States in the early years of the new century, and the pulp romance character Tarzan embody the staged wildness of the animal that had been structured in zoo displays for mass entertainment. The popularity of the bodybuilder's body was fueled by and contributed to Edwardian England's enthusiasm for physical culture: Prowess and fitness were at the core of an overdetermined cluster of meanings that associated the image of a strong, muscular body with ideals of manliness, health, heroism, and morality, the ideals through which eugenics tried to redress the fear of racial and national decay. The most famous of the Edwardian star bodybuilders, Sandow stood as a prominent example of the perfect male physique, both superior idol and a model within reach of the audience, whose strength could be acquired by anybody through training and willpower. "Hundreds of letters reach me daily, asking 'Can I become strong?'" wrote Sandow in his autobiography. "Yes, you can become strong if you have the will and use it in the right direction."[15] Willpower had to be exercised by the aspiring bodybuilder, but the training could be obtained in one of Sandow's own gymnasia, or by following the suggestions he provided in any of his handbooks. Yet as I will show, Sandow's stress on gratification and the body as spectacle show how the discourse of willpower and that of consumer expenditure could be allied in modern consumer culture.

Sandow, like such other gymnast-entrepreneurs of the time as the French Edmond Desbonnet, reached out to his potential clientele through advertisement and a promotional use of photography. As a self-advertised commodity, erotic image, and healthy physique, Sandow offers the chief example from this period of the male body as consumable and priced spectacle, where the Nietzschean discourse of the natural body as totality is continually displaced, fragmented, and newly shaped by the multiple meanings and desires his image inscribes. As a kitsch object, Sandow's body is produced by an assemblage of different iconographical and ideological parts through which the strongman as entertainer and entrepreneur is recast as the blond beast of prey. These components include Nietzschean vitalism, an overt eroticism subdued by bourgeois respectability, the eugenicist call to health and hygiene, and even the high culture discourse of classicism. All are encoded in Sandow's photographic image of aestheticized muscularity, his advocacy of gymnastics as a practice to be based on a scientific knowledge of the human body, his readiness to consider his bodybuilding efforts in eugenicist terms, and, above all, the sense of his body's value as a marketable image and salable artifact. In Edwardian England Sandow became a famous self-made man, an entrepreneur of the body celebrated precisely because he was capable of turning physical strength into a most desirable commodity for the European and American public.

The story of Sandow's career—from his strongman's stunts in the circus and vaudeville to his fame as a performer in the music hall to his success as owner of athletic clubs, promoter of fitness, and trainer of kings and celebrities—shows how he practiced a canny manipulation of his image and a spectacular staging of his body. His fortune was in fact made more than anywhere else in the photographic studio, where his muscles were disciplined to perform semiotically more than physically. His exceptional prowess was developed through a self-devised training method constantly advertised by the accomplishment of great feats of strength on stage: Ironically, Sandow died at fifty-eight while using his muscles in real life trying to lift a car out of a ditch after an accident. In reconstructing Sandow's career, I want to concentrate on the representation of his body as strongman, classical statue, and bourgeois paterfamilias to show how his image complicated the Nietzschean masculinity of the superman.

Sandow's career as self-made entrepreneur and star can be reconstructed from his own autobiographical narrative in the second part of his handbook *Strength and How to Obtain It,* published in 1897 and immediately a best-seller.[16] By then an idol of the British music hall,[17] Sandow, born Friederich Müller in 1867 in Prussia, showed a great interest in physical exercise and in the circus from an early age. His interest in the human figure had been spurred by the sight of ancient sculptures of heroes and athletes in Rome during a visit with his father. In Germany he was fascinated by the performances of wrestlers and strongmen. After a brief period when he studied "physical culture" and human anatomy at the universities of Göttingen and Brussels, against his father's wishes Sandow decided to try to make a living from his strength. At this point, an episode revealed his most important quality for a successful career: his sense for publicity and his awareness that his body could be sold and bought if properly advertised. He tells of being in Amsterdam, where he wandered the city at night, wrecking each of the Try Your Strength machines he found. The machine owners set the police on the lookout, Sandow let himself be caught, and he was suddenly famous: The newspapers wrote of him and his career began. He went on to perform at such London music halls as the Crystal Palace and the Aquarium; during the 1880s he toured England and Ireland with his own troupe. He became a celebrity and appeared in the major European capitals and in fashionable holiday resorts: In San Remo he met the German emperor, and after beating him in a game of strength and agility (the emperor tore a pack of cards in half, Sandow managed to tear two), he received as a reward one of the emperor's diamond rings.[18]

In 1893 in New York Sandow conquered his audience by bending iron bars, lifting huge dumbbells with one arm, and, on one occasion, holding on his chest a platform with three horses. Yet his real debut, what launched him as the most famous strongman and male physique of his time, took place at the World's Columbian Exposition of Chicago that same year. At the exposition, and in the vaudevilles and music halls of Chicago, Sandow appeared clad in a new costume, and besides his usual stunts, he introduced a new type of performance, a series of poses reproducing famous sculptures in the mode of the "living statues" of British music hall turns. His American impresario Florence Ziegfield, the future producer of the Ziegfield Follies, permanently altered the strongman's image; he removed Sandow from the iconography of the circus and recast him in the more refined and highbrow visuality of classical art. This change is portrayed in the photographs of Sandow taken by Napoleon Sarony, the same photographer who eleven years earlier had portrayed another star in the era when the protocols of stardom were being invented—Oscar Wilde. Whereas in the photographs of Wilde the polished exaggeration that popularized his aesthete's image had been achieved by dressing the subject up, in Sandow's photographs the bodybuilder is shown practically naked, except for a figleaf, in a series of poses that imitated famous classical statues from *The Dying Gaul* to *The Discus Thrower* and even Rodin's *The Thinker.* Sandow performed these poses in the tradition of the *tableaux vivants* of the British music hall, which had mostly displayed unclothed women. In Ziegfield's show *Sandow the Perfect Man,* he posed as "Harmodios" or "Illisos" in tight silk shorts with a garland of laurel on his head and his body covered with a glittering bronze powder under a single spotlight on a darkened stage. The classicism of the poses did not entirely defuse Sandow's gladiatorial image, however: At the end of one show he supported on his shoulders a platform on which stood the entire troupe (Figure 3.2), and in San Francisco he fought and defeated a muzzled lion.

Back in England Sandow had become a public personality: His character became the theme of popular songs, his strength was displayed at work by Edison in a short film,[19] and a plaster cast of his body was commissioned in 1901 by the British Museum.[20] At the height of his fame his name figured in a commonplace phrase: "As jolly as a Sandow" indicated the optimism and virtue attached to the perfect, healthy male body. At the outbreak of the First World War he became an adviser to the British army, and even the pianist Ignace Paderewski asked for his

*Figure 3.2    Eugen Sandow holds his troupe on his shoulders, 1896.*

help to develop a series of finger-strengthening exercises. By 1905 the handbook *Strength and How to Obtain It* had been reprinted three times, and in 1914 Sandow received a royal warrant as an instructor in physical culture, renewed annually until his death in 1925. His audiences in the theater soon became his customers in the hundreds of gymnasia he had opened in Britain, where assistants trained men, women, and even children in how to achieve physical prowess. With his personally devised method of gymnastics, with his magazine *Physical Culture*, and with gadgets such as "Sandow's Combined Developer (One Quality: The Best, One Price: 12/6")," Sandow made available to everyone, for a price, the ideal body of the empire, Sandow's own. His exercises as well as the tools he devised—the dumbbells and the "muscle extensor" to use at home—were known to everybody, including King George V, the poet W. B. Yeats,[21] and the hero of Joyce's *Ulysses*, Leopold Bloom, who, cuckolded, regards physical power as a form of compensation and thinks: "Must begin again those Sandow exercises,"[22] perhaps with the hope of becoming, like Blazes Boylan, a "conquering hero."

Sandow as "the perfect man" is an overdetermined figure whose image splits and multiplies in a series of contradictory portraits according to the locale and the medium in which it is represented: vaudeville and music hall, theater and photograph, advertisement images and texts such as the autobiography. In each site his body stages a continual slippage between heroic and sentimental, high and low, erotic and ascetic, functional and ornamental, brute strength and black-coated gentility. This instability is what defines Sandow's body as a popular icon of masculine prowess. The most striking and most widely known image of Sandow was that circulated by Sarony's "club" photographs, the famous body unclothed and its muscles displayed in classical pose. Yet this superb masculinity, triumphantly flaunting its vigor, power, and self-possessed mastery in the photographs, reveals itself to be a careful construction bringing together iconographic traditions that fragment and contradict the phallic totality that this body claims. For a start, the photographs were sold as *cartes de visite,* cigarette cards, and large-format cabinet cards, that is, as a means of publicity and advertisement. Since the 1860s there had been an increasingly wide circulation of these cards, portraying female and male celebrities: *Cartes de visite* of famous actresses and actors were bought, exhibited, and exchanged in the millions, and photographs of circus strongmen and gymnasts were particularly popular.[23] A new cult of the sports celebrity that the *cartes de visite* helped promote had the effect of creating a familiarity with the perfectly fit athletic body for the ordinary person; the strong male physiques that up to now the masses had encountered at funfairs had been regarded as freaks rather than as the result of an intense regime of fitness. The cards advertised the body of the strongman in a new light, as an image of physical perfection rather than brute strength and, further, as an ideal within anybody's reach. These photographic images of powerful male bodies in turn advertised physical culture and bodybuilding: In the 1880s Sandow's French contemporary, Desbonnet, having devised a method for developing the physique, proved the value of his program by circulating before-and-after photographs of his students.

Furthermore, the tradition of the sports-star cards made newly acceptable the display of the naked male body as an image filtered through the canons of classical beauty. In fact, in Sarony's photographs, Sandow's body is, to all effects, a nude, whose artistic patina does not elude but rather heightens its erotic power. Sandow's popular appeal, as the critic Allen Ellenzweig points out, legitimized the appreciation of the male body as an erotic object: "Sandow's heroic muscular image thereby encouraged the sale of male nude photographs at the turn of the century under a tacit social and artistic sanction, often to men of specialized tastes."[24] The display of muscles in the poses and in the stunts, however, made Sandow's body available both to the hetero- and homoerotic gaze. As the vaudeville star Joe Laurie Jr. affirms in his memoir, "Strongmen acts were liked mostly by women, who admired the physique and the strength of the strongmen, but the men in the audience, especially the tiny skinny guys, resented them, and felt like they were being shown up."[25] In Sarony's photographs the different visual traditions through which the male naked body had been displayed cohere to present this enticing physique: The erotic value of Sandow's image lies in this juxtaposition of genres.

In early photographic studies of the male nude one can trace a collusion between the valorization of classical poses of men's bodies and photography's effort to present itself as a decorous and serious art form. This effort led photographers to imitate attributes and scenes considered conventionally artistic; their portrayal of male nudity, therefore, turned to the tradition of the heroic male nude of Greek sculpture. Thus in photography the male body was ennobled through an aesthetically coded classicism that in turn helped suggest that photography itself was a highbrow art form. Sarony's photographs of Sandow deployed these same classicizing formulas, as is signaled by the props used: the *coturni* (Greek-Roman laced-up sandals) or the shield for the *Dying Gaul,* for example. At the same time, the heroicized male body in classical form also circulated as a form of pornography, the counterpart of postcards of women that circulated in the fin de siècle. Early photographs of male nudes had been taken in the service of painting to allow painters who could not afford a live model to obtain a full view of human anatomy; in 1860s Paris Eugène Durier photographed male nudes in very unstudied poses for Eugène Delacroix.[26] Later, photographic studies of the male nude intended for artists were commercially produced; the so-called *études artistiques* became available as a titillating and exotic curiosity to tourists in the streets of French cities. Their marketability encouraged entrepreneurial publishers: Between 1902 and 1907 in Paris Émile Bayard published a monthly album, *Le Nu Esthétique,* featuring female and male nudes interspersed with commercial advertisements.[27] In the photographs the male models, in languorous poses, wear nothing but a figleaf, the same prop that appears in Sarony's photographs of Sandow.

This thin line between art and titillation meant that in the photograph the classicized male nude continually threatens to become sexual. Its covert status as an object of erotic appreciation is brought to the fore by a further figurative genre in which Sandow's image is imbricated, that of the *tableaux vivants.* In this nineteenth century "proto-performance art," as William A. Ewing defines it, a semi-naked individual or a group of performers appeared on stage "frozen" in the positions of famous sculptures, particularly those of antiquity. The vogue of the "living statues" and of the "living pictures" had been fashionable since the early nineteenth century, when the famous Belzoni appeared in a theatrical performance in Oxford as "the Roman Hercules" and posed in "several striking Attitudes, from the most admired antique Statues; amongst others, the celebrated Fighting Gladiator; with interesting Groups from the labors of Hercules, the instruction of Achilles, and other Classical Subjects, uniting Grace and Expression with muscular strength."[28] Throughout the century the *tableaux vivants* had ranged from equestrian acts (in which the performer posed while bestriding a galloping horse, as the athlete-actor Andrew Ducrow did in the 1830s) to the masquerades of the English circle in Rome during their parties, to scriptural tableaux (like those Professor Keller's Berlin troupe performed at Vauxhall in 1845 during Passion Week) to the representation of famous paintings.[29] In Sandow's time the tradition was carried on by artists such as "la Milo," the Australian-born per-

Figure 3.3    *The Seldoms in "Reaching the Winning Post," 1907, at the London Pavilion.*

former Pansy Montagu, famous for her interpretation of *La Bacchante,* and the Seldoms, performing complex statuary acts in London's music halls (Figure 3.3). Although the *tableaux vivants* were meant as an effort to popularize art, the display of the female and male body appeared to the more prudish members of the audience as a scandalous striptease: The actors' tightly fitting "fleshings" always covered and suggested the bare flesh and became de facto a way of exposing the body. The fashion of the living statues was further spread by mass circulation of photographic cards in which the frozen poses both gave the illusion that what was shown was a real sculpture and suggested too the titillation of living flesh.

Sandow's photographic image partakes of both the genre of the "artistic study" and of the simulative quality of the *tableau vivant* without ever fully replicating their illusory static and inanimate qualities. Sandow never wore fleshings either on stage or in the photographer's study, and his body, suddenly appearing against a dark background or artfully enhanced by a professional use of light and shadow, is portrayed in a way that invites both a sensory and a sensuous appreciation of every muscle of his body. Neither does the classical tone of the photos dispel the subject's erotic charge: The veil of antiquity that was conventionally imposed on the male body in the "artistic studies" and in the *carte de visite* to confer a certain veneer of respectability does not fully reach the expected effect with Sandow: In his image, the classical motif certifies the male nude and at the same time introduces an element of embellishment and of aestheticized decoration in strident opposition to the streamlined manliness of the athlete. By being billed as "the perfect man," Sandow was declared to represent not only prowess and strength but also beauty; that is, he was presented as an edifying object of emulation *and* of desire. As such his body inscribes the "outlaw" juxtaposition of use and ornament, function and decoration, that characterizes kitsch: The sportive athlete's body, decked out in Greek sandals, leopard skins, and a shield, is a kitsch body.

Sarony's photographs also imply a further kind of hybridity: The representation of the bodybuilder as the Greek statue deploys the traits of fin de siècle Salon kitsch, a particular reinterpretation of classicism as exemplified by academic painting of the time that, in Ellenzweig's view, "invoked the antique without understanding or employing its formal equilibrium."[30] This was the classicist style, for example, of Sir Lawrence Alma-Tadema's or of Jean-Léon Gérôme's paintings, in which the sobriety of classical art was anachronistically reinterpreted through a Victorian sensibility with its penchant for decorative props—accessories, draperies, and flowers. This kitsch classicism was appropriated with particular enthusiasm in early homoerotic photography, as in some of the neoclassical photographs of Holland Day, whom I discussed in Chapter 1, or the studies of Sicilian youths by Baron Wilhelm von Gloeden, which he sold to visitors in Taormina. Some of the props from the Victorian classical repertoire appear in Sandow's photographs as well and impart to his body another whiff of that character of bad taste that alarmed Loos. The traces of Salon kitsch recognizable in the iconography of the strongman, therefore, given its particular "artistic" associations in the period, may well have acted for part of its contemporary audience as the clues that most pointedly sexualized Sandow's nudity; paradoxically, as in von Gloeden's homoerotic images of classical masculinity, the male nude was being eroticized precisely while being ennobled through the allegedly decorous power of art.

Kitsch, writes Roland Barthes, "implies the recognition of high aesthetic values like taste, but adding that this taste could be bad, and that from this contradiction is born a fascinating monster."[31] In this perspective the fake, Salon quality of Sandow's Hellenism can be seen as anticipating the stylistic sensibility that, throughout the century, the gay spectator-as-producer appropriated as camp. As a form of taste affiliated with homosexual culture, camp is often interpreted as a means of recognition: "Camp is a conscious response to a culture in which kitsch is ubiquitous. Camp is essentially an attitude toward kitsch," writes Scott Long.[32] Its interest in acts of masquerade, artifice, excess, and self-conscious eroticism capable of exposing the naturalized, rather than natural, character of desire and gender makes camp a form of kitsch with a consciousness and an agenda. In the early twentieth century, when modernist aesthetics, so iconoclastic regarding Victorian taste, was in the making, the visual hybridity, the intersection of classical and popular forms, that kitschified Sandow's image functioned rather as a form of pastiche. As such it allowed a fetishistic sexualization of the male body for, potentially, a number of different audiences through a lowbrow appropriation of a secondhand classicism.

Sandow's poses on the publicity cards no doubt were to some of his viewers poses of pornography. At the same time, the classical attitudes of his unclothed muscles made them more acceptable to the Edwardian audience by veiling their taboo eroticism through the highbrow and would-be desexualized discourse of classical art. However, this act of iconographical and ideological recuperation was always bound to be incomplete. As a classical icon, Sandow's body is in open opposition to principles of Greek art as defined by Walter Pater in *The Renaissance*: Serenity, detachment, and abstraction are conveyed by an unearthly image of the body—represented as a not fully formed ephebic figure—staged against a background of pure light. All these elements are replicated merely through approximation by Sandow's body. When posing as "Harmodios"(Figure 3.4), he appears as a kitsch copy of the original and as a mock reenactment of the Greek ideal. Notwithstanding his statuesque, sculpted shape with muscles illuminated one by one, visually chiseled by the use of light, Sandow's body is very different from the aristocratic and androgynous body of the Greek statue. The leopard skin on which he is standing, a reminder of the world of the circus, the zoo, and the colonial hunting trophy, introduces a trace of lower class entertainment, wildness, and exoticism into the picture. At the same time, the exaggerated bulk of Sandow's legs, the artificial, produced muscularity of the bodybuilder, the veins visible in his calves, suggest effort rather than classical repose. This is not the noble, aristocratically inactive young body of the Apollo Belvedere or of Tadzio in Thomas Mann's *Death in Venice*, but a sexualized image of virility, fetishistically emphasized by the presence of body hairs and by the oversized fig leaf as well as by a disproportionate, short, stocky, and too stout "lower-class" build.

In the image of "Harmodios," Sandow's emphatic gesture, with his arm raised, as well as his nudity, attracts the gaze of the viewer and turns him into an object of voyeurism. Thus revealed, his posing body is always on the verge of occupying the place of the most customary model of Edwardian "art photographs," the female body (an example of such reproductions of art and "smut" is the nymph from the magazine *Tidbits* that hangs over Molly and Bloom's bed in *Ulysses*). However, the specific iconographical conventions through which Sandow's body is represented place him in the position of the object of the gaze without fully and literally "feminizing" him. Only on particular occasions does Sandow's body become eroticized as a female one: At the end of each American performance Flo Ziegfield announced that ladies willing to donate $300 to charity could come backstage and touch Sandow's muscles. The image of women, famous socialites of the time crowded around Sandow, closely watching and touching his body, is a reverse copy of the more usual scene from theaters of the time, the encounter in the green room between the danseuse or the actress-prostitute and her male admirers. This physical contact with the male idol, albeit in the name of philanthropy, on the one hand reconsigns him to his old role as circus and vaudeville freak, and

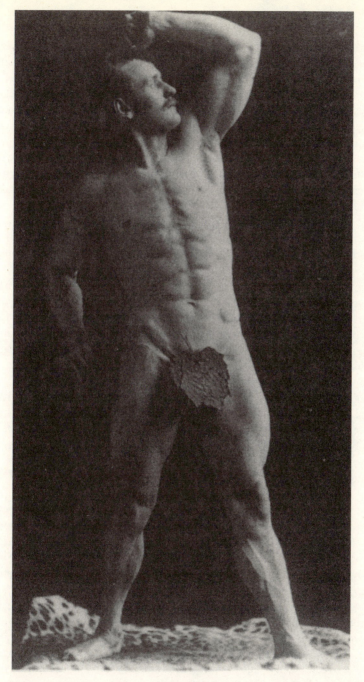

*Figure 3.4    Eugen Sandow as "Harmodios," photographed in New York by Napoleon
Sarony, 1893.*

on the other foregrounds his status as an eroticized commodity. This "feminized" role of Sandow's physique is quickly reabsorbed and turned into the rampant image of masculine active strength when he performs his stunts on stage.

Sandow's prodigious body, represented in an apparently although never completely languid pose on the postcards and as a display of force in the theater, offers itself as an unstable condensation of expenditure, consumption, and labor, which turns him into an icon of excess and self-discipline at the same time. The display of effortless strength on stage—lifting on a board a man playing the piano, for instance—was prepared for with careful and assiduous exercising. The spectacle of excessive, brute strength was the result of a strict and ordered self-discipline. With both his languorous poses and powerful feats of strength, Sandow embodies a complex figuration of male sexuality, enacting a phallic image of totality and plenitude as well as its dispersal. Thus he inaugurates the ambiguous pleasure that the bodybuilder both experiences and provides for his audience by building and flaunting his muscles; as Jonathan Goldberg observes in his analysis of Arnold Schwarzenegger's body, "the pump" (the rigid and repetitive exercise routine through which individual muscles are developed and maintained) in fact works to shatter the image of phallic totality by disconnecting the equation penis-phallus (male body–plenitude–power). When Schwarzenegger describes his working out and weightlifting as a nonstop "coming" ("I'm getting the feeling of coming backstage when I pump up, onstage when I pose in front of 5000 people, so I'm coming day and night. That's terrific, right? So, I'm in heaven"[33]), by dislocating the phallus onto every part of his body, he implicitly decrees its dispersal. This paradoxical dispersal of the phallus in the figure of the bodybuilder also sanctions the crisis of the heterosexual imperative, that is, the crisis of patriarchal definitions of masculinity as phallicly invested in genital pleasure. "If these bodies are the phallus," writes Goldberg, "the phallus has been so dispersed that its proper name is nothing but a scandal."[34]

The same scandal is visible in what Goldberg describes as the shattering of the phallic masculinity predicated by the icon of the superman: "In such dispersal the body itself is shattered, even as it is built. The male bodybuilder's body aspires to other than body limits, to a hypermasculinity that fails, insofar as it exceeds, to guarantee the gender category it means to secure."[35] Although Sandow's bodybuilding was modest compared to contemporary efforts, the theatricalization of his strength gestures toward the same crisis of phallic masculinity that for Goldberg the dispersal of the body's totality signals in the case of Schwarzenegger. A similar fragmentation of the phallic male body is evoked by one of Sandow's feats, moving individual muscles to the sound of music. "Sandow will exhibit his extraordinary command over his entire muscular system by making his muscles dance," advertised a publicity poster for one of his shows. "His four hundred wonderfully developed muscles are exhibited in the following manner: Muscular Repose (all the muscles relaxed). Muscular Tension (all muscles firm as steel). Abdominal Muscles when Tense, producing the wonderful checker-board arrangement of fibers, existence of which modern anatomists deny, being plainly visible at a distance of three hundred feet."[36] The language of control and "command" functions to contain a body whose disintegration simultaneously responds to the call of a centralized power (Sandow's own will) and to the opposite impulse to parcel and expend physical energy in the 400 individual muscles into which Sandow appears to be "dismembered." Furthermore, this hard-gained strength cannot be used as labor: Rather, it is a surplus value upon which the strongman-turned-entrepreneur capitalizes for his own benefit. As such, Sandow's workout reenacts the "work" through which the commodity makes itself desirable and saleable, that of self-display and enticing embellishment.

Within early twentieth century Edwardian culture the figure of Sandow represents an attempt to maintain the beast of prey as a copy of the neoclassical body, and to control the potential excessiveness of expenditure through a stern rhetoric of body discipline. Nonetheless the "gratuitous" excess exemplified by his capability to move each individual muscle, or the element of kitsch excess suggested by the antique props, or the leopard skins in his photographs, are what sexualizes his body as a commodity. Indeed, Sandow's greatest success was not his conquest of the machines in Amsterdam or his struggle with the lion in San Francisco but the way he managed to turn his body into a walking advertisement for himself, his shows, and his clubs. With "Sandow the perfect man" flexing his muscles covered in bronze makeup under the stage lights, the Nietzschean masculinity of the superman, already displayed and desexualized in the "natural" corporeality of the boy scout or the employee-turned-athlete, is reeroticized also qua commodity. Sandow's strength is not labor, and yet it is productive: He made the body into a career and turned himself into the celebrated and fetishized image of the male star. As a walking self-advertisement, he was one step ahead of another modern figure who also used his body to produce value, the sandwichman, who wandered the city streets wearing advertisements for shops and goods on his chest and back. The sandwichman makes his body a scaffold for the advertisement; Sandow instead turns his own flesh into a silent logo for the products that he wishes to sell—the perfect physique as well as the bodybuilding devices he himself designed.

Sandow's commercial shrewdness, his image as a businessman as well as the popular mark of his strength, were mitigated and given a new value in the autobiographical narrative that completes the handbook. The autobiography reproposes all the personae he embodied in his life, thus bringing to completion the careful manipulation of his proteiform image that so much contributed to Sandow's own salability. Here he is portrayed in a frock coat with his wife and children, as well as shaking hands with Theodore Roosevelt or consulting with officers of the British army. His cultural achievements are enumerated: Sandow tells how some musical pieces he has composed have been performed, for example. By explaining the scientific ground on which his exercises are based, he flaunts the education in anatomy received as a young man in Germany and Belgium. Through these details, the figure of the strongman achieves bourgeois respectability. In the first edition of the handbook, none of the "art photographs" of the nude Sandow are shown. Rather, the author wants to stress his social ascent from immigrant circus phenomenon to celebrity promoting physical fitness and contributing to a eugenicist narrative of national health. Onto this conventional plot line Sandow grafts another, casting himself as hero and defender of public order, a socially oriented superman who is vigilant as a good giant, ready to sacrifice himself and his pride to guarantee justice and peace. In Part 2 of his handbook, "Incidents of My Professional Career," Sandow recounts several striking episodes of his life ("I Meet Goliath," "My Lion Fight in San Francisco") whose picaresque tone gives his writing the flavor of an adventure romance. Here Sandow minimizes the body to foreground the spirit: In his own telling, he fashions himself into an image of suffering masculinity, as the sensitive—and self-confident—bourgeois gentleman who never strikes unless provoked. For example he proudly tells of being attacked in a French tavern and letting himself be hit in the face three times before answering the provocation. In the end he gets up, clutches his French aristocratic rival, violently throws him across a table, and then calmly returns to his seat to smoke a cigar. When he meets the man later in London, they become friends; Sandow generously accepts the man's excuses and is even presented with a gold watch: "To-day we are the greatest friends, ... despite the hard knocks that came of our first meeting, it would not be fair to disclose his name."[37]

The autobiography shows its protagonist helping the police locate criminals; Sandow depicts himself as a folk hero, fighting to redress the wrongs perpetrated against him—as did the Count of Montecristo recalled by Gramsci in discussing the mass superman—but also struggling for the common good. He is Sherlock Holmes with a physique. (Conan Doyle, appropriately, wrote the introduction to another Sandow book, *The Construction and Reconstruction of the Human Body* [1907].[38]) At the same time, in his role as the guarantor of justice Sandow strikes a sentimental tone of self-denial that gestures toward the masochistic pleasure in self-exposure and self-loss. The rhetoric of self-sacrifice, the emphasis on humiliation as a result of self-discipline in episodes such as that in the French tavern, for instance, is meant to demonstrate Sandow's "gentlemanly" character, his poise and self-control, as admirable bourgeois qualities. At the same time, this moment of male suffering encompasses both the Victorian sentimentalization of the gentle, brutish freak and the scandalous expenditure of the kitsch male body. This is a body that calls on the audience, male and female, to act out the structure of consumer desire—and in the process new forms of sexual desire. This body celebrates a spectacular physique that masochist discipline and the desire for social advancement described in the autobiography have made beautiful.

## TARZAN AND STRENGTH ABROAD

In detailing the colorful episodes of his life as a lowbrow narrative of romantic adventure centered on his physical strength, Sandow anticipates the fictional figure of Tarzan. The bodybuilder is a historical figure, a real person who turns himself into a novelistic hero in order to sell his larger-than-life body; Tarzan instead is a fictional character whose body is impersonated on the screen by a long series of athletic actors, a series of Sandow-like figures.[39] Yet both their bodies represent the same image of libidinal capital in which the desires and the identificatory energies of the male and female audience can be deeply invested. Whereas Sandow shows the new middle class male who find himself inhabiting a culture of declining masculine power how to represent his body as "artful" and decorous yet flagrantly strong, Tarzan, as a white man inadvertently gone native in Africa, displays his physique while negotiating the necessary wildness of the bourgeois as blond beast of prey.

As a mass culture embodiment of the Nietzschean superman, Tarzan, the figure of a seminaked Aryan body in the jungle, provides an extraordinary example of the masculine effort to "perform" nature in this period: The Tarzan story carries the logic of the zoo into a novel, as it moves from the realm of animals as spectacle to the presentation of the glorified male body. Created in 1912, the Tarzan stories—there were twenty-six sequels written by Burroughs alone—became immediately popular both in America and in Europe, and soon they were transposed to film (1917) and serialized in newspapers, radio shows, and comic strips.[40] Burroughs registered the name Tarzan as a trademark in 1913. From the very first novel the hero's popularity was based unequivocally on the valorization of his wild, strong—and beautiful—body. The transgressive manner in which Tarzan's body reinscribes animality—no longer specifically that of the lion but that of the ape—stages the scene of a further moment of "descent" for the western male body. This body descends not only into the exoticized and feared milieu of colonial Africa and into the ape world (which Darwinism had taught the Victorians that civilization, built on competitive "fitness," had overcome) but, as I will show, into the now animalized realm of massified spectacle.

The ingenuity of the plot of *Tarzan of the Apes* (1912),[41] the first novel of the series, is that Tarzan can be introduced as a creature partly human and partly beast. He is the son of a British lord, John Clayton, Lord Greystoke, who was shipwrecked with his wife on the West African coast. At the death of his parents, the infant son of Lord Greystoke is adopted by an anthropoid ape, Kala, a female whose cub has just been killed. Kala "names" the child Tarzan, which in the apes' language means "strange hairless creature," and raises him as her own son. Thus a British lord grows among the apes like one of them, acquiring all their physical capabilities. Twenty years later, a mutiny takes place: This time, left on the same beach as the Greystokes are Professor Porter and his daughter, Jane, their secretary, their maid, and Mr. William Cecil Clayton, Tarzan's cousin and the usurper of his name and title. Tarzan falls in love with Jane, but a ship rescues the company; after many adventures he follows her to Wisconsin. By now Tarzan is civilized: He speaks fluent French, taught to him by Lieutenant D'Arnot, another European he has met in the forest, and is learning English. D'Arnot helps Tarzan to resolve the mystery of his birth: He is not the son of an ape but of a British lord.

When he finally proposes to Jane she hesitates ("Could she be happy with the jungle waif? . . . Could he ever rise to her social sphere? Could she bear to think of sinking to his? Would either be happy in such a horrible misalliance?" [Burroughs, 235]). Jane decides to keep her promise to Mr. Clayton. At this point, Tarzan could have unveiled his true identity and won Jane. Rather, in "his noble gesture of self-renunciation," at the end of the novel he returns to the jungle.

In *Tarzan of the Apes,* even more than in Sandow's autobiography, the Nietzschean narrative of the male body unequivocally merges with the structure of the feuilleton to produce a romantic, larger-than-life, and yet unstable version of masculinity driven toward an antiphallic self-exposure that contradicts its claim to hypervirility. This contradiction between the image of male corporeality as phallic totality and its disabled version as wounded body is foregrounded by the elements of sentimental self-denial, superhuman self-control, and the masochism through which Tarzan's adventures are plotted. All these are highlighted by the liminality through which Burroughs characterizes his hero.

Tarzan's ambiguous identity as both animal and human, together with the instability of either trait, is one of the chief pleasures of the narrative. By simultaneously inhabiting two worlds and transgressing the boundaries between the jungle and civilization, home and the forest, England and Africa, Tarzan occupies the abject position of the outsider in both. The novel's plot situates the protagonist at an ambiguous distance between man and ape, and this ambiguity is continually fostered by repeated reminders of the beast's civilized quality, his cunning and intelligence. The brutal masculinity of his animal side, his barbaric image as cannibal, for instance, is continually compromised by a more refined aspect that is coded as classical and even mediated by an element of feminine decoration: *Pace* Loos, in the attempt to look "clothed and civilized," Tarzan wears an ornament, his mother's gold chain with a diamond-set locket, and the copper anklet he has stolen from a native tribesman. The reader is alternatively shown the superiority and the "minor" status of the hero. Born in the jungle, Tarzan is perfectly at ease among its fierce beasts: "Trained as an animal," he climbs trees, fights lions, and eats raw meat. Nonetheless, particularly in his youth, he feels inferior to the apes: His body, although agile and muscular, is not as strong, well developed, and hairy as that of the members of his "tribe." As he discovers to his great dismay, he has not at all their same features: "Tarzan was appalled. ... That tiny slit of a mouth and those puny white teeth! ... And the little pinched nose of his. ... He turned red as he compared it with the beautiful broad nostrils of his companion. ... It certainly must be fine to be so handsome" (Burroughs, 39). By looking at Tarzan looking at himself from the point of view of the apes, the reader is offered a defamiliarized view of the human body, and through this defamiliarization the absolute distinction between human and beast is put into question. Tarzan's envy for the apes' beauty relativizes what humanist ideology prioritizes as the sine qua non of man—the mind, the spirit. Once the hero grows up and discovers that he is more intelligent than the apes, the same humanism is invoked to define Tarzan's superiority: It is through reason and cunning rather than through brute force that he manages to kill the lion. Conversely, his animal instincts and their innate morality will be reactivated once he is in civilization. At Father Constantine's mission he is scandalized to discover that men kill for sport without "functional" reason. When asked to kill a lion by civilized Frenchmen, he declines and answers "I am not hungry" (Burroughs, 246).

The contrast of human and animal qualities is made even more evident by geographical dislocation. When in Africa, in an uncanny echo of the anomie of the western urban flâneur, Tarzan feels out of place because he is different from the animals that surround him. While in the middle of Wisconsin he feels "the toll of the jungle," a call to nature and freedom that confirms, in his own eyes, his deeply savage character. In *Tarzan of the Apes* Burroughs continually tries to stabilize and recoup this ambiguity by reclaiming Tarzan's British and aristocratic character: From its very early stages the novel is organized as a detective story whose aim is to solve the mystery of Tarzan's identity. Implicitly, the detective story motif and the question of Tarzan's "real" birth (human and aristocratic) are an attempt to reestablish an Oedipal narrative and to normalize his masculinity by placing it under the sign of the paternal image, suitably described by the narrator as the perfect example of virility: "Clayton was the type of Englishman that one likes best to associate with the noblest monuments of historic achievement, upon a thousand victorious battlefields—a strong, virile power—mentally, morally and physically" (Burroughs, 2). The perfect alignment of Englishness, duty, physical prowess, as well as property and tradition, is both embodied and disavowed by Tarzan, whose jungle adventures significantly open onto the pre-Symbolic pleasures of the maternal body. Animality is uncannily deployed in the novel to fashion an anti-Oedipal masculinity, which by definition disavows the name of the father. What really shocks Jane Porter and makes her decide to keep her promise to the younger Clayton, Tarzan's cousin, is the fact that Tarzan has no name: "Who was he? Who his parents? Why, his very name echoed his mysterious origin and his savage life. He had no name" (Burroughs, 265). Even more strikingly, at the end the hero intentionally renounces his title, property, lineage, and woman to go back to the jungle, a gesture that ambiguously affirms his masculinity as a return to nature. Tarzan's return to Africa nominally consigns him to the "manly" freedom that draws the Nietzschean superman away from feminizing civilization. In fact, nature in *Tarzan of the Apes* carries a more complex value than Burroughs's myth of the American frontier recast as a British colonial fantasy claims: The impenetrable, mysterious, and dangerous jungle is characterized, to all effects, as the "dark continent" of femininity and is represented as the space where a privileged relationship between mother and son, between man and animals, and between man and man can take place.

Although the novel begins with an image of the Oedipal family, Lord and Lady Greystoke and their baby, Tarzan's real parents are swiftly put out of sight: Lady Alice dies one year after having given birth, and Lord Clayton is soon after killed by the apes. All that is left of them is an image, the photograph, and the wooden cabin, which Lord Greystoke built against the dangers of the forest. The cabin, as a signpost of home away from home, is itself a memento of England: Through its image civilization and the Symbolic are represented as the heterotopia of African wilderness. Here Tarzan spends his leisure time, the "afterhours" away from the apes and from his animal life. By studying the children's books his parents brought from England, Tarzan learns to decipher the writing; although he cannot pronounce the sounds, he learns how to read, that is, he acquires a certain form of human language. The influence that the books exert over him ("His attention was soon riveted by the books ... so that he could scarcely attend to aught else for the lure of the wondrous puzzle which their purpose presented" [Burroughs, 54]) has a normalizing effect: From them he learns shame for his nakedness and begins associating humanity with clothing and propriety, in contrast to the nakedness of the animals. As happened with the employee's afterhours, the interpellation into a normative version of subjecthood—national, gendered, racialized—takes place as "play" during Tarzan's leisure time. Later the cabin, as a miniaturized First World, will also be the place where Tarzan's initiation into heterosexual desire takes place: By spying on Jane Porter, who with her father and friends takes shelter in Lord Greystoke's former home, Tarzan falls in love for the first time.

With the disappearance of Lord and Lady Greystoke, a very literal version of the Oedipal narrative comes to be enacted in *Tarzan of the Apes:* As an animal among animals Tarzan kills his hated foster father Tublat to show how great is his strength but also to continue his symbiotic relationship with Kala, his ape mother. By eliminating the paternal figure and violating the incest prohibition, the son threatens the Symbolic (language, gender, and the social law), on which culture is founded. In the novel he can, as an animal, enact these fantasies in ways that would have been impossible in a narrative of "civilization." The relationship between Kala and Tarzan is "humanized" by Kala's "instinct of mother-love," which, according to the narrator, unites the females of all species. At the same time, Tarzan's own attachment to Kala is cast in terms of filial duty and normality and presented as an exact copy of the love he would have dedicated to his own mother: "Upon her he had lavished, unknown to himself, all the reverence and respect and love that a normal English boy feels for his own mother. ... To Kala was given, although mutely, all that would have belonged to the fair and lovely Lady Alice had she lived" (Burroughs, 76). The narrative's insistence on the normality of this filial love is implicitly banking on the pleasures of defamiliarization: An English lord has an ape as his mother, and although she's a beast, she loves him and tenderly takes care of him. In fact, Kala and Tarzan's relationship is more intimate than an English upper class education would have allowed: For a long time he sleeps in his mother's arms, and she cures his mangled body after a fight by licking his wounds. The tearful sentimentality with which these mother-son exchanges are described ("No human mother could have shown more unselfish and sacrificing devotion than this poor, wild brute for the little orphaned waif, which fate had thrown into her keeping" [Burroughs, 52]) does not fully defuse the pre-Oedipal eroticism of this relationship.

The image of Kala licking Tarzan's wounds is only one of the many instances in the novel when Tarzan's body is foregrounded and brought to the reader's attention. The repeated display of his knotted muscles, his "brown, sweat-streaked, muscular body ... supple and graceful" (Burroughs, 61), constructs Tarzan's figure as the object of a voyeuristic gaze. The reader is automatically transformed into a spectator watching Tarzan perform his incredible feats of strength or "posing" as a beautiful sight. Tarzan the replica of bodybuilders and wrestlers of the time—of Sandow himself or of other vaudeville stars such as "the Russian Lion" Georges Hackenschmidt; Tom Connor; or Madrali, the Terrible Turk—with whom the reader may have been familiar.[42] Tarzan's actions and "poses" make available different, even contradictory, pleasures. His body works to consolidate a normative notion of masculinity while disabling the image of the "wild beast" through a sentimentalization and exposure of its wounded flesh. What Jane sees represented in his spectacularly strong body is a primordial condition: "As the great muscles of the man's back and shoulders knotted beneath the tension of his efforts, and the huge biceps and forearm held at bay those mighty tusks, the veil of centuries of civilization and culture was swept away from the blurred vision of the Baltimore girl" (Burroughs, 33). Although this primitive animality is mitigated by what the reader knows to be Tarzan's highly civilized origins, the narrative nevertheless maintains the subterfuge of encoding Tarzan's beauty as wholly the result of natural innocence. His animal masculinity is further mitigated by his very physical features: "The face above her was of extraordinary beauty. ... A perfect type of the strongly masculine, unmarred by dissipation, or brutal and degrading passion ... he killed as the hunter killed, dispassionately. ... When Tarzan killed, he more often smiled than scowled, and smiles are the foundation of beauty"(Burroughs, 36). If this killer's smile recalls the "innocent conscience" of Nietzsche's blond beast, his pure and unmarred masculinity is also a premonition of the ascetic young soldier-hero of the First World War or of the athlete on the cover of bodybuilding magazines. The jungle "nature" from which Tarzan, by association, derives his power is denied its violent Darwinist edge and posited as a well of innocence. In this pulp revisioning of how nature is encoded upon the male body, the strength of the Nietzschean "necessary man" as the hunter is ambiguously blurred by the unnecessary muscles of the gymnast. Tarzan's extraordinary actions are in fact the equivalent of circus stunts. He stabs to death a gorilla after catching it with a noose, he can swing from branch to branch and speeds through the tree tops with his simian siblings: "Though but ten years old he was fully as strong as the average man of thirty, and far more agile than the most practiced athlete ever becomes" (Burroughs, 38–39).

For Tarzan's audience, as we have seen in the case of Sandow, the hero's athleticism could work as an incentive to improve their own physiques, perhaps even to join one of Desbonnet's or Sandow's gymnasia. It might also work as a form of interpellation and indiscriminate identification with the class values attached to Tarzan's figure. Tarzan's seminaked body is presented as an ornament: It is the dream body of the employee as well as an ennobled version of the proletarian's muscles. The less clothing he wears, the more he is dressed ideologically to represent a diluted form of the superman. As the figure of sensational hero, Tarzan verifies Gramsci's ideas about the true nature of Nietzsche's superman: "Much of what is defined as Nietzschean 'superhumanity' has as its origin and ideological model, not Zarathustra, but the Count of Montecristo."[43] For Gramsci the superman is not an original and self-sufficient figure: Ironically, its model is the hero of the feuilleton, the Byronic hero in a cheap edition, popularized for the middle- and lowbrow tastes of a mass readership. The figure of Tarzan deftly inscribes this progression: In his body, the larger-than-life qualities that separate the superman from the rabble ultimately serve the purpose of separating Tarzan from the beast, from tropes of wildness, and in so doing return him to the mass audience, the crowd that Le Bon and others animalized as the herd.

By answering "the toll of civilization" and leaving the African jungle, Tarzan loses his uniqueness: From being the only man in a world of animals, he becomes one-in-the-crowd. *Tarzan of the Apes* plays its narrative of alienation both ways by transmitting a double message regarding class, so that it can be democratic and elitist at the same time: Through the identification in the first instance with his body, the spiritual nobility of this particular aristocratic innocence is presented as accessible to all. Yet what the reader and viewer is in fact valorizing is the *class* quality of this nobility: Tarzan is exceptional and appealing not only because he is a white man alone in the jungle but even more because he is a British lord in the jungle. His body, self-presented as an ambiguous signifier of interclassism, is the site where the demands of the subaltern social classes are answered with the promise of a fictional and fictitious nobility and where an endless leisure seems to substitute and cancel the fatigue of work. In Tarzan's body the proletarian's muscles are ennobled by being temporarily removed from the sphere of production to that of consumption: The worker is flattered when his strength, mirrored in the text and later on the screen, is shown "at work" in exotic, dangerous, and pleasurable adventures.

In the case of Tarzan, as with Sandow, the Nietzschean figure of the "blond beast of prey" as "necessary man" is transformed into a gloriously superfluous image of spectacular excess. As a spectacle, Tarzan promises to be even more gratifying than Sandow: On the screen or in the pages of Burroughs's romances, the heterotopic world that is only synecdochically represented by the leopard skin in Sandow's photographs comes alive as a full-bodied phantasmagoria. This is a recreated space of elsewhere, like the jungle with all its scenarios of imperial adventure from Ballantyne and Rider Haggard, a space where the spectator can imagine himself in the body of Tarzan. In this overdetermined site any hint of work, even of exercise, disappears to fully disclose an already perfect body. Any sign or memory of its production—which Sandow retained with his books of exercises—has now been erased from its visible surface. With ready-made muscles Tarzan's body reminds us both of the commodity, aesthetically staged in the advertisement or in the shop window for consumption, and of the consumer's body, in turn consumed by desire, wanting more and yet living like a lion only vicariously.

There is, however, another way in which this excessive body interpellates its audience. If Tarzan reproduces on the one hand the extraordinary physique of the bodybuilder, whose strength, health, and beauty are the result of a regime of discipline and self-control, the display of his wounds after a fight with his enemy and the detailed description of his pain suggest more unruly pleasures, pleasures that gesture toward the perverse desires of masochism. The narrator over and over again gets Tarzan to "pose" as a Sandow figure, whose brutal power is superseded by the aristocratic beauty and the perfection of his form: "[His] strong and perfect figure, muscled as the ancient Roman gladiators must have been muscled and yet with the soft and sinuous curves of the Greek god told at a glance the wondrous combination of enormous strength with suppleness and speed" (Burroughs, 97). The brutality and gentility simultaneously imprinted in his body ensure that Tarzan is a Nietzschean figure: Animal and noble at the same time, the superman disdains the petty conventions of bourgeois society, proclaiming to belong to an aristocracy of race. The superman's way of distinguishing himself from the herd through the capability of resisting a stimulus is represented in the text by Tarzan's stoicism, his refusal to show any sign of pain after having been wounded. His self-control, however much it suggests the British public school virtue of keeping a stiff upper lip, is ultimately acknowledged by the narrator as an animal quality: "With the stoicism of the brutes that had raised him he endured his suffering quietly, preferring to crawl away from the apes, and he huddled in some clump of tall grasses rather than to show his misery before their eyes" (Burroughs, 52). The image of animality as a form of aristocracy proposed by this passage might have offered a gratifying source of identification for the petty bourgeois or lower class reader by showing that real aristocracy is not a matter of social class but of nature. At the same time the novel demonstrates that upper class identity is not innate but rather can be attained: Nobility is signaled by manners and can be "expressed" through a careful manipulation of one's image. Tarzan, a lord by birth, behaves like an animal. Only by dressing appropriately, showing his refinement by speaking French, and learning table manners can he be transformed into an aristocrat. The physical and moral beauty that the novel valorizes as aristocratic can, it shows its readers, be cultivated, and the manners of the upper classes can be learned as exterior signs.

The radiance and power of Tarzan's perfect physique is not the only image of the male body that *Tarzan of the Apes* provides. Equal attention is dedicated to the spectacle of its disabled condition and to its maiming. The image of "Tarzan's torn and bloody form," of his body "lame and sore" after a fight, is displayed in long and detailed descriptions: "A portion of his chest was laid bare to the ribs. ... One arm was nearly severed by the giant fangs and a great piece had been torn from his neck, exposing the jugular vein, which the cruel jaws had missed but by a miracle" (Burroughs, 52).

The narration of the wounds is always graphic and sensational: "Tarzan was torn and bleeding—his scalp in one place half torn from his head so that a great piece hung down over one eye, obstructing his vision" (Burroughs, 105). Here the gladiatorial act of the circus lion tamer culminates in and merges with the spectacle of hurt masculinity. The way the narrator's gaze lingers on Tarzan's wounds turns him into an eroticized object of that gaze, an image that offers the reader a voyeuristic pleasure as compelling as the pleasure produced by the hero's intact physique. In these moments, the self-possessed Nietzschean masculinity of Burroughs's character is superseded by an image of self-exposure and of masochistic exhibitionism—a spectacle centered on the pleasure of abjection, the same pleasure that had characterized the perverse erotics of the aesthete's body in its Saint Sebastian pose.

These scenes of self-exposure, where Tarzan's body is shown as punished, are made acceptable and normalized through their sentimentalization. It is precisely the sentimental turn of this narrative of masochized masculinity that allows a further antipaternal transgression on the protagonist's part: Tarzan's powerlessness allows him to take shelter not only in the maternal body but in the tender care—brotherly, parental, and nebulously erotic—of another man, D'Arnot. After the fight with the gorilla Tarzan is again consigned to maternal love in a scene reminiscent of a pictorial version of a pietá: "With a low cry Kala rushed to Tarzan's side, and, gathered the poor, blood-covered body to the breast, listened for a sign of life. Faintly she heard it—the weak beating of his little heart. Tenderly she bore him back … and for many days and nights she sat guard beside him, bringing him food and water" (Burroughs, 51–52). In this scene or in the moment when D'Arnot "went about bathing the blood from Tarzan's face" (231) after accidentally shooting him, Tarzan's "minority" is reaffirmed as a means of reconquering the pleasures of the maternal and of deferring, or even disavowing, his submission to the law of the father. In the novel, however, this masochistic function of Tarzan's body works intermittently, with the result that the disturbing tear it causes in the phallic image of the hero's glorious and wild body is continually reabsorbed. Thus Tarzan's "ruin of the paternal heritage," to use Kaja Silverman's description of the chief effect of male masochism, is temporary. As Paul Smith suggests, the perverse denial of the law of the father can be sustained only provisionally.

In general, therefore, Burroughs's narrative deploys the discourse of male masochism only to finally reaffirm the phallic power of the male hero. Masochism here is a means of staging gestures of possible disruption only to triumphantly contain them. Smith's account of the uses of masochistic scenarios in film describes the implications of this simultaneous exposure and containment:

> Male masochism can be seen, finally, as another way for the male subject to temporarily challenge his desire for the father and to subvert the phallic law, as ultimately another step in the way … of guaranteeing the male subject as origin of the production of meaning. … Crucially the lessons of masochism do not last, they come and go

as part of the subject's history of struggle in learning how to reach symbolic empowerment triumphantly.[44]

For Smith, the son's transgressive desire for the father, his will to be both sexes at once, is only a stage in the formation of normative masculinity, and the masochistic male body is hystericized as it is normalized. Burroughs's descriptions of Tarzan's mangled body might be read in this vein as an instance of this hystericization of sexualized, and ultimately homoerotic, masculinity. The descriptions of Tarzan's wounded body show moments of powerlessness and incoherence that signal what the Oedipal law has made unsymbolizable; thus this can emerge only as an inexplicable excess—an excess that Tarzan's gruesome and even grotesque wounds aptly represent.

At the same time, Smith's theory only partly explains the function of male masochism in the novel. If it is true that the final submission reinstates Tarzan as Lord Greystoke and fully places him under the name of the father (the mystery of his identity is resolved; he *is* the son of Lord Clayton and Lady Alice), his final, sacrificial self-denial does more than situating him within the Symbolic. In fact his final renunciation of power, property, and title is a further gesture of disavowal of the paternal function: "Here was the man who had Tarzan's title and Tarzan's estates, and was going to marry the woman whom Tarzan loved. A single word from Tarzan would make a great difference in this man's life. It would take away his title and his lands ... and—it would take them away from Jane Porter also" (Burroughs, 275). This is a residual moment of Victorian sentimentality as well as a display of Nietzschean aristocratic manhood. Tarzan shows that he can resist a stimulus and at the same time gives his self away for the love of another. But his apparently disinterested love is in fact a gesture of masochistic submission to the female figure, as Tarzan's claim to have given everything up for Jane illustrates: "I have come across the ages out of the dim and distant past from the lair of the primeval man to claim you—for your sake I have become a civilized man—for your sake I will be whatever you will me to be" (Burroughs, 274). This gesture of submission and the promise to change into whatever Jane wants recalls the masochism through which Severin submits to Wanda in Sacher-Masoch's novel *Venus in Furs*.[45] By implicitly representing Jane as a cold and all-powerful figure— the cause of Tarzan's phallic demise—the novel turns the "Baltimore girl" into the double of Kala, as an image of the terrifying and loving figure of the pre-Oedipal mother, dispenser of pleasure and pain, source of protection and of self-loss for the male subject.

With the image of Tarzan's submission to the romance novel's version of Sacher-Masoch's cold mistress, the normality of the English boy—which Burroughs posited to describe Tarzan's relationship to the maternal figure—is compromised. The taboo pleasures of incest are tacitly invoked and simultaneously relinquished in the image of the lonely male hero escaping the "feminizing" effects of civilization to go back to nature. *Tarzan of the Apes* ends in the name of the mother and with the hero's radical denial of the Symbolic: "My mother was an

Ape, and of course she couldn't tell me much about it. I never knew who my father was" (Burroughs, 276). The final sacrifice, flaunted as act of Nietzschean spirituality, is in fact a stratagem to return to the jungle, the space of savagery par excellence where Tarzan can get rid of his upper class self-control and even, as the fin de siècle aesthete had preached, resist a temptation by yielding to it rather than showing his self-possession by resisting a stimulus. Tarzan's romantic wildness, recovered through a disavowal of phallic masculinity, situates the image of the Nietzschean superman—the model for early twentieth century heroic virility—under the sign of gender undifferentiation; thus, his romantic escape into nature turns out to promise the pleasures of abjection rather than guaranteeing a perfect and self-contained masculinity.

回      回      回

Whereas the new century ideology of Nietzschean virility as popularized by eugenics and the discourse of nationalism used a language of essence and originality, founded no longer on the logos but on a hypostatized image of the body, the popular culture transposition of the superman as wild beast shows that his virility is a cultural fiction. As we have seen in the case of Sandow and Tarzan, this cultural fiction, arising in the period of mass consumerism, was reclaimed as a pervasive form of commodity fetishism. The final version of the "blond beast" may have been the fashionable fur coat of the interwar years, worn by both men and women, nothing more than a commodity, an expensive costume that bespeaks the natural but that signals social status rather than nature. Such an image of nature as costume—in fact as a real garment—might be seen as the ultimate displacement of animality onto the bodies of men and women in mass culture and as the culmination of a process that begins with the production of wildness in the zoo. There is only a short distance from the tiger displayed in a cage to the "specimen" killed for sport in the colonies and exhibited as a carpet (as one sees in Sandow's photographs) to the fur coat that the businessman or his wife desires. In all these examples the wildness signified by the animal—tropes that contributed to the image of the excessive corporeality of the superman—is reified and colonized as the space of consumption. No longer functional, this excess of the animal turns into a spectacle, a substitution of the part for the whole, a fetish-object replacing the absent phallus.

By partaking of this spectacularity, the examples of Sandow and Tarzan show that the image of the male body as a totality is a fabrication, producing, in turn, an unstable notion of masculinity. This gender instability, however, is only one symptom of perhaps the most far-reaching crisis in the representation of male bodies in the new century: the changed relation between the body and ever more pervasive machines. As technology became a constant presence, the "prosthetic culture" that I consider in the next chapter reflected a new set of anxieties. These centered, in the first place, upon the role of the "natural" in any version of embodied subjectivity viable in the machine age. Scattered texts of this period were already beginning to suggest the inadequacy of the "beast" imagery altogether in the age of technology. In Luigi Pirandello's novel *The Notebooks of Serafino Gubbio* of 1915, for example, which I will consider briefly to show how the beast imagery had always been prone to exposure, a comic and domesticated tiger becomes the central motif through which the image of the male body as totality is thoroughly questioned. The novel's setting, a film studio, and its plot make for a scenario in which performance and imitation, "nature" and reality, continually change places. As a cameraman, the hero is the medium for the transformation of reality into fiction. Gubbio is the modern man at the service of the machine: His passive role, his mediocre life, and his marginality in the process of reality-making through film can no longer be transfigured by the image of the blond beast. The wild animal in the novel, the tiger, first appears as a domesticated pet and then shreds to pieces, literally and metaphorically, the male body.

Gubbio works at the Kosmograph, a film production company; day after day at the studios he witnesses the transformation of life into images. An already illusory reality is "eaten up" by the machine ("this shrieking little machine, which, on its tripod ... looks like a big black spider ready to attack"[46]) and turned into meters of celluloid. Gubbio's relationship to the machine is ambivalent: By turning the handle and lending his eye to the camera, Serafino makes possible the miraculous effect of cinema, yet he perceives his body as a mere prosthetic extension of the apparatus, the means of this miracle rather than its author. He is, he concludes, at the service of the machine and even foresees the day when "it'll get to the point of suppressing me. The machine ... will work by itself."[47] His anxiety at being suppressed and made superfluous by technology cannot be assuaged; nothing in the vicarious after-hours life of this new version of the technician-clerk can turn him into a protagonist, an author. He feels wholly incorporated into the apparatus that, furthermore, is responsible for annihilating any possibility of reality, and he knows that even this denial and destruction is not his own.

The only sign of real life Gubbio finds at the Kosmograph is the tiger. Sold by a zoo, the tiger waits in a cage to become the protagonist (and the victim) of the last scene of *The Woman and the Tiger,* a film being made of the story of an English "miss" traveling in India, followed by her suitors. For Gubbio, the tiger, now tamed and made apathetic by months of imprisonment, represents an image of life "before the fall": The animal appears to him as unreified nature destined to die a gratuitously true death in a completely fictional (and again, predictably colonial) background: "India will be fake, the jungle will be fake, the journey will be fake; fake are the "miss" and her suitors: only the death of this poor beast won't be fake. ... In the middle of a general fiction, only its death will be real."[48] Yet something goes wrong. During the climactic scene, the main actor intentionally shoots his unfaithful mistress (a real-life person standing outside the cage) instead of the tiger. In turn, the beast attacks and kills the actor. The tiger's wildness has reemerged unexpectedly, causing a final demise of the actor as strongman.

Throughout the scene, the cameraman keeps turning the handle of the machine, thus displaying at its best "the specific quality demanded from one practicing my profession," impassivity.[49] Everybody else on the set is paralyzed by this action; this scene had not been predicted, it was not in the script. Paradoxically, what is shocking and surprising is the spectacle of a beast being "beastly" while the supposedly "animal" body of the strongman-tamer loses all its power.

Pirandello's plot provides a paradoxical reversal of the process through which the male body is reimagined as being as wild as that of the beast. With the novel's comically unexpected twist, the tiger—the only element of reality in the midst of cinematic fiction—does not perform the "magic" of fetishistic substitution but rather strikes a man dead. While the fake hunter, the actor, gets killed by a tame tiger turned wild, Gubbio remains behind the camera, impassively shooting a scene of murder and recording a staged fiction gone real. In contrast to the mangled body of the actor, Gubbio remains safe and intact behind the camera. And yet he suffers the same, although less gruesome, tearing apart as the actor. As he laments, he is no longer a powerful, free-willing individual; rather, he has become a mere spectator while his body is reduced to only what is necessary to operate a mechanical apparatus—a hand and an eye. Gubbio's anxiety about his enforced "spectatorship" and the metaphorical mutilation of the male body is symptomatic of the modern relationship of masculinity and technology. The mass culture display of the male body, whether as Nietzschean blond beast of prey or as masochized and wounded corporeality, might continue to be enjoyed and consumed as excessive spectacle; it turned out to be threatened less by contact with real wildness than by contact with machines. In the culture of the early twentieth century the parceling of the human body into separate organs adapted to technology produced different responses and, in turn, new ways of imagining masculinity. The machine age promised to radically streamline the body and its emotions. Futurism, in particular, thrived on imagining the "metallization" of the body and recuperated the fusion of nature and technology as the defining character of a newly modern and unsentimental virility. It is to this robotic body that I turn now.

# 4  A TEAR IS A MECHANICAL THING: AUTOMATON MASCULINITY

In the nineteenth century men were confident, the women were not but in the twentieth century the men have no confidence and so they have to make themselves as you say more beautiful more intriguing more everything and they cannot make any other man because they have to hold on to themselves not having any confidence.

—Gertrude Stein, *Everybody's Autobiography*

B ETWEEN THE TURN of the century and the First World War, an array of new machines came into everyday use in European culture, dramatically altering how people thought of the body and its relation to effort and expenditure. Given that Nietzschean corporeality—whether in the form of the proper and chastely natural body offered to the rising middle class or of the more excessive and masochized body of mass popular entertainment—was to a large degree premised on a display of superhuman energy, the new sense of the machines' pervasive and extraordinary power had a profound effect on the imagining of the body's strength. With Tarzan such energy was imagined, archaically, as animal rather than mechanical; with Sandow, the grossly muscled male body was displayed with a certain pathos in the spaces of leisure at the moment when physical strength was being outmoded in the workplace by the machine. Masculine corporeality had been structured to signify strength and energy in the very period when these qualities were being appropriated by machines—hence the modernist desire to signify the body as a mechanical apparatus, to not simply emulate and challenge technology but instead to identify with it. In the effort to imagine a new relation between bodies and technologies, two discourses intervened. First, in the space of work, the cult of efficiency wished to remake the body itself as useful

129

rather than spectacular; second, in that of high art, various modernisms dreamed of an ever more energized corporeality based on a fusion of male body and machine-metal. In this chapter, I focus on these modernist fantasies, and argue that their scenarios of robots and automatons, of metallic bodies made more alive by a partnership with the mechanical, are made possible first by a denial of the worker's body and second by a fantasy of "male motherhood" as the organizing trope of male sexuality.

The factory in the new century was no longer the chief site of technology: By leaving the sphere of industrial production to enter the home (in the form of household appliances), the street (as vehicles of transportation), and leisure time (as new means of entertainment), technology became an unavoidable experience, shaping the imaginary of masses of people and of modern writers and artists as well. Machines such as the car, the bicycle, and the airplane represented an image of freedom in the form of speed and acceleration; others, such as the mass-marketed pocket watch,[1] the conveyor belt, and the escalator,[2] suggested images of order, rationalization, and efficiency. This image of order and rationality became, in turn, a principle of management for the workplace, the state, and the bodies of the citizens themselves.

Spurred by the example of the United States and by an ever more productive Germany, a cult of efficiency developed in Edwardian England. Aimed at making the country function as a gigantic mechanism, "National Efficiency" came to inform practices as different as industrial organization, imperial management, and personal and collective hygiene.[3] Resolutions in favor of simplification and acceleration and against "waste" and "muddle" became staples of the political and social programs of the time. The same principles came to inform both modernist aesthetics and the masses' everyday life. Ezra Pound, who arrived in London in 1908, wrote in the journal *The New Age* of the need for a new, streamlined language in poetry, and Arnold Bennett wrote guides that taught people how to make the most of their time in both their working and private lives: *Mental Efficiency* and *How to Live on Twenty-Four Hours a Day* appeared in the same year, 1912.

The Edwardian cult of efficiency was one response to a perceived decline of England's imperial and economic strength. The outcome of the Boer War and the loss of commercial hegemony to Germany and the United States were attributed by numerous commentators either to the malfunctioning bodies of the working classes, lacking adequate housing and medical care, or to the waste of time and human energies in the backward and mismanaged organization of labor in factory and office. The great models of how to successfully manage the labor force were the American movement for national efficiency under Roosevelt and Wilson and the system of assembly-line production newly introduced in Henry Ford's factories.[4] The "streamlined" movements of the worker at the assembly line had been carefully studied by F. W. Taylor in *The Principles of Scientific Management* (1911). In his motion studies Taylor had considered the capabilities of the human body as motor, observed the productive process in the factory, registered the worker's most precise and direct movements, and arranged them in a fixed sequence of actions that the worker now *had* to perform. This enormously influential tract showed how productivity could be accelerated by fragmenting the labor process into single tasks to be performed according to a calculated and rigorous standard of time.

Taylor's system of time management was deployed mostly in factories and offices, but the principle of speed and rationalization encoded in this mechanized work process also spread from the space of production and came to organize the citizen's life in the city as well. The newly zoned city was represented both as an icon of ordered and rationalized movement (as for example in Walter Ruttman's film *Berlin, Symphony of a Great City* [1927]) or conversely as a spectacle of spasmodic and revolutionary chaos (as in Giacomo Balla's painting *The City Rises* [1912]) or in Georg Grosz's crowded urban scenes. In each case the city stood as the space of human and technological energy, representing both the freedom of acceleration and the calculable regimentation of the masses. In his famous essay "The Metropolis and Mental Life" (1911), Georg Simmel explained how the accelerated rhythm of city life produced a new type of subject characterized by a certain hardness and by a matter-of-fact blasé, attitude. At the same time, "metropolitan man," as Simmel defined him, was a split subject: His newly accumulated nervous energy had sharpened his intelligence ("He reacts with his head instead of his heart. . . . Metropolitan life, thus, underlies an heightened awareness and a predominance of intelligence in metropolitan man"[5]), but the speed of city life threatened him, and gave him the impression of "being levelled and worn out by a technological mechanism."[6] The sense of alertness that for Simmel characterized the psychological structure of modern metropolitan man was required by the frenzy of street life: Once cars appeared in the metropolis, the city seemed as dangerous as a battlefield. One of the first fatal car accidents caused a sensation in 1914 England; the death of a child, the son of the newspaper magnate Lord Northcliffe, led to much campaigning for speed limits.[7] In this new traffic, the pedestrian became a marginal character and the flâneur—for Walter Benjamin a chief figure of nineteenth century modernity—whose predecessors in Paris had walked turtles at the Palais Royal, was practically obsolete. His *flânerie* was endangered and superseded by the speed of the automobile, and his body, as Adorno suggests in *Minima Moralia*, became a moveable target for the homicidal instincts of the driver: "And which driver is not tempted, merely by the power of his engine, to wipe out the vermin of the street, pedestrians, children and cyclists?"[8] Incapable of keeping up with the machine, the pedestrian's body becomes that of the designated victim, a sign of the older order powerless before the modern driver.

This new urban and industrial panorama gave an enormous impetus to intellectual and cultural innovation. William M. Beard, for example, described the dangerous effects of the new technologies (the telephone and the train) in *American Nervousness* (1881), coining a medical term, neurasthenia, that was immediately popular in early twentieth century Europe. The sculptor Jacob Epstein instead represented "the sinister armored figure of today and tomorrow"[9] in his bronze sculpture *The Rock Drill* (1913–1914), and Adorno himself, a few years later, lamented a "withering of experience" that he attributed to the invasion of technology: "Technology is making gestures precise and brutal, and with them men. ... It subjects them to the implacable ... a historical demands of objects."[10] At the same time, artists from Fernand Léger to Marcel Duchamp, from Gino Severini to Sonia and Robert Delaunay, took the machine and its "dehumanizing" speed and rationality as a principle of aesthetic innovation. Between 1900 and 1920, the technological imagination of European modernist avant-gardes came alive in the aesthetic experimentation of Cubism, Italian Futurism, Russian Constructivism, the Dutch movement De Stijl, and the Bauhaus and, after the First World War, Swiss and German Dada. All these movements launched a new modernist aesthetics organized around the qualities of the machine: linearity, functionality, impersonality, dynamism, violence, and fragmentation of the human figure. The technologies of modern life taught the artist, as Léger affirmed, "the beauty of the fragment."[11] In this chapter I concentrate on Futurism, in particular on the work of Filippo Tommaso Marinetti and Umberto Boccioni. For Futurism the machine was not simply a means, as for Cubism and Dada, of aesthetic and social innovation; the movement's members also saw themselves as organizing a new form of masculinity founded on the fantasy of a mechanical body.

Combining the Nietzschean ideology of the superman with the early twentieth century cult of the machine, the Futurists in their writing, painting, and sculpture engineered the image of a mechanized male body characterized by the lack of emotions and recognizable human features. Like Umberto Boccioni's dynamic figures or Marinetti's image of "man multiplied by the motor," the male body envisioned by Futurism bears little resemblance to the classically harmonious body of the subject of western humanism; its brutal dislocation of the human form, the development of new, machine-like qualities and even of new limbs (the wings of an airplane), turns the male body into a dehumanized automaton, the product of the interfusing of metal and flesh. Even more than a new human type capable of functioning in the modern city and of promptly reacting to its sudden and violent stimuli, like Simmel's metropolitan man, the Futurist man-machine is the model of a new technological-military body devoid of individuality. By virtue of his mechanical qualities he is capable of accomplishing more incredible and heroic deeds than a normal human being, particularly the mediocre and adipose bourgeois, could ever achieve.

The claim of Futurism's "planned" male body to be a fully mechanized version of the corporeality of the athlete—steeled, drilled, and unsentimental—is founded on the displacement of two elements: its similarity with the body of the Taylorized worker, and sexuality and desire. In this chapter I read the Futurist male body in the light of this maneuver of displacement to show how both the mechanized laboring body and a sexualized masculinity are integral parts of the image of the Futurist man-machine, and as such compromise his claim to a "naturally" technological virility.

The robotic body of Futurist man—juxtaposing the Nietzschean virtues of power, amorality, and antisentimentality and the cold rationality of the machine—relies on an almost imperceptible occlusion of the political economy of the modern automatized body. The qualities of the machine that Futurism deployed to debunk the passé culture of the bourgeoisie were the same that fragmented and dehumanized the worker's body at the assembly line, but it is this similarity that the Futurist artist wanted to elide from his text and with it, his dependence on the material conditions that mechanized and rationalized the human body in the new Taylorist regimentation. It's not by chance that the technologies appearing in the Futurist manifestos are unproductive machines: With the image of the car, the tank, and the human and animal automaton, the Futurist tried to dispel any hint of the actual function of "man multiplied by the motor" in the capitalist scenario of the time. In turn, the unfinalized mechanical power of the Futurist man turned his body into a territory where sexuality could be once again reinscribed, often through the visual tropes that had defined the handsome and martyred male physique in the fin de siècle. At the core of a metallic and rationalized image of masculinity that seems to be denying any kind of pleasure to both itself and its spectator, the final interpenetration of metal and flesh produces a monstrous masculine subject who masochistically rejoices in his loss of any human character, as well as in the painful process through which this loss takes place—for instance, the car accident.

This sacrificial pleasure in being wounded, which supplies the climax to a number of Futurist writings, translates the image of the fin de siècle aesthete's martyred body into technological terms. Moreover, the violence of the accident is interpreted by the Futurist as a moment of mystical fusion with technology ("the divinity," as Marinetti calls it) that places the notion of the sacred at the center of an avant-garde project of absolute modernity, while also invoking the pleasure of self-loss that sanctions the ruin of masculine subjectivity in the case of the aesthete. This masochistic desire for a fusion with the car or the plane proposed by the Futurists is central to their vision of a new relationship of the male body to technology. For them, man does not try to dominate the machine; instead, by assuming its "automatic" qualities, he relinquishes his traditional order of humanity and individuality. Rather than measuring up to technology to demonstrate his own superiority, he performs an act of self-production as self-annihilation not simply by submitting to the machine but by becoming it. This strategy, as it came to be worked out, was used by the Futurists to establish and reinforce a notion of excessive, apparently antibourgeois, virility.

At the same time, the image of Futurist man as the subject of his own objectification into mere matter turns this hypermasculinity on its head and cracks its carapace to present a view of the male body articulated through a number of contradictions: rationalization versus an almost decadent sexuality, the impassivity and hardness of metal versus the "softness" of wounded flesh, the ascetic streamlining and geometrization of the human form versus the exuberant eroticism of the male body, and fragmentation versus fantasies of motherhood and creation.

The metallic corporeality of the robot depicted in the Futurist manifestos contrasts with the erotically charged masculine beauty displayed in Marinetti's romances. In the manifestos the Futurist superman is represented as a self-controlled automaton whose hygienic norms of self-preservation, renunciation of sexuality and feelings, turned him into a fully efficient body, no longer an individual but a weapon. In the romance *Mafarka* (1909), which I will discuss in detail, Marinetti deploys the metaphor of birthing and maternal creation, although accomplished by a superman, to disavow any dependence of the mechanical male body on the material conditions of its production. Nevertheless, the metallized body of Futurist man remains the counterfigure of the worker: He uncannily exhibits the same qualities of discipline, self-restraint, and efficiency that Gramsci describes as necessary attributes of the modern worker in "Americanism and Fordism" (1929–1935). The anxieties about masculine power, originality, and agency that Futurism tried to elide from the male body become fully visible when we read both the manifestos and the romances in the context of other early twentieth century representations of the mechanized body of the automaton. Futurism excluded sentimentality, sexuality, and labor from the scene of reproduction and production (Mafarka's son is a machine) in the attempt to affirm the male body's independence from the material conditions that had automatized the human body in the period: Like Minerva, born from Jupiter's brain, Gazurmah is infused with life exclusively through his father's will. In Fritz Lang's *Metropolis* (1926), which I will briefly consider as a further version of the worker's relation to the automaton body, sexuality, as well as women and workers, whom Marinetti had excluded from the privileged father-son relationship, are reintegrated only to be more deeply interpellated by capitalism's demands: Whereas Mafarka causes the death of his workers in Marinetti's novel, in *Metropolis* they are treated instead to the ideological seduction of a sexualized and sentimentalized maternal figure.

Both Mafarka's son, Gazurmah, and Maria in *Metropolis* are automatons. Automatons, at least since the time of Vaucanson's mechanical duck in the eighteenth century,[12] are part of a long history of machines that imitate organic bodies. The automaton is an image of self-propelling matter that aspires to appear human or animal, and alive. The representation of Marinetti's new man as a robot rather than as a purely abstract form or a deeply dislocated shape (like Boccioni's barely anthropomorphic sculptures of speeding bodies, for example) betrays a desire for individuation on the Futurist's part and evidences a barely suppressed eagerness to return to figuration. The winged, metallic, and classically beautiful body of Gazurmah, paradoxically an image of Icarus or the *Victory of Samothrace* and of the passé classicism that the Futurist claims to have overcome, implies that although the body was fragmented into unrecognizable parts and then reassembled in a totality that bore no resemblance to the human figure, individuality and mimesis were by no means entirely ruled out by Futurism: The ornamental beauty of the man-machine implicitly transforms him into another spectacular body. In many Futurist texts, the Futurist man's decorative qualities are not that far removed from those of the strongman in the style of Sandow. The ideological collusion of the Futurist male body with that of the spectacular and eroticized strongman-bodybuilder had already been brought to the fore in the final text that I will consider, Alfred Jarry's novel *The Supermale* (1902). In this futuristic and protofuturist novel set in 1920, Jarry anticipated and mocked in advance Futurism's puritanical and militaristic construction of masculinity: His novel ends, as a tragic-comic response to the modern frenzy over the machine, with an image of the final shrinking of the vitalistic superman into a jewel-like tear.

# FUTURISM AND THE
# SYNTHETIC MALE BODY:
# THE EROTICISM OF DANGER

In the narrative of the *Founding Manifesto* of Futurism (1909), Futurism famously begins with a car accident and an injured body—Marinetti's own. "We went up to the three snorting beasts, to lay amorous hands on their torrid breasts. I stretched out in my car as a corpse on its bier, but revived at once under the steering wheel, a guillotine blade that threatened my stomach."[13] The drive through the Italian countryside is interrupted by the sudden appearance of two cyclists who cause the accident:

> Their stupid dilemma was blocking my way—damn! Ouch! ... I stopped short and to my disgust rolled over into a ditch with my wheel in the air. .... Oh maternal ditch, almost full of muddy water! Fair factory drain! I gulped down the nourishing sludge; and I remembered the blessed black breast of my Sudanese nurse. ... When I came up—torn, filthy and stinking—from under the capsized car, I felt the white hot iron of joy pass through my heart! We, bruised, our arms in slings, but unafraid, declared our high intentions to all the living of the earth. (Marinetti, *Selected Writings,* 41)

Marinetti's narrative features all the elements of Futurist discourse: a tone of rodomontade (spoken with a Nietzschean accent), love for the industrial landscape, the cult of the machine, the virility of hard metal (both steeling and threatening the softness of flesh), all contained within a triumphalist autobiography. However, the passage features two elements that appear in strident contradiction to the declamatory rhetoric of Futurism's technological enthusiasm: an image of masculine suffering and the allusion to the soothing maternal body. In the first instance, Marinetti's pose as the aggressor, about to injure the cyclists, is reversed into the role of the victim, a body wounded by the accident. The piercing steering wheel, "a guillotine blade that threatened my stomach," and the metaphor his feeling the "white hot iron of joy pass through my heart" evoke once again the body of Saint Sebastian, the fin de siècle cult figure of male masochism. At the same time, in the midst of the Futurists' all-male company, the image of the maternal breast appears unexpectedly. At the moment of their symbolic baptism in the dirty waters of an industrial Jordan, the factory drain's "nourishing sludge" is transformed by association into maternal milk and into the memory of Marinetti's Sudanese nurse.

Both images are promptly dispelled, however, through a rhetorical move that characterizes both the manifestos and Marinetti's fiction. On the one hand, Marinetti's nostalgic memory of the maternal body is displaced by the image of woman as sexualized prey, here represented by the car itself; he wants to place his "amorous hands" on her "torrid breasts." On the other, the Saint Sebastian–like image of masculine masochism implicit in the male body in pain is superseded in the instantaneous healing of the wounds. Through a cut, with almost cinematic speed, from the scene of the accident we are moved to the moment when the protagonists appear with their arms in slings and the neo-Futurists begin declaiming their credo. In the first section of the manifesto, Marinetti's narrative has the fast-moving pace of comic strips where, through fast editing, the story is rapidly forwarded for the audience's enjoyment. The Donald Duck–like resilience of the Futurist body confirms his superhuman quality and his identity as an automaton, a fantastic machine that tries in vain to imitate the organic: The impossibility of pain and death proves that the body, for the Futurists, has achieved the status of a technological apparatus, a thing.

The remainder of the *Founding Manifesto* expresses the Futurist affirmation of energy, audacity, danger, speed, and the exaltation of urban life against "literature" and the serene repose of classical beauty as represented by Greek sculpture: "A roaring racing car, rattling along like a machine gun, is more beautiful than the winged victory of Samothrace"(Marinetti, 41). The racing car and its speed represent for Marinetti an image of power and violence that will be fully realized in war. By praising war as "the world's only hygiene," Marinetti embraces an exclusionary program of social cleansing that, through an attack on women, human feelings, and liberal parliamentarism, posits itself as a blueprint for the creation of a new race of men—a new race, the Futurists prophesied, that would renovate the backward culture of their time. The dynamism of the machine was assumed by Futurism as a model for a corporeal aesthetics centered on aggression and for a cultural practice founded on mass agitation and violent interventions in the spaces of the everyday. Speed and synthesis were to take over every level of aesthetic experience: from language ("parolibere," "wordsatfreedom") to the theater (now to be a mixture of political assembly, drama, and riot) to the figurative arts, where Art Nouveau's curves were to yield to the geometry inspired by machines.

The interest in geometrization and linearity assumed a particular poignancy in the Futurist representation of the human form: Futurist sculpture was characterized by an interpenetration of planes and by a fascination with the violent "mixing" of objects and bodies. As Boccioni explained in *Technical Manifesto of Futurism* (April 1909), such sculpture brings objects to life by showing how they prolong in space and how they intersect with other solids. Boccioni's aesthetic program involved a dramatic redefinition of the human figure. The body, in his view, no longer maintains its anthropomorphic shape but rather becomes an ag-glomeration of matter in space: "Thus from the armpit of a mechanic there could protrude a gearwheel, the line of a table could slice through the head of a man reading, and the fanned pages of the book could section his stomach. ... We pro-claim the absolute and complete abolition of determinate lines and closed statues. We split open the figure and include the environment in it."[14] In Boccioni's theory and practice the human form is denied the stability that anchors the subject to a specific, individual body in order to privilege a drama of fusion with the sur-roundings. This machine-like and reified body is the visual translation of Marinetti's new man; the aim of the Futurist enterprise is to produce a new human subject, a man modeled on the machine, "fed by electricity," and capable of responding to any challenge. Marinetti's "man multiplied by the motor"(Marinetti, *Selected Writings*, 120) described in *War, the World's Only Hygiene* (1911–1915) is a man without memory and individuality whose body is organized according to a contradictory impulse to reason and impassivity on one side and "the lust for danger and daily heroism" on the other (Marinetti, *Selected Writings*, 121).

By identifying with the motor, the Futurist male body goes beyond his human, organic possibilities to develop new capabilities and even new organs: "One must imitate the movement of the machine with gestures: pay assiduous count to the steering wheel, ordinary wheels, pistons, thereby preparing the fusion of man with the machine, to achieve the metallicity of the Futurist dance. ... The Futurist dance can have no other purpose than to intensify heroism and to fuse with the divine machines of speed and war" (*Manifesto of Futurist Dance*, July 8, 1917; Marinetti, *Selected Writings*, 75). The visionary tone of this passage announces, implicitly, that the new man is no longer an individual but a type and that his body, replicating the different functions of the machine, is nothing more than plastic, transformable material. Human psychology, now obsolete, must be re-placed with "the lyric obsession with matter" as the *Technical Manifesto of Futurism* (May 11, 1911; Marinetti, *Selected Writings*, 87) makes clear. The free-dom from bourgeois sentimentality and psychology that Futurism claims as its founding principle is visible in the image of the subject turned animated matter in Boccioni's bronze *Dynamism of a Form in Space* (1912) (Figure 4.1). Propelled forward by the efficient energy of its tight muscles, this body is an aerodynamic shape suggesting continuous movement. Individuality has been abolished from it: The head is a combination of skull, helmet (that still, however, retains a memory of the classical), and machine part; facial features have been erased.

As mechanized matter, the Futurist man-robot must be devoid of any sign of individuality and humanity. The multiplication of man by the motor takes place through a process of synthesis, condensation, and elimination of the superfluous. To become a body without a residue, the Futurist type must divest himself of all emotions ("moral suffering, goodness of heart, affection and love, those sole cor-rosive poisons of inexhaustible vital energy," [*War: The World's Only Hygiene,*

138

*Figure 4.1*    *Umberto Boccioni*, Dynamism of a Form in Space, *1912.*

1911–1912; Marinetti, *Selected Writings,* 81]), and at the same time distance himself from the excessive, redundant, and useless elements of society, "women, the
sedentary, invalids, the sick and all the prudent counsellors" (*Let's Murder the
Moonshine*, April 1909; Marinetti, *Selected Writings,* 46). The elimination of
"erotic alcohol"—the drink of revel and carnival—by "the caffeine of Europe" (47,
46, respectively), as Marinetti defined himself, points to a juxtaposition of Futurist
asceticism and the protestant ethic of capitalism. Both feminine sentimentality
and lust must be banned from the "naturally cruel, omniscient, combative
Futurist"; Marinetti affirms that virility is preserved at the cost of self-control and
sexual renunciation. In *War: The World's Only Hygiene*, he advises young men, in
a peremptory tone, to stay away from "the double alcohol of lust and sentiment"
(Marinetti, *Selected Writings,* 83). In an exercise of willpower, youths must learn
how to dominate their feelings and how to turn sex into a detached, almost therapeutic, practice. The ascetic underpinnings of many Futurist harangues, however, meant that their visions of excess were still generally recontained in rhetoric
that served "progress" as defined by the established order.

Once he has eliminated affect and expenditure, the subject can finally become
matter that can be refunctioned ad infinitum. This is a body whose use and re-
sourcefulness does not end with death; the evolutionary transformations of the
human subject, his plastic capability of assuming new shapes, continue also after
life, as Marinetti describes in an ominously prophetic story. His tale of the "recy-
cled" corpses from the Chinese battlefields anticipates a rumor that circulated in
England during the First World War about German military efficiency, according
to which the Germans were said to transform the dead bodies into oil and pig fod-
der.[15] Marinetti's story, introduced in one of the manifestos, is presented as a laud-
able example of Futurist synthesis. In Japan the coal made from human bones is
used as a new explosive substance and sold at a commercial price: "Day after day,
the merchants search the Manchurian battlefields. ... One hundred tsin (seven
kilograms) of human bones bring in ninety-two kopecs. ... The Japanese merchants who direct this absolutely Futurist commerce buy no skulls. It seems that
they lack the necessary qualities." From the Transiberian railway, the passengers can
see piles of bones arranged into gigantic pyramids, "skeletons of heroes who do not
hesitate to be crushed in mortars by their sons, their relations and their fellow citizens, to be brutally vomited out by Japanese artillery against hostile armies. Glory
to the indomitable ashes of man, that come to life in cannons! My friends, let us
applaud this noble example of synthetic violence!" (*War;* Marinetti, 82).

It is by turning himself into matter, this narrative implies, that man achieves
immortality. This modernist parable of eternal life brings into focus the ideological dynamics at work in Futurist discourse: In the course of the narrative, the initially foregrounded information that the bones are *for sale* is gradually reabsorbed
and blurred by Futurist bombast. The system of abstraction and equivalences
through which the bodies of individuals are turned into value—a metaphor for
the way in which capital turns live men into dead labor—is celebrated as Futurist

synthesis. Notice that here too, as in Boccioni's sculpture, Futurist man has no face, in fact no head. The skulls are not bought because they lack the "necessary qualities": The seat of individual reason has been eliminated. Above all, these fragments of the body produce a new whole that has nothing to do with the coherence of the human figure: The scattered bones no longer belong to one individual, recognizable body but are rather pulverized to produce a missile of war and destruction, the cannonball. What we witness in this narrative is an ideological slippage from the materiality of the body to its marketability and hence to its fetishized version as object of blind and destructive force. The slippage occurs behind the Futurist rhetoric of heroism, in which political economy is reencoded as myth and tall tale.

What remains unsaid in the flamboyant and decisive rhetoric of Marinetti and Boccioni and is invisible in the image of the male body they present is its sexuality. This returns as an aesthetic and political unconscious in Marinetti's fiction. In *Mafarka le futuriste* (1909), the figure of the eroticized automaton and tropes of motherhood and of masculine suffering introduce the issues of male desire, the scope of individuation, and the potential creative power of the man-machine into the text. These issues are considered in relation to the hero, Mafarka, to produce an image of the male body that, as I will show, exists in opposition to that of the impassive and cruel machine presented in the manifestos. In the manifestos Marinetti had manufactured the image of a robot, a fearless man of iron identified with the motor and beyond "muscular possibility"—a man whose playground is the battlefield and who, after his death, becomes himself a weapon. The Futurist man-machine, faceless like Boccioni's dynamic forms and devoid of interiority and psychic drives, seems to replicate the image of the soldier male whom Klaus Theweleit describes as "a machine for the persecution of pleasure."[16] In his analysis of the Freikorpsman's unconscious, Theweleit attempts to elucidate the mechanisms that propel this soldier's disciplined and self-contained body and that provide his pleasure in destruction. Theweleit concludes that the soldier's rationalization and inclusion into the totality of the troop functioned to block the productivity of the unconscious. In this process, as he describes it, while "the natural machinery of the human unconscious is abandoned, and the periphery of the human being artificially mechanized, the machine, on the other hand, abandons its natural element of production and is artificially anthropomorphized."[17] The body of the Freikorps soldier becomes a human mechanism with no ego and no desire, its instinctual energies completely made functional by war. This soldier-male, given his self-denial, his renunciation of pleasure in order to function efficiently in the battlefield, and his effort to suffocate affect, would seem to embody the physical type whose characteristics the Futurist hero of the manifestos strives to achieve. However, as it becomes evident in the reading of *Mafarka*, two key elements distance the man envisioned by Futurism from the Freikorps man-machine. Marinetti's new man *strives* to attain but does not fully achieve the perfectly robotic condition Theweleit ascribes to the Freikorps soldier. Second, Marinetti's figure, as the product of a technological aesthetics embedded in the social and cultural scenario of the early twentieth century, exists as the epitome of, rather than claiming no relation to, the productive logic of monopoly capitalism.

Theweleit does not emphasize a connection between the machine body of the Freikorpsman and the increasing technologization of the means of production; in his view, whereas the fascist utopia of a mechanical male body finds a new venue in the modern imagery of the machine, the elements of this political direction had already been implanted in the masculine self. Such a politics, he suggests, "has nothing to do with the development of machine technology. ... The mechanized body as conservative utopia derives instead from men's compulsion to subjugate and repulse what is specifically human within them—the id, the productive force of the unconscious."[18] He reads the mechanization of the male body not as a historically contingent strategy through which the male subject, "learning" from the machine and at the same time becoming engulfed by the logic of capital, tries to reaffirm his authority and privilege but rather as a transhistorical condition ("men's compulsion to subjugate ... the id") made sharper and more evident in the fascist soldier. I wish to argue, however, that the Futurist man-machine and the texts that represent him suggest instead an interdependence between the image of "man multiplied by the motor" and the political economy of the machine on which this body relies. The ways in which the Futurist man and his body function in an economy of consumption and production become more than once visible on the surface of Futurist discourse, as in the parable of the bones turned missiles, for example; this visibility is merely obscured by the manifestos in their attempt to demonstrate the originality and almost mystical—and, as I will show, fetishistic—quality of this version of the male body.

It is precisely the Futurist anxiety about demonstrating autonomy from the material and historical conditions shaping the modernist technological imagination that structures Marinetti's romance *Mafarka le futuriste,* in which the male protagonist "gives birth" to a colossal automaton. Written in 1909, the same year as the publication of the *Founding Manifesto, Mafarka* was, in its author's own words, "a lyrical song, an epic, an adventure novel, and a drama all at the same time."[19] Mafarka is a warrior, a storyteller, and the most exuberant lover. His eleven-meter-long penis, which the protagonist rolls around himself before going to sleep, cost Marinetti a trial for obscenity in 1910. *Mafarka*'s romance structure combines a series of narrative genres, from the boys' adventure story to pornography, to the orientalist tale on the model of travelers' reports from exotic lands, to early science fiction. Alice Yaeger Kaplan sees the romance as a protofascist fantasy; she suggests that it "exists in juxtaposition to the manifestos as Freud has described a daydream existing in relation to a work of art."[20] The North African setting allows Marinetti to refashion a colonial milieu with which he was familiar into a mythic otherworld depicted as a sultry landscape where the Futurist fascination with technology is played off against a typical imperial fantasy of exotic nature. This world of palm trees is populated by figures who either are dressed in

*Figure 4.2    Vaslav Nijinski as the Gold Slave in* Scheherezade, *1911.* Photo: Bert, courtesy of the Dance Collection, The New York Public Library for the Performing Arts.

ways that recall the dancer Vaslav Nijinsky's performance in Fokine's ballet *Scheherazade*, where he appears covered in veils and precious fabrics(Figure 4.2), or, à la Tarzan, are flaunting their glistening muscles in the African sun.

Marinetti's Africa is a heterotopic fantasy space where the gym and the theater stage merge. The inhabitants of Mafarka's kingdom are bizarre and fantastic animals, such as the winged "war giraffes," gigantic mechanisms that need to be wound up before they attack the "celestial unicorns." The picaresque plot, full of adventures, dangerous encounters, and struggles, begins with the victory of Mafarka over his uncle and the defeat of his enemies. The tenor of the text is suggested by the account of how he conquers the most powerful of these: Dressed as a beggar he penetrates the enemy camp, and by telling arousing stories he incites Brafane's men to orgies that lead them to excess and self-destruction. He then prevents a mass rape of native women with his brother and gives proof of his supernatural sexual power by possessing all the young women of a town in one night. Throughout, the Kurtz-like imperial male fantasies of omnipotent rule and going native are taken to the ultimate extremes through the western technological fantasy of an all-powerful mechanized body.

At this point Mafarka the warrior, lover, and storyteller becomes Mafarka the engineer and grows absorbed in the most important enterprise of his life, having a son. Mafarka wants to "make" a son without the intervention of a woman. The misogyny of this exclusion is evident also in several of Marinetti's manifestos; he declared that women's calls for suffrage reflected only their awareness that they had become useless "mothers, wives and lovers" and admitted in *Against Amore and Parliamentarism* (1911–1915; Marinetti, 75) that "We have even dreamed of, one day, being able to create a mechanical son, the fruit of pure will, a synthesis of all the laws that science is on the brink of discovering." To understand Marinetti's replacement of a narrative of heterosexual reproduction with a father-son story that wishes to forgo the mother's role altogether, one needs, however, to consider the interplay of the organic and the technological—in which the body of this fantasy father is made to operate.

The manifestos propose the image of an ascetic, almost puritanical, masculinity; Mafarka's male body, in contrast, becomes oversexualized in Marinetti's romance. *Mafarka* presents a hybrid scenario that combines technological streamlining with a Nietzschean celebration of male corporeality, as seems appropriate in a modernist science fiction text that luxuriates in the kind of decadent opulence familiar from Aubrey Beardsley's drawings to Wilde's *Salome* or D'Annunzio's fin de siècle novels, particularly *Il piacere* (1900). Although Mafarka is, above all, a warrior, his body is described in highly sensuous terms:

> He had the agility and the strength of a young athlete, invincible, well equipped to bite, strangle and immobilize his enemy. His body—too compact, too lovely and almost frantic under a red hairiness and a skin patterned like that of a snake, seemed to be painted with the colors of fortune and victory, like the prow of a beautiful ship.

And light certainly worshipped him passionately because it would not stop caressing his broad pectorals, all knotted up in impatient muscles, as well as his biceps, which seemed to be made of oak, and his arresting legs, to which the sweat gave a metallic glare. (Marinetti, *Mafarka*, 21)

More than once the narrator indulges in these close-ups of the male body: Often portrayed seminaked, showing off his arms covered in "bird tattoos" (20), Mafarka is more an animal than a machine. He is simultaneously described as Loos's tattooed and decorated savage and as a Nietzschean blond beast ("his eyes, golden-black like licorice, violently sparkled under the sun, too close to each other, like those of the beasts of prey" [21]). This warrior body is not quite the physical type that Theweleit, via Junger, describes as "exploding" in battle, releasing all its repressed instinctual energies in war, but rather is the seductive, sensuous male body that haunted the aestheticist boudoirs of the turn of the century. In *Mafarka*, the clattering of the metallic Futurist body is replaced by the rustle of precious fabrics slipping off the sensuous skin of a male body. The pleasures that "man multiplied by the motor" ascetically renounces in the manifestos are recuperated here through the representation of Mafarka's body as a sensuous and at times even languid form.

The sexualization of the male body in the romance takes place through the formulas of adolescent porn fantasies, schoolboy pranks centered upon and obsessed with the male genitals. An example of this fixation is provided in one of the tales that Mafarka, in the garb of a beggar, tells Brafane and his men of the legendary genesis of Mafarka's supernatural powers. Mafarka the warrior was once a horse dealer; one day the devil, disguised as a rich merchant, asked to buy a black stallion with red mane and tail. The focus of attention in this part of the narrative is the horse's "zeb," his penis, which Mafarka describes as "red in color ... with its tip covered in diamonds, like the one which the girls of Tell-el-Kibir dream of the night before their wedding" (75). The devil-merchant immediately bought the horse, but it turned out to be an unfortunate purchase: The horse was magical; each time its mane was ruffled by the wind, it caught fire. Further, as it was the mating season, the horse managed to copulate with all the animals of the forest, always unsaddling his rider. The devil decided to take his revenge by castrating the horse, and after stuffing its penis, he served it to Mafarka as a savory "stuffed fish." By eating the magic phallus, Mafarka becomes insane, throws the devil out of his palace, and, like the horse, starts displaying his animal masculinity. At this point, the Futurist anxiety about phallic power takes a grotesque turn: After eating the magic fish, Mafarka's penis grows so huge that some sailors nearby mistake it for a rope and roll it around the mast of their ship. Thus Mafarka is taken by sea to another city, which he conquers singlehandedly. The experience of eating the horse's penis, an act that transforms Mafarka into a man out of control, can be read as a moment of fusion with the paternal body, an act of "communion" with the phallus that explodes rather than normalizes Mafarka's subjection into Oedipal masculinity. The paternal body is metonymically presented in this tale as an object to be introjected, literally eaten, by Mafarka. Thus it invokes both the pre-Oedipal relation to the maternal body and the male masochist's desire for, rather than normative identification with, the paternal figure.

The supernatural sexuality of the protagonist is expended in voluptuous love-making *and* preserved through a "swift casual contact with women," as Marinetti prescribes in the manifestos. Although Mafarka enjoys the bodies of many women in the text, the female body is phobically despised and represented through the decadent formula of the femme fatale, uniting the image of beauty and impure, rotting flesh, sin and seduction. The most Futurist moment of the entire novel is that of "The Futurist Speech," which Mafarka delivers to his adepts upon his brother's death. The death itself leaves Mafarka untouched ("Contemplate my hardened soul, my agile nerves, vibrating under my implacable and lucid will. My metallic brain sees everywhere precise angles in rigid geometrical systems." [240]), and he explains how he has managed to reach such sublime impassivity by re-nouncing his juvenile pleasure in and love of women. Although the pleasures of the affectively charged female body are thus allegedly abolished by the protago-nist, they do not disappear from the scene of the romance. Rather, they are dis-placed onto the image of the masculine-maternal body and onto the hero's am-biguous desire to "make" a son without the intervention of a woman.

After renouncing sexuality and "the female ovary," which he uses as a synonym for organic reproduction, and brutally sending away his bride, Colubbi, Mafarka literally builds a son with the help of two different types of workers, the black-smiths and the weavers. While the blacksmiths are building the metallic structure that supports the colossal body of Gazurmah, Mafarka's son, the weavers "weave" his flesh with a magic mixture concocted by Mafarka that turns vegetable fibers into living flesh. In Marinetti's narrative, the organic and the inorganic juxtapose to produce an image of the protagonist as engineer-mother: "I build and give birth to my son, undefeatable and gigantic bird, with his big flexible wings made to embrace the stars" (233). The son is the product of the masculine "soul" and is brought to life by Mafarka's will; nevertheless, the "absolute power of will" that the protagonist cultivates through a program of strict discipline and self-renunci-ation, soon yields to a highly poetic and sensuous moment of parental pride. Tenderly Mafarka imagines his son's beauty: "I will transmit my soul to him with a kiss; I will inhabit his heart and his lungs, and I will reside behind the glasses of his eyes; I will lean out of the red balconies of his lips. ... He is more handsome than all the men and the women of the earth!" (236). This sentimentalized list of beautiful attributes speaks not only of paternal pride but also of desire: Here Marinetti's romance inadvertently touches an ambiguously homoerotic chord. The handsome male body is exposed, visually explored by the protagonist, and proudly offered to the reader's gaze.

In his act of creation, Mafarka plays simultaneously the role of God the Father, plastically shaping matter in every possible form he wishes, and that of a mother, whose son is born from her self-abnegation, from her will to transfuse her energy from her body into his. However, the maternal production of this colossal and winged robot, which Mafarka attributes entirely to himself, equally relies, in fact, on the efforts of the blacksmiths and weavers. The production of Mafarka's great masterpiece is founded on a precise division of labor. This division relies, in turn, on an implicit class distinction: While the blacksmiths do the heavy work of laying the foundations for Gazurmah's frame and the weavers prepare his external semblance, Mafarka performs the intellectual role of engineering the robot. The proletarians are elided from the scene of Futurist creation in a plot twist that makes their disappearance seem natural and inevitable: The blacksmiths are suppressed by the weavers after an internal fight, and the weavers are sent away without being paid while Mafarka mysteriously gives life to his son-machine through an act of pure will. Although the disappearance of the workers is not as theatrical as the exclusion of women, it is not less remarkable. The banning of labor from the scene of Futurist creation (actually a production) reproduces the mechanism through which the "sale" and the commodification of the Manchurian corpses is dispelled in the passage I previously discussed: The political economy of the body is always forgotten by the Futurist. Notwithstanding its investment in the industrial landscape—the "faces smeared with good factory muck" of the *Founding Manifesto*—the factory itself and the workers are absent from Futurist prose. All the machines Marinetti glorifies—the car, the plane, the camera, the *intonarumori*—are unproductive ones that work rather to speedily and prosthetically catapult or reproduce images of the heroic male body; the Futurist "mechanical man" is the aviator, the warrior, the engineer, and the athlete, but never the worker. The machine and its indestructible metal must compensate for the body's own fragility, for the softness of the flesh. It functions as a prosthetic device whose characteristics are gradually absorbed by man to become "lively, pugnacious, muscular and violently dynamic" (*Futurist Democracy*, 1919; Marinetti, *Selected Writings*, 78)[21] and to make him fit for war.

Through the ideal of the metallic man, Marinetti wanted to produce a new subject: male, coldly objective, his musculature enhanced by mechanical prostheses. Both in the manifestos and in the romance *Mafarka*, he claimed that the new Futurist man was a war machine and as such bore no relation to the rationalized body of the Taylorized worker. In fact, both the Futurist superman and the worker were produced by the same culture of technological modernity: "This phase will itself be superseded by the creation of a psychophysical nexus of a new type, both different from its predecessors and inevitably superior." These are not Marinetti's words, however, but Antonio Gramsci's in *Prison Notebooks* (1929–1935), from the section "Americanism and Fordism."[22] Gramsci saw Fordism—the new form of organization of production based on Taylor's principles that Henry Ford had been putting into practice in his automobile plants since 1915—as an effective way of maximizing industrial production and therefore as the means of Italy's potential economic modernization. The echoes between the Marxist Gramsci's and the Futurist Marinetti's texts are surprisingly numerous; in the first instance, both oppose bourgeois humanism with the intent of producing a new man, a new human type that can function in the machine age. Yet whereas Marinetti looks at this new subject as the creation of human will, of which Mafarka's son, created by his god-like and technically adept father, is an example, Gramsci is well aware that the new individual is constituted as a response to the demands of intensified capitalist production.[23] The management of labor studied by Taylor demanded a new type of individual, fast and pragmatic and capable of performing "automatically" the gestures dictated by the assembly-line process. For Gramsci, this man had to be capable of "a new mode of living and thinking and of feeling life."[24] He understood that creating a new type of worker for capitalist society meant creating a new man.

## AUTOMATONS, WORKERS, AND THE LURE OF TOTALITY

Although speaking from two different perspectives—Marinetti against what he saw as the moral hypocrisy of the bourgeoisie, Gramsci against the immorality of the modern division of labor that had reduced sexuality to the status of a "sport"—the Futurist and the Marxist reach uncannily similar conclusions: Lust, passion, and excessive feelings would be eliminated from the body of the new subject in the name of an ascetic ideology of functionalism. Gramsci saw that the kind of efficient production processes that had been pioneered in America implied the "streamlining" of the modern worker to produce a "stable, skilled ... and a permanently well-adjusted" labor force more invested in production than in consumption. To maintain such a force, he realized, it was necessary first to eliminate excess, now recognized through the new sciences of production schedules as the inefficient workers of the old, un-Taylorized working class, and second to rationalize any "sexual instinct" that might interrupt this dream of smooth mass production. Marinetti recommended a "swift and casual contact with women," but Gramsci saw clearly why capitalism advocated monogamy:

> New industrialism wants monogamy: it wants the worker not to squander his nervous energies in the disorderly and stimulating pursuit of occasional sexual satisfaction. The employee who goes to work after a night of "excess" is no good for his work. The exaltation of passion cannot be reconciled with the timed movements of productive motions connected with the most perfect automatism. ... It is necessary for the worker to spend his extra money "rationally," to maintain, renew, and if possible increase his muscular-nervous efficiency, and not to corrode and destroy it.[25]

This acknowledgment—that for the worker in the newly efficient order of production, temperance and self-control in the afterhours are the corollary of Taylorism in the workplace—is couched in the observant, mildly ironic tone of materialist analysis. Yet what is striking is that Gramsci is clearly also impressed by the promise of Taylorist efficiency—in his case, its potential to sweep away the last vestiges of archaic and "feudal" practices in European capitalism, which he saw as a brake on the inevitable history Marx had outlined. Thus although apparently advocating the exact opposite of Futurism's celebration of occasional, unaffected sex, Gramsci in his observations is not so distant from Marinetti's advice to Italian young men to stay away from the "alcohol of *amore* and lust." In both texts, the culprits of male inefficiency are assumed to be women and the feminizing effects of sexuality. These are the women who stopped men from going to war in Marinetti's manifestos: "Yes, our nerves demand war and despise women, because we fear supplicating arms that might encircle our knees on the morning of departure!" (*Founding Manifesto;* Marinetti, *Selected Writings,* 46). They reappear in Gramsci's *Prison Notebooks* as those who stop him from working efficiently.[26]

What this juxtaposition of Gramsci's interest in the new workplace and Marinetti's in a "new man" underlines in the first place, however, is the ideological move through which Futurism deletes the labor of the worker and the reification of the relations of production from its discourse altogether. The Futurist man is in fact built on Taylor's principles: His body must become a machine not in order to fight and conquer, as Futurist bombast purports, but primarily to function better in the workplace. Conversely, in not taking into account this juxtaposition of labor and war, of the ways the factory system matched that of the battlefield, Gramsci's surprising suggestion toward the end of his essay that Taylorism might even be a means of freedom and redemption for the worker reveals the utopian edge to his argument. Gramsci proposes that once the new worker has become adjusted to the entirely calculated movements and schedules of modern rationalized labor, once he has completely automatized his body to the point that he can work without thinking about what gesture to perform and what muscles to move, then he has the potential to reach a state of total freedom. He notes that only the body is mechanized and kept busy in the intense and repetitive rhythm of work, whereas the mind is free: "One works automatically and at the same time thinks about whatever one chooses."[27] Gramsci, therefore, here represents the worker as a "head without the body"; his faith in the inevitability of technological capitalist progress in the ultimate service of the proletariat allows him to ignore the fact that the modern rationalization of labor was as likely to increase the worker's alienation, transforming him, rather, into an exhausted body "without the head"—of which Boccioni's almost faceless dynamic body may be read as an image.

Marinetti does not admit that the utopian man-machine engineered in the manifestos and the modern worker are two different personae of the same subject; thus he never stops elaborating strategies capable of dispelling and occluding this analogy. In *Mafarka* he deploys and recasts a partly romantic, partly Nietzschean fantasy of male motherhood to affirm the Futurist power of self-creation: The modernist monster Gazurmah owes allegiance only to the father who made him, himself a superman. In this sense, Mafarka represents the counterfigure of the

Futurist artist himself, trying to affirm his originality and aesthetic independence from the logic of capital, in which the machine is imbricated. Marinetti disavows this imbrication through two further strategies: the implied classlessness of the Futurist superman and the suggestion that his fragmented body is reabsorbed into a new form of totality.

The contiguity between the Futurist new man and the modern worker is further denied and dissimulated by Futurism's deletion of class as a category of social analysis. Marinetti's "social theory" ultimately amounts to a caricature of petty bourgeois conservative common sense. He refuses the class divisions that marked the social scene of his day and redraws them in general and impressionistic terms: "Rich and poor exist; poor from bad luck, illness, incapacity, honesty; rich from fraud, cleverness, avarice, ability; exploiters and exploited; stupid and intelligent; false and sincere; so called rich bourgeois who works more than the workers; workers who work as little as possible; slow and fast, conquerors and conquered" (*Beyond Communism*, 1917; Marinetti, *Selected Writings*, 151). By blurring class distinctions into psychological categories, Marinetti's theory can envision a social structure governed by a meritocracy, "the vast proletariat of gifted men." The aim of the Futurist utopia is certainly neither to appropriate the means of production on behalf of the proletarians nor to favor and reinforce bourgeois hegemony but rather—and here the Futurist's debt to the aestheticist movement via D'Annunzio is evident—to aestheticize the political sphere by turning everyone into an artist. Instead of the militarization of the proletarians, described more recently by the French theorist Paul Virilio,[28] here we have the aesthetization of the working class through the nominal and bohemian avowed proletarization of the artist. Once the burden of manual labor is transferred onto the machine, the realm of consumption, "the freedom to think, create and enjoy the arts" becomes accessible to any "intelligent person."[29] While for Gramsci manual labor can continue to exist as a valid occupation because Taylorism has mechanized and automatized it to the point that it does not need any mental energy on the side of the worker, Marinetti fantasizes about the disappearance of labor, which he seems to find degrading. Only when the need for manual labor is overcome will the life of the masses become a work of art. Again, Futurist discourse proceeds through a series of ideological displacements: The proletarian is transformed into the "intelligent person"; the artist (at least nominally) identifies with the proletarian and in fact is substituted for him in a clever phrase ("the proletariat of talented people") that deletes any connection to the proletariat's real conditions of existence.

By attributing the qualities of the machine—linearity, impassivity, efficiency— to the human body, Marinetti is capable of producing an image of fiercely antibourgeois masculinity that is in open opposition to the principles of humanistic reason. The most evident visual sign of this new formation of male subjectivity is the violent fragmentation of the Futurist body, whose form can, as Boccioni made clear in the *Technical Manifesto of Futurism*, be violated and freely dislocated. Yet this fragmentation of the body, advocated by Boccioni and practiced, for instance, by Severini in one of his first paintings, *Bal Tabarin* of 1911, is simultaneosly accepted and rejected by the chief ideologue of the movement. On the one hand, Marinetti flamboyantly affirms the need to disperse the self and considers art as the terrain where the Futurist can get rid of the "I," the principle of subjective cohesion, by subverting the harmonious figure of the classical body: "Art is needed to destroy and to scatter oneself, a great watering can of heroism that drowns the world" (*Technical Manifesto of Futurist Literature*, 1911; Marinetti, *Selected Writings*, 89). On the other, the scattering of the self and of the body implies destruction and self-destruction, and as such, it must be circumvented. Marinetti's anxiety about the "loss," the reification, and the excessive automatization of the male body is visible in the way in which he negotiates the relationship of the fragment to the totality; in the way, that is, in which Futurism's destructive iconoclasm, of which the "body without a residue" is a key example, turns into a will to wholeness.

In Marinetti's writing the fragmented Futurist body is made whole again through its identification with images that signify solidity and totality. An example of this totality is the automaton Gazurmah, whose anthropomorphic shape gives coherence to the single inorganic elements that "make" his body—iron and the vegetable fibers. Another is Marinetti's grotesque and morbid fantasy of the perfectly recyclable body in which each corporeal fragment is continually reinvested in a new totality, as in the case of the corpses on the Manchurian battlefields. Marinetti's most famous image of wholeness, through which the fragmentariness of the Futurist body is once again displaced, is the prosthetic oneness between the driver and his car. In *The New Religion-Morality of Speed* (1916) Marinetti notes the synthesis of soft flesh and the hard metal, the merging of body and machine as a mystical event: "The intoxication of great speed is nothing but the joy of feeling oneself fused with the only divinity. Sportsmen are the first cathecumens of this religion" (*Selected Writings*, 94). This "fusion with the divinity" is also represented by the accident in which the monad is literally "integrated" into the divinity-car through the violence of the wound. As in ancient sacrifices, the unity of individual and totality takes place through the flowing of blood. Theweleit exposes the military underside of this "mystical" fantasy of compenetration: The male fascist soldier abandoned individuality to become part of the military machine by conceptualizing both his body and his ego as a totality, a steel armor that can be relinquished and exploded only in war. As in Marinetti's text, Theweleit shows how the fascist fantasy of an intact body is produced by the elimination of emotions and sexual desire. Through the conflation of the male body and the machine, sexuality is channeled toward destruction and can, literally, explode in all its violence.

In Futurist discourse violence is sexualized not only through the eroticism of danger but even more by transforming the physical aggression of war, as well as of the accident—the violent compenetration of metal and flesh—into an orgiastic and orgasmic moment of identification with the totality. In this sense, Marinetti's description of the fusion between the car and the human body in religious terms is striking. As in the fantasy of the fragmented and subsequently reconstructed body of the Freikorps soldier studied by Theweleit, here the identity of fragment and whole is a transcendental, antiempiricist process whose dynamic is graspable only through intuition and not reason. Futurism positions itself vis-à-vis this relationship of body and machine, part and whole, with the same irrationality. The relationship between fragment and totality is not represented by the Futurist as a dialectical opposition: No *Aufhebung* is produced by this conflict but rather undifferentiated identification. By abolishing mediation, the Futurist bridges the distance between the part and the totality so that the subject becomes an embodiment, an emanation, of the whole.

Futurism's technological reason manages to refigure the relationship of individual and machine, then, in mystical and mythical terms. Mafarka's ascetic-scientific renunciation of love and of aesthetics ("the putrefaction of poetry") was blatantly contradicted by Marinetti's religious discourse of the fusion of man and "the divinity." The almost imperceptible moment of exchange between reason and myth—the contradiction between geometrical fragmentation and the mystical fusion with the machine that Marinetti passes over in silence and seems to affirm simply as a gesture of Nietzschean antirationalism—is made fully visible by the Weimar critic Siegfried Kracauer in the essay "The Mass Ornament" (1927), where he critiques modern precision dancing in the light of technological rationalization. The operation through which the fragmented male body is made part of the totality—which in Marinetti's writing is represented, for instance, by the car, the winged automaton, or the corpse-turned-cannonball—does not give integrity to Futurist man. Marinetti's man-machine remains a dislocated body whose fictitious wholeness, suspended between rationality and technological mysticism, is not an innate quality but rather is prefigured by two historically contingent images of mechanistic totality, that of the newly visible body of the soldier inextricably encapsulated in the totality of the troop and that of the dancers described by Kracauer.

For Kracauer the synchronized movements of the Tiller Girls—a group of British ballerinas popular in 1920s Berlin—represents Taylorist regimentation made into a pleasurable spectacle by associating it with female bodies. The perfect synchronicity of their movements, the geometrical patterns they formed, stand as an aestheticized image of the worker's movements at the assembly line. The male spectator is asked to recognize himself in the women on stage, who, as unaware as the workers in the factory, partake of a process they cannot dominate. At the same time, he is asked to deny this recognition through gender difference in order to reaffirm his at least nominal control over the process of production and consumption in which he is involved both in the workplace and in the theater. Part of the pleasure produced by the mass ornament lies in its gender, in the spectacle of symmetrical movements performed by glittering and costumed *female* bodies. Yet because they function as fragments of a pattern, the dancers' bodies, for Kracauer, have no erotic meaning. Their "severed" legs do not signify the individual female form but rather point to the whole, the figure to which they give shape on stage— an opening flower, a square turning into a circle or triangle. The dances of the Tiller Girls, dislocating and fragmenting their bodies to form always new ornamental patterns, refigure the process by which the parts of the Futurist body are reabsorbed into a new totality.[30] As such, the Tiller Girls illustrate how the fantasy of fusion with the whole, which in Futurist discourse takes on a mystical-masochistic value, comes to function as a form of regimented loss of self. Such a loss of self in the crowd was staged in different sites of culture from the stage to the stadium to the military and fascist parade.

To be a human tessera in an ornamental, geometrical whole means one's loss of self-consciousness as an individual and implies the definitive loss of autonomy of the individual body, now recruited merely as a component in a larger spectacle. Just as the Futurist body—mechanized like that of the worker and similarly dislocated—is the counterfigure of the precision dancer, her body in turn recalls the military precision of the troop's symmetrical marching. The troop, too, as Theweleit notes, is a totality in which the body of the individual soldier ceases to exist: "The soldier's limbs are described as if severed from the bodies. ... The leg of the individual has closer, functional connection to the leg of his neighbor than to his own torso. In the machine, then, new body-totalities are formed: bodies no longer identical with the bodies of individual human beings."[31] The perfect fusion of man and motor advocated by Marinetti, which is analyzed in its military context by Theweleit, is lucidly disavowed and shown as aleatory by Kracauer: "Hereafter the Tiller Girls can no longer be reassembled as human beings. Their mass gymnastics are never performed by whole, autonomous bodies whose contortions would deny rational understanding. Arms, thighs, and other segments are the smallest components of the composition."[32] The bodies of the Tiller Girls are the space where the rationality of technology reveals itself as "a mythological cult wrapped in abstractness."[33] The abstractness to which the dancers' bodies are reduced brings together the image of the Futurist body in Severini's paintings and in Boccioni's sculpture. In these works of art the human form is reduced to a simulacrum of speed and to the abstraction that Georg Lukács, in his 1924 essay "Reification and the Consciousness of the Proletariat," identified as the chief effect of the reification and commodification universally spread by modern capitalism, in which both human relations and the body of the worker are abstracted and quantified in monetary value.

The term "cult," used by Kracauer to elucidate the ideological value of the claimed rationality represented by the movements of the Tiller Girls, also brings to mind the logic through which Marinetti explains the relation between the Futurist "scattered self" and the machine-totality in terms of a mystical interpenetration. Kracauer's words are an appropriate commentary on Marinetti's claim to a scientifically religious rationality: "The rationality of the ornament is an illusion. … In the mass ornament we see the rational, empty form of the cult stripped of any express meaning. As such, it proves itself to be a regression to mythology … a regression which once again reveals the intransigence of capital to reason."[34] The Tiller Girls are a spectacle of capitalist abstraction disguised as totality and packaged as a means of expenditure: The audience consumes their abstraction "emotionally," reading as pleasure what in fact represents their own functionality in the process of mass production. This is the reality that one glimpses through the stage glitter: The image of the Tiller Girls represents for Kracauer a venue through which to consider in depth the corporeal logic of capitalist reification. The dancers, their bodies an icon of mass mechanization, indirectly also expose the Futurist artist's disavowal of his stake in the instrumental value of technology: The technological reason that Marinetti recognizes as the point of departure of Futurist aesthetics, at work both in the rationalized movements of the ballerinas and in the streamlined gestures of the workers, is founded on the postulates of Taylorism, which advocates a perfectly functioning body to optimize production. Without ever losing its instrumental value, technology functions simultaneously as a signifier of aesthetic subversion in Futurist discourse and as a means of material oppression in the social text. In order to maintain his autonomy as a subject and the coherence of his aesthetic and social program, Marinetti needed to dispel the memory of the other function of technology, and he did so by turning the machine into an aesthetic object and by "freezing" the fragments of the body into the totality of metal. Nonetheless, the metal "armor" of the Futurist superman melts to reveal a fleshy, desirable male body, eroticized and obsessively described by Marinetti himself.

For Kracauer, the spectacle of the Tiller Girls, an image of popular culture that other intellectuals would refuse to take seriously, reveals a fundamental truth about modern culture and its fascination with the machine, a truth that bourgeois culture is incapable of recognizing: "No matter how low one rates the value of the mass ornament, its level of reality is still above that of artistic productions which cultivate obsolete noble sentiments in whitered forms, even when they have no further significance."[35] Although Futurism as an avant-garde movement continually ridiculed these "noble sentiments" as bourgeois, the Futurist artist himself behaves exactly like the "privileged intellectuals" attacked by Kracauer—the intellectuals "who do not accept the fact that they are an appendage to the prevailing economic system, have not even understood the Mass Ornament as a sign of the system."[36] Perhaps the Futurist has understood that as an "appendage of the prevailing economic system," he is no better than the worker or the ballerina—hence his embrace *and* disavowal of technology. His fear of not being able to dominate the machine and, like the Taylorized worker, of becoming subjected to it is continually defused in his text, especially by staging its presence in the space of aesthetics and leisure within the fictionality, pleasure, and consumption associated with the stage, as happens both with the "mass ornament" and with the *serate futuriste*—Futurist soirees that mixed entertainment with propaganda.

Marinetti attempted to affirm his agency as a writer and his authority as a male subject through two strategies: first, by negotiating the relationship between the fragmented Futurist body and the totality of the machine and second, by excising sexuality and labor from his text. Taking as my departure point Mafarka's claim to creative autonomy through the exclusion of women and workers, I will now turn to another modernist work, Fritz Lang's film *Metropolis*, to elucidate the terms of the exclusions on which Futurist masculinity is founded.

## MAKING MEN OF MACHINES

Almost twenty years after the date of publication of *Mafarka le futuriste*, the film *Metropolis*, a document of Weimar culture, uncannily reproposes the ideological scenario of Marinetti's romance by reenacting the same triangular relationship between the father-son dyad, the rebellious workers, and the sexualized maternal figure. If we focus on the way these three elements are articulated in Lang's film, it is possible to reconstruct the mechanism of occlusion through which Marinetti displaces the image of technology from the sphere of production to that of modernist science fiction and spectacular consumption—the sphere inhabited by the fantastic automaton Gazurmah, a combination of man, machine, and bird. In his anxiety to prove and affirm his independence from "manual labor" and the logic of production, Marinetti does not realize that the symbolic exclusion of women and workers from the scene of Futurist production is utopian, or at least idealistic. In *Metropolis*, the feminine figure and the workers denied by Mafarka are once again reintegrated and made useful: The maternal body is desexualized to guarantee the stability of the symbolic order (patriarchal and capitalist), and the workers are thought of and represented as automatons whose repetitive and frantic productive rhythm propels the modern Taylorized factory.

Thea Von Harbous's 1923 novel *Metropolis* was made into a film in 1926 by the corporation UFA (Universum Film Aktiengesellschaft) with financial backing from the German government and industry and from American sources. The producers considered her novel an exemplary parable of order and discipline for the unruly social scenario of Weimar Germany. In *Metropolis* social rebellion is translated in sexual terms and, as Futurism had preached, resolved "aesthetically," or more precisely, emotionally, that is, not through the intervention of art but through that of feelings, represented by the female protagonist, Maria. The taming of unruly female sexuality puts an end to class conflict and convinces the proletarian "men-machines" to return to work. At the same time, the father-son relationship, sexualized in *Mafarka*, is brought once again under the safe umbrella of the Oedipal narrative.

In the opening scene of *Metropolis* the social-spacial boundaries through which order and hierarchy are maintained are violated: Maria, a woman belonging to the underground world of production, enters the garden where the son of Fredersen, master of Metropolis and owner of the means of production, is playing with his friends. When she enters the garden with a crowd of poor children, Maria's image is connoted as maternal: This is sharply contrasted with Freder's frolicking with his female friends, which suggests, instead, sexuality. Seeing her in the garden, Freder is immediately attracted to the young woman and later follows her to the underground, where for the first time he experiences the slave-like conditions of the workers. When a man frantically moving the arms of what seems to be a huge clock collapses, Freder rushes to continue his work so that the machine can keep functioning, and catastrophe is avoided. This scene, one of the film's most famous moments, conveys a double message about perceptions of technology in Weimar culture. On the one hand, it represents the machine as a dangerous and enslaving force, subjecting the workers and overpowering their bodies; on the other, it depicts it as a pulsating apparatus signifying dynamism, energy, and speed. The first meaning is signified by the exhausted inhabitants of the underground: The resigned submission of man to the machine is allegorized in the moment when ordered rows of workers climb a stair into a tunnel whose entrance appears like an open mouth, the mouth of Moloch eating its victims. However, when the camera pans on the whole cave-like interior of the factory, one is offered an aestheticized and painterly composition, a geometrical arrangement of straight and curved lines that combine and mix to please the eye. In this context, the mechanized gestures of the indefatigable workers of Metropolis resemble the stylized steps of modernist dance, evoking both the decorative synchronicity of the Tiller Girls and the abstract purity of dance movements in such modernist ballets as *Relâche* (1924), in which marionette-like bodies, costumed by Léger, danced to Satie's music.

After his first visit in the underground world of Metropolis, Freder follows Maria into the catacombs, where in a space arranged like a church she preaches to the workers. Although Maria's preaching really serves the cause of capital, she constitutes a threat to Fredersen. On the one hand, the secrecy of the meetings and her influence over the workers elude Fredersen's panopticism and weaken his power; on the other, by revealing to young Freder the injustice upon which Metropolis is built, she jeopardizes the father-son bond—the continuity on which the Symbolic order, as well as production and meaning itself in this science fiction city, are founded. When Fredersen himself finds out about the secret meetings in the catacombs, he asks Rotwang, the scientist of Metropolis, to help him put an end to a situation threatening chaos. Rotwang has created a robot, a metallic body waiting to be given an "electrical" soul (and Maria's features) through a scientific experiment. The robot will be sent among the workers to instigate a rebellion—a chaos that will give Fredersen the opportunity to drastically repress the malcontented workers.

Whereas the human Maria is a modest, maternal, and subdued figure, her mechanical double is a femme fatale who arouses men's desire and, by unchaining their libido, incites them to sexual and social insubordination.[37] In Fredersen's mind the robot ("A machine that can be made to look like a man—or a woman— but never tires ... never makes a mistake") is a substitute for the worker. Rotwang's futuristic human machine will allow Fredersen to do without man. His dream, "the dream that it might be possible to go a step beyond making machines of men ... by making men of machines,"[38] is both a sci-fi dream and the Taylorist fantasy of the automatization of the human body pushed to the extreme, to the point when the body can be actually eliminated and disposed of. Lang's film reverses the gender connotation of the Futurist superman, turning Marinetti's "cruel and combative" man-machine into a seductive female body. Why must the man of the future be a woman and at the same time a machine gone crazy whose mechanism produces the exact opposite of the order and functionality it was programmed to reestablish? This gender reversal can be explained by considering the history of the production of *Metropolis*, but it must also be theorized vis-à-vis the Futurist attribution of both the "inhuman" qualities of the machine and the creative function to the male body.

The inconsistency of the male worker becoming a female robot was produced by the cuts (almost one-quarter of 3,421 meters of film) the film underwent for its American version of 1927. An important motive, the rivalry between the scientist Rotwang and Fredersen for the same woman, Hel, was eliminated: After marrying Fredersen, Hel dies in giving birth. In the original version, *Metropolis* was the story of Rotwang's hatred for Fredersen and of his revenge through a robot that brings chaos and subversion. When the character of Hel was eliminated because, as Enno Palatas notes, "it would create a guffaw in the English-speaking countries,"[39] Rotwang becomes a tool in the hands of Fredersen and inexplicably creates a robot that does not help defuse a conspiracy but rather starts a rebellion. While for Lang the man-machine becomes a woman through this serendipitous process, for Marinetti, instead, the man of the future is a father who, to nourish his dream of absolute power over the process of production, becomes a mother and "gives birth" to an automaton.

The means by which gender, sexuality, and technology are articulated in Lang's film repeats and at the same time exposes the utopian value of technology in Futurist discourse. The film poses the collapse of technology and sexuality as a threat both to established definitions of gender and to social hierarchies. However, this threat can be reabsorbed: Sexuality is integrated into the metallic body of the robot, but at the same time it is demonized as female. The fear of not being able to control the machine is defused by replacing it with the highly controllable body of the femme fatale, the centerpiece of phallocratic representations of femininity. The robot Maria is produced as a male fantasy; under the male gaze, she changes from the "reasonable" maternal figure exerting her power of persuasion over the workers, a power that ultimately legitimizes capital, into a vamp. Her newly acquired outlaw sexuality, set up by patriarchy itself, and the political revolt it generates, become the reasons for her death on the pyre. In *Metropolis* capitalist and patriarchal power, as it is embodied by Fredersen, seems to set up its own transgressive other in the figure of a "straw woman" whose outlaw body is literally burned so that she can be once again disciplined into obedience. The insubordinate female subject is not eliminated from the scene of organic and industrial production but rather is tamed into an image of sentimental motherhood. In the end, converted again into a mother figure, Maria speaks the language of love, brotherhood, and forgiveness and as such can be used to interpellate the workers.

When Maria turns into the selfish and unproductive vamp, however, alluring both bourgeois men and proletarians to their own perdition, and the maternal function disappears, the world of Metropolis falls into chaos. Production stops and the workers begin to destroy the machines. Only in the end, when the vamp is sacrificed and burned by the crowd of workers, can the real Maria escape from Rotwang's house and reassume her maternal and salvific function. With Freder she sets out to save the children of Metropolis from the flood provoked by the crazed workers themselves. As in Marinetti's *Mafarka*, the absence of real mothers calls into question the realm of organic reproduction, the structure of the family romance, and with it the phallic organization of the real. The abjected maternal body is the necessary condition through which the Oedipal relationship between father and son can take place. By eliminating what he termed "the female ovary," that is, the maternal female figure, from the scene of reproduction, Marinetti poses an almost counter-Oedipal link between father and son—a relationship of desire for the son—which is severed when Gazurmah kills Mafarka to follow his Icarus-like dream of subjecting the sun. Lang's film instead restores the classical Oedipal scenario by reinstating a hierarchical father-son relationship predicated on the exclusion of the sexualized maternal figure, here represented by the robot-vamp.

The crisis of the maternal body as site of reproduction and birthing that Mary Ann Doane sees as the consequence of contemporary technologies of reproduction is visible, in its modernist version, both in *Mafarka* and in *Metropolis*. "These technologies," writes Doane, "threaten to put into crisis the very possibility of the questions of origins, the Oedipal dilemma and the relationship between subjectivity and knowledge that it supports"[40]—and, it may be added, the social and political hierarchies implicit in such a relationship. In other words, the entire symbolic economy of capitalist patriarchy relies on the Oedipal structure; if the chief actor in this structure does not function properly, if the mother turns into a sexualized vamp or a rebellious machine, this order is in jeopardy. The vamp must metamorphosize again into a mother so that Oedipalization, the Symbolic, language, gender definitions, and, last but not least, the submission of labor to capital can be maintained. Indeed, it is Maria's tamed sexuality, as exemplified by her return to the maternal function when she saves the children from the flood, that ensures both this submission and the final reconciliation between father and son. In order to become the "mediator," the heart that reconciles mind and hand, Freder's own desire for Maria must change into pure love, the chaste, desexualized relationship that links the mother to the son in the Symbolic order. Lang's film proposes a "peaceful" solution to a conflict that Marinetti resolves with violence: Mafarka's vain attempt to substitute himself for the maternal figure and thus separate Gazurmah from his father's bride, Colubbi—who refers to the automaton as "my son, my lover"—culminates in an act of violence in which Mafarka brutally sends Colubbi away.

In the intentions of its producers—the private capital that paid for the making and distribution of *Metropolis* had among its sources Krupp Steel, AEG, and Deutsche Bank—Lang's film figured as a predecessor of the *Traufilm* of the Nazi era, a didactic parable supposed to defend the status quo against the red danger.[41] In *Metropolis,* the appearance of the "heart," represented by Maria's reconciling power in the melodramatic conclusion of the film and at the core of the discourse of technological reason and economic exploitation, sutures the division between labor and capital in emotional terms. Marinetti, who drastically excluded feelings and human emotions because he considered them effeminate, did not grasp *the use* of feeling or realize that feelings can be useful even to the superman. In fact, in *Metropolis* they turn out to be instrumental to Fredersen's hegemony by becoming a chief means of interpellation of the workers.

It is capital that writes the conclusion to the modernist narrative of the avant-garde. The same emotional surge that at the end of *Metropolis* converts the hand to the sovereignty of the mind may win the consumer to the sex appeal of the commodity, for example. Marinetti's romantic fantasy of creation is a mere utopia. The image of the man-machine, which in *Metropolis* becomes inextricably enmeshed in the image of the worker's body, is an anxious response on the Futurist's side to the historical imbrication of modern technology, the "matter" of Futurist masculinity, into the discourse of efficiency sustained by early twentieth century practices of labor management. The miraculous body of Marinetti's male automaton, born from his father's will, is itself an aestheticized image of technology, an unproductive body whose strength recalls Sandow's eroticized muscles. Futurism's sexualization of the male body as a machine through the eroticism of metal and danger, and in particular the traffic between the functional and the ornamental that this body suggests, is fully disclosed and brought to the extreme by another avant-garde text, Alfred Jarry's *The Supermale,* in which Futurist bombast is turned into a sarcastic tragicomedy of wounded masculinity.

## A TEAR IS A MECHANICAL THING

In the years preceding the First World War, the technomechanic fantasies of Futurism represented the culmination of a new aesthetic and cultural interest in the machine. Novels such as H. G. Wells's *The Time Machine* (1899) testify to the spreading of a new, often cautious enthusiasm for the scientific and technological progress of the period. Futurism transformed such cautious enthusiasm into a triumphalist celebration and looked at the machine as the chief means of attaining

the ultrahuman qualities of the Nietzschean superman—an amoral and antisenti-
mental pose combined with a steeled body that could be easily assimilated to the
automatism of the machine, as well as to the "headless body" that Gramsci read as
industry's version of the ideal worker. It is such an unconditional and flamboyant
celebratory tone that is missing in the articulation of the relationship between
man and technology prior to Futurism. In his novel *The Supermale* (1902) Alfred
Jarry explores, in an absurdist and comic vein, the dangers of a too close proximity between the male body and the machine and as such offers a highly cogent critique in advance of the first Futurist dreams of male automatons, turning the
image of "man multiplied by the motor" into an object of a ferocious satire.

Jarry's novel brings to a conclusion my narrative of the mechanized male body
in this chapter by fully exposing the eroticism and the contradictions inscribing
the Futurist ideal of masculinity. The novel purports to prove the Futurist as-
sumption upon which the version of the new male body was constructed: As long
as sexuality and "the heart" are defined as feminine—as happens in *Metropolis*—
the male subject can fantasize about his identity with the machine. But when both
the erotic and the realm of feelings are referred to the male subject, his body-
armor disintegrates and flesh and metal are again structured by a relationship of
domination and submission that causes a literal demise of the male body.
Significantly, *The Supermale*, the story of a man-machine becoming human again,
ends with the image of a male body in ruins. Reduced to an irredeemable fragmentariness, in the end the hero's body turns into an inanimate object (a jewel) in
which the hard and utterly functional Futurist male body exchanges place with
the most useless and decorative of objects.

Jarry was a central figure in the Parisian turn of the century avant-garde. His
proto-Dada attitude of provocation, abrasive buffoonery, anarchism, and
grotesque humor influenced such younger writers and artists as Apollinaire,
André Salmon, Max Jacob, Picasso, and Breton. The quality of Rabelaisian excess
that infused his characters, Ubu King, Dr. Faustroll, and the supermale, was in the
first place autobiographical. "The original legend centered," as Roger Shattuck
writes, "about his attire (a cyclist costume with pistols), his habits (drink practiced
as a discipline), his lodging (a double cell literally on the third-and-a-half floor)
and his daily fare (fish he caught at will anywhere in the Seine)."[42] Jarry was an eccentric figure even in fin de siècle Paris, part dandy, donning costumes and revel-
ing in idiosyncratic habits, and part sportsman, as he appears in several photos,
riding his bicycle and flaunting his muscles in a sleeveless jersey. In his work he
pays particular attention to the body: Through carnivalesque deformations of the
human form, he offers a comic critique of the tics and habits of the bourgeoisie.
His most famous character is Ubu King, the villain-hero of a series of plays staged
in Paris; Ubu's monstrous and overgrown body, modeled on Monsieur Hébert, a
much hated teacher of Jarry's at the *lycée*, represents an amplified version of bourgeois greed and human cruelty. The character, created by Jarry in 1896, was the
reverse image of Monsieur Teste, another famous figure in modernist French lit-

erature. Monsieur Teste was invented that same year by Paul Valery and was the protagonist of the novel of the same name. Whereas Teste (head) is nothing but brain and reason, Ubu is a sanguine brute whose trademark is an enormous belly. Ubu Roi became the model for Marinetti's only satirical character, the protagonist of his *Roi Bombance*.[43] Jarry and Marinetti knew each other: Jarry published two articles in Marinetti's journal *Poesia* in 1905, a year before his death.

Among the monstrous creatures that populate Jarry's books, the protagonist of *The Supermale*, André Marcueil, is the one who more than any other embodies the mechanistic qualities of the Futurist man. Written in 1902 and set in 1920, the book structures the relation between body and technology in prefuturist terms: Man's desire to challenge the machine, to measure up to it, shows that the two are separate entities as yet unidentified. Thus the novel could be read as a cautionary tale in which Jarry may be seen to sarcastically explode in advance what will become Marinetti's technological credo. In so doing, he lays bare the contradictions and some of the unexpressed fears that will be features of Futurism: its anxiety about the fragmentation of the body and the way this fear is inextricably enmeshed with questions of gender, the gynophobia underlining its aggressive macho technophilia, the danger and pleasure of resexualizing the male body, and its disciples' fear of losing power vis-à-vis a changing economic and political reality.

André Marcueil breaks the Futurist rule: He is not a superman, that is, a figure beyond the traps of gender identity and the weakening temptation of sexual desire; rather, he is a supermale endowed with an ultrahuman virility. In the novel this hypervirility offers itself to both the erotic and scientific gaze. He believes in the infiniteness of human possibilities and wants to exceed the physical limitations of mankind; to show his unlimited faculties he turns himself into a machine of sexuality. Any trace of emotion or personal involvement is deleted from his view of love, and even sexuality is perceived as an act of "mechanical reproduction," "of no importance since it can be performed indefinitely."[44] The serialized image of the erotic act reminds one both of Futurism's mechanization of the human body and of Benjamin's argument in "The Work of Art in the Age of Mechanical Reproduction" (1936): Once it comes to be performed "indefinitely," love, like the work of art, loses its aura to become one type of physical exertion like any other. Once quantity is privileged over quality, as happens in the supermale's reasoning, the lover's experience becomes agonistic, and his aim is to compete, be the champion, break a record. However, the story moves from an image of masculinity as a scientific curiosity—pleasure is used as a means of measuring Marcueil's mechanical power—to a spectacle of male sexuality in which the aseptic logic of the scientific experiment allows an exhibitionist self-display that in the end culminates in a comic destruction of the male body. At the beginning Marcueil sets out to perform an exceptional deed. To a group of friends gathered at his château, he announces his intention of breaking the record of the Indian, a semimythological figure "so celebrated by Theophrastus, Pliny and Atheneus, who, Rabelais reports after these authors, with the aid of certain herbs, did it in one Day three-score Times and ten More" (Jarry, 9). The mention of Rabelais's name among the classical-scientific sources and authoritative references quoted by Marcueil is a clear hint of the comic grotesquerie of the supermale's enterprise: By giving a veneer of classicism to what otherwise would be a juvenile prank, Jarry satirizes the exasperated virility that at the turn of the century was inscribed both in Nietzscheanism and in the new mystique of the machine.

With the figure of Marcueil, the text appears simultaneously to endorse and resist the idea of the mechanization of the human body. Marcueil's relationship to technology is ambiguous. On the one hand he affirms his identity with the machine and, like the Futurist man, turns himself into one. On the other, he demonstrates his will to be distinguished from the mechanical apparatus by challenging it in order to show that man is as good as if not better than the machine. Notwithstanding Marcueil's "mechanical" performances—the bicycle race against the locomotive and his prodigious lovemaking—the novel is dominated by the awareness that man is not a machine but rather, as one character observes, that he might need to become one in order to survive: "In these days, when metal and machines are all-powerful, man, if he is to survive, must become stronger than machines, just as he became stronger than beasts" (Jarry, 75). In modern times, when the term of comparison for human strength has become the machine, Marcueil diligently tries to improve his chances of survival by challenging and showing his superiority to technology.

The first of Marcueil's challenges is his struggle with the dynamometer, the machine to measure one's strength that had became common at popular fairs around the turn of the century. In this episode, the image of technology is collapsed with that of woman; thus to overcome the mechanism means, for Marcueil, also to affirm male superiority: "Break it? Oh no," said Marcueil, "I want to kill it"—and he inserts the coin in the dynamometer. The dynamometer's slot listed vertically. "It's female," said Marcueil gravely, "but a very strong one" (Jarry, 26). This scene repeats Eugen Sandow's action in Amsterdam when in one night he broke all the dynamometers of the city in order to gain notoriety as a strongman. Marcueil seems to imitate Sandow also on another occasion: Setting out to break the record of Theophrastus's Indian he covers his body, as the bodybuilder did before his stage appearances, with a bronze powder; this allows him to signify exoticism and to flaunt his muscles in a way that makes his body seem simultaneously metallic and hence machine-like and also an erotic object. Marcueil's fetishistic masquerade contradicts the coldly scientific logic of the experiment: In his orientalist costumes and oiled muscles he looks more like a music hall star than a sportive machine-body. (Since Sandow was touring the theaters of Europe at the time when Jarry was writing *The Supermale*, it is conceivable that Jarry even knew about Sandow and that Marcueil is more than uncannily evoking the image of the German-born strongman.) The "female" dynamometer that Marcueil wants to conquer with his strength is the counterfigure of the female protagonist of the novel. The actual "strong female" of the story is Ellen Elson, the American woman with whom Marcueil will try to break the record of the Indian. Ellen, "a little slip of a woman," is described as both embodying and dominating the machine, "a monstrous automobile, a racing model" (Jarry, 25), and because of her power *over* the machine, she becomes the villain of the story, the type of technological femme fatale against whose power Marcueil must continually prove himself.

The next challenge to technology in the text is the bicycle race, the Perpetual Motion Food Race, in which Marcueil races for 10,000 miles from Europe to Asia against a locomotive and a five-man bicycle team. Strapped to a five-seat bicycle and exclusively fed on Perpetual Motion Food, a concoction intended for mass consumption and invented by one of the sponsors of the race, the team is part of both a scientific and a commercial operation. During the five days of the race, one of the five men dies, but the others decide to go on pedaling and do not stop: "The man was kicking backwards, counterpedaling, seizing up. It is extraordinary how this term, which is applied to the function of the machines, was marvelously applicable to the corpse. And it went on doing what it had to do" (Jarry, 34). Jacob's death and the refunctioning of his body is at the same time a memento of Marinetti's image of the "functional corpse" of the soldier on the Manchurian battlefields and the ominous anticipation of the outcome of Marcueil's final sexual-mechanical experiment at the end of the book. The darkly comic image of Jacob pedaling to death and continuing to efficiently "serve" the machine even as a corpse is also a caveat with which Jarry seems to warn the reader: To become a machine-man means to be subjected to technology; or, less ominously, to be "incorporated" into the machine, dead or alive, means to lose the contours of one's own individuality and become the counterfigure of the mass ornament.

By winning the Perpetual Motion Food Race, Marcueil demonstrates that he is as good as the locomotive. The episode of the bicycle race anticipates the supermale's final challenge to technology, in which he transforms himself into a sexual mechanism. After having proved himself as a superman, stronger than beasts and machines, he wants to show his capabilities as a supermale and as such dominate the powerful American woman, Ellen Elson, car driver and daughter of an engineer. In a tone of absurdist satire, Jarry narrates the tragicomedy of a modern, clockwork sexuality turned scientific experiment. To perform his extraordinary deed, Marcueil arrives at the castle incognito, disguised as the Indian and in the sumptuous and exotic garb of Theophrastus's character. This masquerade can be considered one of Jarry's quirky *boutades* and as such need not be overread; yet particularly in the light of my discussion of sartorially produced identities in the next chapter and the pleasure of "posing," enacting a newly fashioned identity as in the experiments of the fin de siècle aesthetes, it is worth noting that Marcueil's costume is a disguise and therefore both a means of protection against the spectators' curiosity and a means of self-exposure. By impersonating a mythological figure, Marcueil excises his real identity from the scene of the experiment: It is not André Marcueil who turns himself into a dehumanized sex machine, but someone else. At the same time, through his fetishistic costume and his flaunted and made-up body, Marcueil turns himself into an actor on stage or a sports star who is aware that he will be performing for others and who narcissistically enjoys the pleasure of being watched. Dressed in the exotic costume, his skin covered with golden red powder, Marcueil makes love to Ellen eighty-two times in one day and breaks the record of the Indian. But his mechanized virility does not save him from his own feelings and ultimately from his own self-destruction in an appropriate death by electricity. When, after breaking the record, Ellen asks him to make love "for pleasure," he realizes that he is in love with her. At this point he starts composing sentimental poems and discovers that the very axiom on which his whole enterprise had been founded is wrong: "The act of love is of no importance since it can be performed indefinitely. ... Indefinitely. ... Yet there was an end. An end to the woman. An end to love" (Jarry, 63). Marcueil is admitting that there is a limit to the allegedly limitless powers of the supermale. His feelings make him human, but his newly found humanity will become his ruin. Sentimentality does not become the superman: Not only does kitsch compromise his claim to efficiency and self-contained manliness, but, in the end, it kills him.

Marcueil is known to his friends as a ruthless rationalist: Nobody believes that he could be in love, particularly Mr. Elson. When Ellen confesses to him that she is in love with the supermale, her father, who is not aware of Marcueil's sentimental side and does not want his daughter to be hurt, decides to submit the man-machine to another mechanical apparatus, "the machine-to-inspire-love," which is supposed to test his feelings and to rehumanize him: "Since this man had become a mechanism, the equilibrium of the world required that another mechanism should manufacture a soul" (Jarry, 77). But Marcueil already possesses a "soul." In fact, his poetry writing and his uncontrollable feelings show that his newly acquired humanity has been pushed to the extreme. At this point, the protagonist is strapped to something that resembles an electric chair: "A strange object was placed on his skull, a sort of cranellated platinum crown, with its teeth pointing downward. In front and in the back it had a sort of tubular diamond" (Jarry, 78). But it is the supermale's nervous system that in an unexpected turn exerts power over the machine, which, as it turns out, falls in love with Marcueil. The man-machine is stronger than technology, but rather than dominating it, he wins it over by seducing it.

The exchange of roles between the male body and the mechanical apparatus reaches a climax at the conclusion of the text. At the crucial moment when man has apparently succeeded in overpowering technology both with his body and with his mind, the machine breaks down and makes the supermale the victim of a mortal accident: "Drops of molten glass flowed like tears down the supermale's cheeks. On contact with the floor, several exploded violently like Prince Rupert's drops. The three hidden spectators distinctly saw the crown tatter and like a pair of incandescent jaws, sink its teeth into the man's temples" (Jarry, 80). The accident, in which the hard metal penetrated the softness of the flesh, is another protofuturist element of Jarry's novel and a motif that was becoming more and more common in the cultural imaginary of early twentieth century Europe. This accident, however, functions differently for the supermale than it does in the

*Founding Manifesto*. For Marinetti the car accident was a rite of initiation, an experience that steeled the masculine body into technological manhood, and at the same time the occasion for a masochistic pleasure in being wounded. Whereas the Futurist emerged from the accident regenerated and ready to declare his intentions to the world, the conclusion of Jarry's novel represents an anticipatory repartee to Futurist bombast: After the accident, with the machine "biting" into his temples, Marcueil rushes in pain to the door of the castle, showing, in the narrator's words, "how lamentably tragic can be a dog with a pot tied to his tail" and dies at the monumental gate, "twisted into the iron work" (Jarry, 81). The comic hyperbole of this finale both confirms and reverses the Futurist utopia of the man-machine. Jarry's novel advocates a distinction between the human and the technological; yet when man tries to measure up to and show his superiority over the machine, he loses. In Jarry's story, it is not the machine that makes the human body powerful but rather the opposite. Both in the bicycle race and in Marcueil's last ordeal, man is killed by technology and the human body is annihilated.

In his depiction of this masochized male body at the end of *The Supermale*, Jarry does not allow the protagonist any time to indulge in the pleasure of flaunting and exposing his mangled body—in contrast to Burroughs's descriptions of Tarzan. Instead, Marcueil loses his human shape and turns into a beautiful object. At the end, the supermale's corpse is taken out of sight, and all that is left of him is a solidified tear. This Ellen wears on a ring: "[She] found an adroit jeweller to set, in place of a pearl in a ring that she faithfully wears, one of the solid tears of the supermale" (Jarry, 81). The tear is a polysemous object. On the one hand it recalls the hardening and the condensation of the soldier's pulverized bones into the cannonball, described by Marinetti; on the other, it is a grotesque mockery of modern Taylorized efficiency, which on this occasion "streamlines" the male body to death. And yet this image of masculine efficiency in a nutshell does not signify the virile "cruelty and combativeness" that will soon be envisioned by Futurism but rather suggests two elements that belong to the sphere of femininity: The tear is both a sign of lacrimose sentimentality, that is, a symbol of the "heart," and a jewel, a sumptuary object that has no other function but that of an ornament. As such, it points to the "deviant" pleasures of expenditure. One could say that the male body, through its final sacrifice, has turned into a tangible image of Bataillean excess. Marcueil's tear remains the most apocalyptic and yet faithfully realistic modernist representation of the male body in the context of the early twentieth century relation of technology and masculinity. Jarry's parable makes clear that the body cannot be refunctioned indefinitely, as Marinetti claims in his bombastic Futurist theory of reincarnation. Marcueil's tear, a fragment where the organic and the inorganic, function and ornament, compenetrate and clash, shows that the male body, notwithstanding its claims to phallic masculinity, has become an expendable object of consumption inscribing a dangerous and disturbing excess, not a totality but a fetish.

# 5 THE FASHION TOUCH: PRIMITIVIST BODIES, NATIVE CLOTHING, AND WESTERN MASCULINITIES

I explain to my mistress how necessary it is to construct a wall around oneself by the means of clothing.

—Michel Leiris, *Manhoood*

Take yer clothes off an' look at yerselves! Yer ought ter be alive an' beautiful, an' yer ugly an' half dead. —So I'd tell 'em. An' I'd get my men to wear differ-ent clothes: 'appen red ... trousers, bright red, an' little short white jackets. Why, if men had red, fine legs, that alone would change them in a month. They'd begin again to be men! ... Because if once the men walked with legs close bright scarlet, and buttocks nice and showing scarlet ... then the women 'ud begin to be women. It's because th'men *aren't* men, that th'women have to be.

—D. H. Lawrence, *Lady Chatterly's Lover*

As a witty prophecy by one of the chief forerunners of the European modernist avant-garde, Alfred Jarry's fable of Marcueil's body grotesquely unravels *avant la lettre* the implications of Futurism's ideal of the ro-botic male body. *The Supermale* demonstrates that the attempt to merge the Nietzschean ideology of masculinity with the modernist cult of the machine can have unexpected and paradoxical consequences: The beast of prey, which was supposed to overturn narrow-minded bourgeois morality, can suddenly reveal it-self as a well-oiled mechanism whose functioning reenacts rather than subverts the middle class ideals of duty, productivity, and self-preservation. The Futurist notion of mechanical virility mocked by Jarry further perverts the Nietzschean ideal of a powerful and natural masculinity by removing the superman from the space of nature: His sense of duty and self-restraint turns out to make him the perfect metropolitan subject, capable of functioning in an orderly fashion whether on the assembly line or queuing at the cinema. The Futurist collusion with the established order meant that the movement not only contributed enthusiastically to the rhetoric of the First World War but also became the harbinger of a postwar aesthetics that would privilege rationality, geometrical linearity, and functionality over the ornamental.

For modernist writers and artists who had been taught—partly under the influence of Pater and aestheticism—to look upon contemporary culture as a wasteland, a desiccated landscape of industrial ruins that decreed the atomization of the individual and the degradation of the body, the Futurist fantasy of the man-machine might have appealed for its post-Nietzschean vitalism, but it ultimately repelled in its celebration of the mechanistic. This "last romantic" modernism (Yeats's self-serving phrase) turned once more to nature—now thoroughly recognized by the urban writer-flâneur as a space elsewhere, chronologically preceding civilization—in search of an alternative symbolic order in which to imagine a new means of cultural and individual renovation. The specific natural scenario that this modernist desired was not Zarathustra's impervious alpine landscape, a space representing verticality, ascent, and the amoral superiority of the superman, but rather the luxuriant and exotic landscape that had been painted by Paul Gauguin and described by R. L. Stevenson at the end of the nineteenth century, suggesting a movement of "descent," the return to a precultural condition comprising sensuous innocence, violence, and magic. This represented a late-imperial, imaginary version of the colonial encounter: The conqueror-explorers of Victorian imperialism (Gordon, Livingstone) had been recast as administrator tourists by 1900 (Stevenson, Leonard Woolf) and as fans of primitivism by the 1920s (Nancy Cunard, D. H. Lawrence). These primitivist fantasies signified a western desire to return to elemental sensations and to an antirational structure of affect centered on the body. In a range of transgressive representations in the 1920s, the body of the native came to represent the spontaneity, freedom, violence, and sexuality that the western subject had supposedly been deprived of in the name of capitalist efficiency.

This chapter shows how the "native" as represented by the early twentieth century discourses of aesthetic and ethnographic primitivism was deployed by a heterogeneous strand of modernist writing in the years following the First World War to resexualize western versions of masculinity and to covertly display the male body as an object of homoerotic desire. In the two modernist literary texts that I analyze in detail, the French ethnographer and writer Michel Leiris's autobiography *Manhood* (drafted in 1933, published 1946) and D. H. Lawrence's novel *The Plumed Serpent* (1926), the eroticization of the white male body takes place by proxy: By describing and gazing upon the primitive body seductively unclothed, dancing, or performing sacrificial rites, Leiris and Lawrence can fantasmatically identify with the native and reconquer the natural state that he or she represents. Both writers suggest that the exoticism and savagery of the native other do not rely on mere nakedness, which had been the usual trope of "savagery" in standard nineteenth century versions of the colonial encounter, but on the operation of costuming, exposing, and decorating the body. In Leiris's and Lawrence's imagination, these rituals of clothing and unclothing enacted the native sensuousness to which the modernist aspires through "fashioning" the body with ornaments and clothes.

By writing about and identifying with the decorated and unclothed body of the native, Leiris and Lawrence transgress the laws of sobriety that regulated the appearance of western bourgeois men. The display of the native body and, even more, of its tribal marks that fascinates both writers was, predictably, anathema for such spokesmen for modernist functionalism as Adolf Loos. In "Ornament and Crime" (1908) Loos described the act of decorating and exposing one's body as an act of degenerate backwardness performed by savages and women and therefore as a sign of cultural inferiority inadmissible in men. Loos's critique of the ornament was informed by specific precepts of sartorial propriety that became the norm in Europe at the end of the eighteenth century. Since the time of what historians of costume define as "the Great Masculine Renunciation"[1] men customarily wore sober and dark clothes to signify the dignity and the authority attached to the masculine public position in bourgeois society. Whereas the desexualized and plainly wrapped male body pointed to qualities of rationality, productivity, and self-restraint, ornamentation was displaced onto female clothing to signify desire, expenditure, and sexual availability. Women dressed up to attract and charm men and, as Loos explained, to secure a safe place in society for themselves through marriage. Both Leiris's and Lawrence's costuming of the male body, therefore, situates the masculine subject in a liminal position that threatens traditional definitions of gender and endangers notions of phallic masculinity.

For the western male subject under threat and seeking to recover phallic plenitude, the encounter with the primitive promised to be both rewarding and dangerous: His immersion in tribal culture and his identification with the native could produce a further dissolution of his rational subjectivity, and with it, of his masculinity. Therefore he needed to elaborate textual strategies that allowed him to signal his attack on traditional gender definitions and to resexualize the male body. Both Leiris and Lawrence in their writing use clothes, and specifically the clothing of the native, both to signify masculine exhibitionism and to stage an ambiguous display of the male body. Both of these writers treat the sexualization of the male body as a dangerous operation producing dissonant effects. In *Manhood* masculine sexuality turns into a violent fantasy of identification on the part of the author with the "savage" female body; Lawrence instead exposes and veils masculine homoerotic desire through clothes that are both carnival garb and military uniforms so as to fasten the body as securely as he can to a heterosexual ethos of combative masculinity.

## THE PLEASURE OF THE OTHER

The prominence of primitivism on the Parisian artistic scene—in particular during the first three decades of the twentieth century, when it radically changed western figurative art—had both overtly political and voguish dimensions; ultimately it might be read as a premonition by the European avant-garde of the decline of western imperial power. The interest in African culture and art shown by artists such as Picasso, Derain, and Maurice de Vlaminck and by writers such as Alfred Jarry and Guillaume Apollinaire was charged with political meaning: Their often vaguely socialist and anarchist backgrounds tended to turn their art into anticolonialist statements in the context of ongoing debates over imperialism. Press revelation about European atrocities in the French and Belgian Congo and government scandals in Paris and Brussels provoked international protests, of which primitive modernism partook.[2] In the period between the wars the interest in *les choses nègres* continued more as a vogue and also as a scientific-ethnographic area of study than as a political stance. The 1920s marked the beginning of academic ethnography; scholars such as Marcel Griaule, Marcel Mauss, Bronislaw Malinowski, and Leo Frobenius regarded the cultures of Africa and Oceania not as curiosities or aberrations, in the terms of ninteenth century colonial ethnography, but rather as objects of scientific study in their own right.[3]

This modernist enthusiasm for "things native" and for primitive cultures also produced new social figures: the collector of African artifacts, such as socialite Nancy Cunard showing off her ivory bangles in a famous photograph by Man Ray, and audiences in Paris who appreciated Josephine Baker's performance of *la danse sauvage* in La Revue Nègre at the Théâtre des Champs-Elysées.[4] Fashionable primitivism in 1920s Europe included an interest in African art and in African American music, jazz, and spirituals played and sung in European "negro bars," where the urban bourgeoisie looking for transgression went to consume a version of modernity and what they took to be as the liberatory wildness of African, Asian, and South American culture. In all these instances, from the modernist fascination with African art to the ethnographic field trip to Africa or Oceania (even Rupert Brooke had traveled in the South Seas) to Baker's convulsive dances, "tribal" culture did not signify an idyllic, precivilized state of innocence but rather an imaginary source of irrational violence and cruelty. Appearing as another form of Nietzschean antirationalism, another disruptive force threatening notions of bourgeois order, this tribal vitality was deployed by avant-garde modernists as an attack both on bourgeois propriety and on the colonialist claim of white superiority.

This usefulness of primitive imagery as an apparent weapon of opposition to the bourgeois categories of order, morality, and reason and to the aesthetic principle of mimesis that upheld them is openly acknowledged by two male modernists whose fascination with such imagery came from opposing political impulses, Picasso and D. H. Lawrence. In 1937 Picasso told André Malraux about his first encounter with African art in the Musée d'Ethnographie in the first years of the century: "The masks weren't just like any other piece of sculpture. ... They were magic things. ... They were against everything—against unknown, threatening spirits. I always looked at fetishes. I understood; I too, am against everything."[5] Picasso perceived the masks as magic objects and as a vehicle for a polemical attack on conventional art, a way of imposing an aesthetic chaos on the fixed orders of western representation. Lawrence attributed very much the same oppositional value to the African fetish that appears in *Women in Love*, published in 1920.

In *Women in Love* the "African idol" is introduced as the occasion for an exchange between the chief male characters, Rupert Birkin and Gerald Crich. "The carved image of the savage woman in labour"[6] presides over a scene of male nakedness—a group of men, undressed, chat in the morning—in a fashionable London apartment. Gerald watches the carving through the eyes of "the stark naked figures": "It was a terrible face, void, peaked, abstracted almost into meaningless by the weight of sensation beneath."[7] For Birkin the sculpture is art, and as such it contains an image of truth, the faithful representation of a savage culture of the body, "Pure culture in sensation, culture in the physical consciousness, mindless, utterly sensual."[8] Gerald Crich, instead, feels threatened by what he regards as "a sheer, barbaric thing": "But Gerald resented it. He wanted to keep certain illusions, certain ideas like clothing. 'You like the wrong things, Rupert,' he said, 'things against yourself.'"[9] Birkin's appreciation of the African statuette is not merely aesthetic: The distorted female body (distorted in terms of the classical female poses familiar to the London viewers) of the woman in labor points to a metaphysical experience of authenticity that transfigures her as well as her public. It is her "cultural nakedness" that makes her, for Gerald, "a wrong thing to like"; the barbarity of this figure, he feels, requires that its viewer also shed his clothes to return to a precivilized, unconscious state. Gerald's and Rupert's different reactions to the idol illustrate the double value that the primitive assumes for "cultivated" westerners, as both emancipatory and threatening experience. Whereas the clothing metaphor used by Lawrence suggests the possibility of reaching, by means of the primitive, "down to the hidden core" of human truth, this revelatory experience takes place as act of self-effacement; the "pure culture in sensation" founded upon the body calls for the dissolution of meaning, reason, and individuality. The Lawrentian naturalist utopia implies immersion into a nebulous past-in-the-present that situates the subject in an ahistorical realm of primitive essences.

Whereas in Picasso's words the fetishes are invested with a magic-anarchic meaning that makes their oppositional value absolute ("They were against everything"), Lawrence, through the character Gerald Crich—who is blond, Aryan, and a businessman—is more cautious in embracing the primitive. Yet if the desire to reconquer an atavistic plenitude at the cost of self-effacement remains unsatisfied for Crich, the scene in which Gerald and his friends view the idol fulfills another desire, Lawrence's own, to display the naked male body and thus allow a moment of physical freedom and scopophilia both for the characters and for the reader. In this sense, the scene in the London apartment is a key, emblematic image for my discussion. By showing the verbal and scopic exchange between unclothed male bodies "under the eyes" of the African fetish, this scene recapitulates metaphorically the process through which the modernist uses the primitive to reflect narcissistically upon himself. The culture of physical sensation represented by the statuette allows a return to the body and at the same time structures a specific triangulation of desire that makes the male body the object of scopophilic pleasure for another man. The image of the woman giving birth is at the center of attention, but the way the gaze works in this scene demonstrates that hers is a false centrality. In this moment of double voyeurism (Crich is watching his naked friends, who in turn are contemplating the carving), the female figure serves to stage a display of the western male body. The scene tellingly reproposes one by one all the elements that partake in the dialectic of primitivism: the recentering of the other, her disintegration through the discourse of aesthetics, the spectator's pleasure in the "savage horror," and the parasitical endowing of significance to the other's body by the bourgeois male subject trying to resolve the crisis of his own shaken identity. In the discourse of primitivism the specificity of cultural identity is recuperated under the sign of western universality: The native body and her pain, reinscribed as a primeval state of the "human condition," is in fact used by Lawrence to attract attention to the western male body.

Lawrence acknowledges that "the pure culture in sensation" symbolized by the African carving can be threatening for the western subject: The erotic spectacle of the male body, the masculine pleasure in becoming the object of the gaze, removes this subject from the territory of phallic masculinity into an abject space that bourgeois culture understands as feminine. Incapable of resolving this contradiction, Lawrence chooses to remain unaware of how his writing sexualizes the male body and implicitly inscribes homoerotic desire. Both in *Women in Love* and in *The Plumed Serpent,* as in much of his fiction, same-sex desire and the spectacle of masculinity are passed over in silence and presented as something that he wishes to display and dissimulate at the same time. The savagery of the native body provides the perfect site to stage this double operation. The spatial and temporal dislocation implied by the body of the native, inhabitant of a faraway and "archaic" culture, makes the sexualization of western masculinity more acceptable. Savage desires can also assail the western subject, but in a world elsewhere, as in Lawrence's novelistic Mexico in *The Plumed Serpent.* Furthermore, the native body allows the modernist to perform a double gesture of exposure and denial through which he can disguise his own desire, because savagery itself is a costume, an artificial construction, a theatrical disguise with which colonial power "dresses up" the native. Whether as a radical and avant-garde aesthetics or as a vogue, primitivism relies on the discourse and practice of colonialism. What was considered as a signifier of authenticity and spontaneity—the "wildness" of the black body—was in fact produced and circulated in the West through particular technologies such as tales by explorers and missionaries, the popular press, boys' adventure novels, museum exhibits such as that which fixated Picasso, and even zoos, where during the nineteenth century colonial natives were at times exhibited together with wild animals.[10]

Hence in the following discussion in this chapter I show how "black savagery" was fabricated in the heart of the European metropolis through the display of the native body at the turn of the century Imperial Exhibitions. In particular, the vicissitudes of Peter Lobengula, a black man from South Africa who went to London in 1898 to take part in the Greater Britain Exhibition, demonstrate that "wildness" was, literally, nothing but a costume. Lobengula ended his life working as a miner in England, claiming to be an African prince in disguise. His story, I will show, destabilizes the assumptions of primitivist discourse: The fact that a "native" was placed on display in the imperial center, affirmed himself to be a civilized aristocrat, and died a western proletarian clamorously contradicts the classless innocence that had characterized the image of the colonial subject.

Lobengula's masquerades serve the purpose of hiding and at the same time fashioning his various identities. This costuming, this fetishistic marking of the native body, is what attracts both Leiris and Lawrence to the primitive. The theatrical barbarism discerned on the body of the native enables the male modernist to gesture toward a sexuality and a desire that had never been "lost" but rather, at least since Oscar Wilde's trials, had seldom been allowed to emerge. Leiris's and Lawrence's works illustrate two different ways of resexualizing the male body through primitivist discourse. The difference in their position, simply put, lies in the use they make of clothes as symbolic properties. *Manhood*, the first volume of Leiris's autobiography, based on notes taken between 1931 and 1933 when he was working as an ethnographer in Africa, is centered on the author's masochistic fantasy of identification with the female body as figured in a painting by Cranach and by the image of an Ethiopian woman Leiris had met during his African travels. As in the case of the displayed body of Lobengula, clothes—African, western, women's, and men's—allow Leiris to play multiple roles and to linger in a liminal territory where gender marks are no longer clearly defined.

For Lawrence instead, clothes, which he never misses the opportunity to describe in detail, function to simultaneously flaunt and hide the masculine homoerotic body. There is no clear identification with the female body as such in Lawrence, but rather the erotically displayed male body violates the borders of traditional bourgeois masculinity to become the object of a female and male desirous gaze. In *The Plumed Serpent*, a protofascist fantasy of masculine authoritarianism and male bonding set in rural Mexico, native savagery is acted out through semireligious rituals and atavistic costumes worn by the members of a revolutionary movement. This mythological-political mise-en-scène of homoerotic desire culminates in a moment of sexuality between two men. However, this revelatory moment is immediately contained through narrative strategies that affirm heterosexuality: Through its clothes, the desirous native body is turned into the phallic masculinity of the totalitarian subject.

## PRIMITIVIST BODY POLITICS

The British male modernist who, like Lawrence himself, lamented the loss of a more spontaneous and even sacred dimension to the mechanical quality of modern life looked with diffidence at the massified new century culture of the body. He enjoyed holidays at the beach (or even better in the countryside at Garsington Manor) while looking askance at organized sports, mass holidays, and so on, which—with a strong dose of snobbery—he considered vulgar and an integral part of modern clockwork existence. This elitist modernism did not reject the masculine vitalism of the body per se but rather its class determination, which it readily discerned in the populist messages of nationalism and consumer culture. In high modernist aesthetic discourse the natural immediacy of the Nietzschean male body of the blond beast and its mass culture icons—from Eugen Sandow to Tarzan to Baden-Powell's Rovers—was recuperated instead through the exotic body of the colonial subject. For European modernists from Roger Fry in his essay "The Art of the Bushman" (1910) to Man Ray to Lawrence and even to Ronald Firbank in *Prancing Nigger,* the body of the native became a site onto which they could displace their fear of class contamination, of losing individuality and becoming part of a mass, and through which they could reaffirm social boundaries not in terms of class but rather in terms of "race" and "civilization." At the time when class distinctions were becoming weaker, the epithet "barbarian" gave the besieged high bourgeois subject as well as the modernist a way of denigrating and therefore marking his distance from the "vulgar" lower classes.

The parallels between the western urban crowds and colonial "savagery" was foregrounded by the Spanish social critic José Ortega y Gasset in his analysis of what he saw as modern cultural decay, *The Revolt of the Masses* of 1930. Ortega y Gasset relates the disempowered condition of the modern subject, his loss of individuality and authority, to the decline of the aristocratic elites and to the emergence of the masses. In his description of modern culture he discerns none of the excitement Simmel noted in the crowded metropolis; for him the images of human crowds besieging hotels, trains, theaters, and beaches ("Towns are full of people, houses full of tenants, hotels full of guests, trains full of travelers … "[11]) are a sign of modern decadence and of social disorder; the multitudes are visible because they are taking over the spaces formerly reserved for the aristocracy. The average man ("the football fan") is spilling into the sites of the educated elites and dangerously spreading his subaltern and massified condition to the rest of society. In his social analysis Ortega y Gasset exchanges—to use a phrase of Walter

Benjamin's—"the illusion of the crowd" for "the reality of class."[12] He presents the social facelessness of the crowd as "barbarity"; describing the modern masses more than once through the rhetoric of savagery, he refers to them as "tribes," "primitives," and "modern barbarians." In this late-imperial economy of metaphors the notion of race readily substitutes for that of class. The working class bathers are reduced to a homogeneous mass of indistinct flesh; class identity itself is replaced by an image of racial or ethnic difference, a difference formerly attributed to the native. By assimilating the urban masses with their plebeian culture of the body to the image of the savage, this modernist critic assuages his own anxiety vis-à-vis the threat to individuality, order, and hierarchy posed by the modern masses and their "democratic" culture.

In such texts primitivism produced the centering of the body of the native in the universe of western signification. In modernist discourse from Kipling to Evelyn Waugh's *Remote People* (1931) on Ethiopia, the colonial "savage" takes the place of Ortega y Gasset's bathers, the modern urban barbarians. The idea of the average person's "barbarism" tapped the discursive repertory developed by colonial ideology and provided polemicists with a ready-made rationale, accompanied by the anthropometric and ethnographic knowledge needed to define racial and cultural difference as inferiority. It was the presumed inferiority of the native that was attached to the modern masses when they were called barbarians. Conversely, when both "primitive" cultures and the European "barbarians"—the average man or "the football fan"—were referred to as savage, the purpose was to elide from the body of the native any mark of his position in the cycle of production and consumption.

By collapsing one barbarity into the other, the high modernist erased the discourse of class through a celebration of the "classless" native, who was going to be not only exploited economically but also consumed aesthetically by the West. Through this strategy, the western modernist glossed over the position the African individual actually occupied in the economy of the colony. Thus the native's material conditions of existence, his role as cheap labor often exploited in near-slave conditions—as revealed, for example, in Roger Casement's reports on the Congo and Putumayo of 1903 and 1907—was displaced and dispersed onto an archaic past, a time of prehistoric consciousness of which the native came to be the sign. The substitution of the body of the colonized for the working hands of the proletarian was articulated in aesthetic terms: The effigy of otherness, the native body as well as the African mask, collected and imitated by western artists, became the foundation of a new aesthetic, a new art whose formal aspect, highly stylized and antimimetic, made it undecipherable to the majority. Put forward by modernism to enable its own aesthetic production and covertly to mantain class divisions, the primitive body was subjected to a progressive process of abstraction and effacement. In 1890s Paris there were African models who posed for paintings; by the 1930s, Man Ray was photographing a white model with an African mask. Fixed on the native's ritual tattoos, on patterns and on forms, western artists paid little attention to the less decorative and more brutal scars of imperialism, the signs that civilization had imprinted on his body.

Not only did the modernist discourse of the primitive and the colonial other help to elide the presence of the proletarian but, by aestheticizing the native's otherness, it obscured a very important analogy between the "barbarians" at home and those in the colonies. While exchanging class with race, the modernist passed over the fact that the European proletarian and the African savage occupied similar positions in the social formation and in the mode of production of which each was part: that of the labor force. A focus on racial otherness allowed the modernist to think of himself as part of an undifferentiated West—"civilization" as opposed to savagery—rather than as an upper middle class subject seeking to distinguish himself from the lower classes. He could then occupy a space outside existing class definitions and ultimately represent himself as part of that fictitious aristocratic and intellectual elite described by Ortega y Gasset, an imaginary and nostalgic replacement for a class that was historically in decline.

## IMPERIAL EXHIBITIONS AND THE POLITICS OF DISPLAY

Even when committed to primitive cultures—nostalgically, as in the case of Lawrence in *The Plumed Serpent,* or quasi-politically, as with Picasso and the Fauves in pre–First World War Paris, or through colonial administration, as with Leonard Woolf and Joyce Carey—the modernist's perception of the native relied very much on colonial discourses and spectacles generated by the imperial centers. Hence, the modernist accepted as real what was in fact an ideological construction; besides visiting museums of ethnography, where they could observe African artifacts, most modernist writers, like millions of people in Europe, learned about colonial life in Africa in particular from such popular sources of information as the music hall, adventure novels, films, and radio broadcasts.[13] The zoo and the numerous Imperial Exhibitions were spaces where colonial life could be experienced firsthand by the urban audience of European cities and where the "savagery" of the native could be closely watched. While in the zoo the natives might simply be exhibited next to the caged animals, in the exhibitions they were displayed among commodities from the home country and with products and raw materials from the colony, testifying both to the homeland's industrial progress and to the colony's rich but backward state.

The British exhibitions changed from international industrial fairs in the mid-nineteenth century to colonial displays in more modern times. After the Berlin Conference of 1884, which marked the beginning of a period of aggressive colonial competition among European states, the fairs became vehicles of imperial ideology, selling "the scramble for Africa" as popular entertainment and propaganda. Two of the grandest were the Great Empire Exhibition at Wembley in 1924–1925 and the Paris Exposition Coloniale Internationale of 1931.[14] At these exhibitions the decorated and unclothed body of the native, implying his "natural" spontaneity, was staged in the light of self-interested colonial knowledge. The distinctive qualities of the savage as described and transmitted by missionaries, explorers, traders, and ethnologists who had taken part in the colonial enterprise in the nineteenth century were his wildness, suggested by the cruelty and ferality of his customs, and his lack of intellectual capability, compensated for by his physicality, his existence as nature, pure body. These traits were used to represent the African as the negative of the colonizer, to confirm the superiority of European life against the "darkness" of the colony, and to highlight the rationality of the westerner as opposed to the instinctuality of the other who was put on view.

At the exhibitions the physical energy of the native was displayed in two spheres: either as the racist stereotype of the male native required, in tableaux of war and fighting, or in suggestions of an unrestrained, excessive, and immoral sexuality, which the Victorians had attributed to the female savage as well as to the prostitute at home.[15] A third sphere in which the native's energy was displayed was labor. His incorrigible deficiencies, it was insisted, made him an innate laborer, perfectly fit for work. Explorers such as Richard F. Burton had written of the African as an acceptable worker: "I unhesitatingly assert—and all unprejudiced travellers will agree with me—that the world still wants the black hand. Enormous tropical regions yet await the clearing and draining operations by the lower races which will fit them to become the dwelling place of the civilized man."[16] This racist picture of the other as born worker constitutes the imperialist fantasy of a natural division of labor and of a submissive and totally obedient workforce; as such, it betrayed the empire's own anxieties about its loss of hegemony over the British working class, which was gaining power with the growth of labor in the early years of the century.

Although imperialist racial discourse described the colonial native in terms of absolute distance and difference from the white colonist and his superior civilization, the increasing economic dependence of the homeland on the colony and its resources demanded that the colonial real be made accessible, knowable and brought closer to the western subject. Once the colony became more necessary for the economy of the homeland, it assumed a new role in the western imaginary, that of a threat *and* of an object of desire. Getting to know the colony, being able to imagine life there, became a way for the European subject to bridge "the spatial disjunction" between the metropolis and the colony that Frederic Jameson defines as characteristic of early twentieth century imperialism. "What is determined by colonialism," Jameson notes, "is now a rather different kind of meaning loss; for colonialism means that a significant segment of the economic system as a whole is located elsewhere, beyond the metropolis, outside of the daily life and existential experience of the home country."[17] For the West, the loss of its absolute centrality and independence in the economic process implied a loss of power over the process of the production of meaning. Since the homeland was incapable of producing meaning "by itself," national life and national identity could not anymore be understood immanently. The empire now found itself involved in another kind of colonial war, this time in order to reconquer the lost territories of its own imaginary. Thus by familiarizing himself at the exhibitions with the life in the colony, the Englishman or Frenchman at home could feel that he was able to master ideologically what was in reality determining the direction of the empire's economic welfare. Thus the succession of Imperial Exhibitions from the 1880s onward became one setting where the colonial unknown was reintegrated into the metropolis through the presence of the native. In these sites of modernity the European empires spelled out their ideology to the masses and worked to maintain the upper hand in the production of meaning by deliberately manufacturing the image of the other.

The major attractions of the exhibitions were the native villages, where different aspects of colonial life were enacted by the natives themselves, and shows managed by professional impresarios. The 1899 Greater Britain Exhibition in London, for example, featured "Savage South Africa: A Vivid, Realistic and Picturesque Representation of Life in the Wilds of Africa";[18] besides watching reenactments of Boer War battles on stage, the audience could see enactments of "everyday" life in the colony. The show included a tour of a reconstructed "Kaffir kraal," where about 200 Africans of different ethnic groups crowded in four villages complete with exotic animals such as cranes and giant tortoises. In the Kaffir kraal the natives were not represented as individuals or as tribes but as a crowd of savages indistinguishable from each other in the eyes of a British audience—an image that in turn recalls the undifferentiated masses critiqued by Ortega y Gasset.

The visibility of the native in these mock villages was regulated by imperial surveillance and ideologically mediated in two ways: through the discourse of science and through the theatrical staging of what seemed to be authentic and spontaneous behavior. Submitted to the same regimes of inquiry as the criminal, the proletarian, and (in studies of evolution) prehistoric man, the native was similarly constructed as an example of social, biological, and racial deviance. In the Science Pavilion at the 1908 Franco-British Exhibition in London a special section, "The Life of Primitive Man, with Particular Reference to the Stone Age People, Prehistoric and Contemporary,"[19] assured its audience that the Senegalese dancers and even the Irish colleens standing in front of their reconstructed cottages could be identified by the public as primitive and inferior. The arrangement of another display in the same pavilion established a link between the colonized, the criminal, and the working class: The data collected by the anthropometry section of the

Imperial Bureau of Anthropology were shown together with drawings, photos, and casts of "native skulls" and next to a fingerprint apparatus. The physiognomic principle of anthropometry, in which the physical measurements of the subject's body were used as a test of his deterioration or progress, were shared by ethnography, criminal anthropology, and eugenics. The Imperial Bureau of Anthropology had been established in 1903 by the Physical Deterioration Committee; that committee had been originally set up in response to the medical reports on the poor health of British working class men at the time of the Boer War.[20]

The Science Pavilion at the 1908 exhibition did not attract as much attention as the villages, but its displays gave the audience an interpretative key to read the spectacle of the native. This spectacle, produced through both scientific measurement and naturalistic display, was that of a potentially dangerous individual captured and now shown in his natural environment. Paradoxically, the empire wanted the colonized person to be peaceful and savage at the same time (that is, similar and simultaneously different); he must represent himself as he was *before* the coming of the British (as he *really* was) and *after* their civilizing intervention. Yet these "savages" were not spoils of war, reduced to captivity, although this was how they were represented to the western public; rather, they were actors, engaged by a manager to perform "themselves" in a simulated African village—and even on stage. The troupe of "Savage South Africa," for example, had been brought to Europe by Frank Fillis, a London showman who managed a network of circuses in the Dutch and British parts of South Africa in the 1880s.[21] Once in London, the troupe was engaged to appear in the Greater Britain Exhibition by Imre Kyralfi, a Hungarian-born impresario who with his company produced all the major shows at the exhibitions. In 1899, the troupe members from South Africa appeared both in the Kaffir kraal and in a theatrical reenactment of the Matabele Wars of 1893, where—while acting out their former resistance against the British—their "authentic," ferocious, and dangerous nature was put on show.

This image of savagery was becoming increasingly untenable historically. By 1910 natives of many African colonies were assimilated into the economic structures of the colonial system as the subaltern and necessary "black hand" of the empire: as tea pickers in Ceylon, as farm labor in Kenya. Because of his position in the system of capitalist production, the colonized became a proletarian; as cheap, underpaid labor, he was one of the main "products" of the colony, ultimately its chief commodity. This knowledge was elided not only at home, in the exhibition, but even in the colony itself, where the native was not recognized as a worker. As the historian Terence Ranger puts it, "In South Africa, African employees were not defined as workers, but instead controlled and disciplined under the terms of the Master and Servant Act."[22] A material relation of economic exploitation was thus represented in terms of master-servant paternalism. This substitution of a fictitiously organic and almost feudal social model for the mechanistic social relation of capitalism was the basis of a white identity formation in the colony. Through the imagined classlessness of the colonized, the master-colonizer could in turn transform his image from that of unscrupulous entrepreneur to genteel aristocrat.

The invention of a stereotypical, homogeneous African identity, where the servant replaced the worker and the image of the tribe covered a more complex and fluid social reality, was useful to the empire in at least two ways: It enforced the colonial surveillance of the native by fixing him into easily recognizable social categories, and it enhanced a self-congratulatory white identity. The display of the "dark races" at the exhibitions aimed to consolidate the British nation in an interclassist unity by implying that *all* the British were equal as a race. Displayed to the public behind iron railings, the natives' seminaked bodies in their tribal costumes were structured so as to be enjoyed by the audience as an image of picturesque and unselfconscious childishness; traces of work and sexuality were only obliquely suggested. As the guidebook of the Franco-British Exhibition explained, the native's energy was rechanneled into productive and pleasant activities: "Unlike the Indian, the South African native is a restless, active savage, and he will be seen grinding corn, making native drink, working beads and, most attractive of all, particularly for the fair sex, the manufacture of Kaffir bangles, which are said to be lucky amulets."[23] Thus while male physical prowess was reabsorbed into these forms of apparently unexploited domestic labor, the actual underpaid labor offered to native workers could be ignored. The African women meanwhile were shown dispelling their "savage energy" in dance, although the guidebook hastened to note that "in all their dances the natives of the villages observe the greatest decency and good conduct, naturally and without prompting";[24] in passages such as this, native "lasciviousness" was simultaneously invoked and contained.

## PETER LOBENGULA'S SHORT JACKET: NATIVE STRATAGEMS

The guidebook's painstaking effort to establish the dancers' morality was aimed at avoiding any apparent violation of the sexual and social order, as in the sensation that had been whipped up by the new yellow journalism at the 1899 Greater Britain Exhibition. On that occasion scandal had arisen when the male black body, already "degraded" as the object of the western gaze, had actually become the object of female touch. The troupe of "Savage South Africa" put on display for "six pence a look" in the Kaffir kraal was immediately popular and, as the press noted, attracted the curiosity of both the populace and the "elegant crowds" of London. This display of African male bodies was tolerated by public opinion as long as the natives, kept at a "safety distance" from the audience, were observed as nothing more than an ethnological curiosity. When one of the Africans married a white woman in the same year, however, the response of the press, until then benevolent, became hysterical. Peter Lobengula, the bridegroom, was a "well-mannered" member of the troupe who also appeared to have had a western education: he claimed to be a prince, the son of the king of Matabeleland. His father, he told the reporters, had him raised "as a civilized man" by the Wesleyans at Bloemfontein. In 1891, on the collapse of his father's kingdom, he had gone to South Africa to work as a valet for a white colonist. There he had met the impresario Frank Fillis and Kitty Jewell, the white woman who was to become his wife. Jewell, the daughter of a Cornish mining engineer who had emigrated to South Africa, had followed Lobengula to England.

The couple tried on three occasions to get married in London and were prevented, in turn, by the manager of "Savage South Africa," by the local vicar, and by Kitty's mother, who had read about the marriage in the Paris papers. Each day a great crowd gathered in front of the church to enjoy the spectacle. A newspaper reported that "the Royal South African was dressed in a short jacket and a straw hat. ... Loben is a presentable looking gentleman and Jewell was even more presentable."[25] Although a marriage certificate was finally filled out on the second day, no civil ceremony took place. The couple then went "into hiding" in a house in Kensington.

The story of Peter Lobengula and Kitty Jewell was made to appear by the newspapers as the outcome of the immoral spectacle of masculine sexuality at the kraal. The public's curiosity about the natives was demonized as unacceptable, and the interest on the part of women, already remarked upon ("how our womenkind fairly mobs the Africans in their anxiety to see them near"[26]), was presented as an explicitly sexual response, inadmissible for white, and particularly British, gentlewomen.[27] Lobengula's marriage was openly condemned as an act of miscegenation and therefore as a threat to racial integrity. Yet the fear of racial decay in fact mobilized masculine anxieties related to the increasing instability of traditional gender hierarchies. By constructing a story of "hurt pride" in which white men are ignored by white women who choose instead to gaze on the bodies of black men, the British male subject could displace the real source of his insecurity from women onto natives and thus avoid a direct confrontation with female power. The episode of the Kaffir kraal provided a disturbing image of female independence that excluded British men and reversed the traditional sexual roles: It was women who "chose" men as objects of their desire, and the African men were displaying their bodies, it was inferred, to attract the sexual attention of women. Whether real or fantastic, this scene implied a subversion of the patriarchal structure of the gaze and of desire: The women, actively engaging with a "passive" male body transformed into a spectacle, were subjecting men, turning them into the object of the gaze and even of touch. This reversed relation of specularity between the male and the female subject created anxiety because it stood as a memento, at the level of the imaginary, of the social and sexual independence that western women were increasingly claiming, just as they claimed the right to vote, in precisely this period.

In press commentaries, the kraal episode was seen as a shameful act of feminine misbehavior, a matter of manners and not of power: The female visitors to the kraal had discredited "civilization" even in the eyes of the natives themselves by behaving like savages. A characteristic slip of the tongue in one report reveals, poorly concealed behind the female figure, masculine insecurity: "The tales that these black men will take back to their land about the white men in the capital city of Europe … in that mysterious city that they have always connected with the power of the Great Queen and of a superior race … will be a precious result of a show supposed to help the empire."[28] The women's misbehavior had the effect of exposing the white male's powerlessness in front of the colonial subject, and ultimately of shortening the distance between the inferior male native and the supposedly superior colonial power.

The memory of Lobengula and Jewell's marriage was a lesson for the organizers of early twentieth century shows: At the Franco-British Exhibition in 1908, no contact with the natives was allowed to the public. The image of the Senegalese dancers, male and female, was rigorously shorn of any possible eroticism, and the male native body was moralized as a source of artistic inspiration, its sexuality exchanged for aesthetic value: "In no part of the British dominions are there more handsome men from the sculptor's point of view, than among certain types of Nilotic Negro or Negroid," wrote one reporter.[29] This clothing of the native's nakedness, and with it of the "pure culture in sensation" that this nakedness signified, was a central trope in the discourse of primitivism deployed by high modernist writers. As a representation, the body of the other is always ideologically clothed; the absolute nakedness of the African carving that in *Women in Love* troubles Gerald Crich existed only within western discourse.

Peter Lobengula disturbed Edwardian England so much because his was a story of racial travesty. If Lobengula had kept to the feathers, wild animal skins, warlike decorations, and ostentatious nakedness of his Zulu costume in "Savage South Africa" Figure 5.1, if he had let himself be clearly identified as the primitive—as his theatrical role at the exhibition required—his story would have been less scandalous. Instead, the gentlemanly figure of the black man "in short jacket and straw hat" stepping into a church to marry a white woman came to signify social and racial disorder. It meant that when wearing the proper clothes, a "savage" could pass as, and in fact even take the place of, a white gentleman; ultimately it meant that the difference between the white man and the native was not a matter of skin but of garments. Thus the vicissitudes of Prince Lobengula demonstrated to the British audience that both the savagery of the "dark races" and the civility of the British gentleman were not "natural": One's identity was not written on the body by one's skin color or by anthropometric measurements but signified rather by the ephemerality of clothes.

Lobengula's life story—fostered as a "strange case" by the new penny journalism—refused to disappear from public attention. Eventually this exile's narrative,

*Figure 5.1  "Prince Lobengula with a Troop of Matabele," 1899 postcard.*

as a contradictory and disturbing case, turned into an unsolvable mystery and reemerged a decade later as the occasion for a further inquiry into colonial otherness. On September 12, 1913, "a frail looking negro wearing a band of crepe on his arm"[30] appeared in a court in West Salford, demanding, as a British subject, his right to vote. He was "Prince Peter Lobengula," the oldest son of King Lobengula of Matabelelend, and his country was now incorporated into Britain's dominions. The barrister accepted his story; to the *Salford Chronicle* reporter the quiet, unpretentious man claimed to have personally led the Matabele uprising of 1896 and afterward had come to England engaged to appear in a show. When the show had flopped in Manchester, Lobengula had earned a living as a miner, caught tuberculosis, and was now seriously ill. Married to an Irishwoman and with a family of five children, he and his wife survived on a state pension of ten shillings per week. "Lacking the comforts—to say nothing of the delicacies—which are normally enjoyed by a man of his birth,"[31] he hoped for a higher pension. The case of "the prince in poverty" acquired such a resonance that the Colonial Secretary asked the British South Africa Company in Salisbury to check the prince's eligibility for a such a pension, that is, he asked the Company to ascertain his identity. Through the media's intervention, the image of the "pitiful savage" became more complicated. Lobengula had already been famous: When in 1899 he had married Kitty Jewell he had been defined as "a dusky savage mating a white woman,"[32] but even the reporters then had, to their surprise (or perhaps their disappointment), found him not a savage but a gentleman.

Always exceeding the roles that the empire had created for him at the same time that he played along with them, Lobengula's identity flickers in and out of a series of contradictory personalities: loyal British subject and rebellious colonized; black villain and lovable savage; educated primitive; upper class black man; an actor playing himself; an aristocrat *and* a proletarian. In England Lobengula discovered, at his own expense, that there was no space for him outside the role into which he had been interpellated by colonialism, that of the ethnological curiosity. Every time he tried to affirm his identity in terms of class rather than race, he encountered a rejection: He could be neither a British gentleman nor a British worker. When he became a worker—his true condition as a colonized—his identity was resented by his white fellow miners, trained in the ideology of racist nationalism that Lobengula's own impersonation at the exhibition had helped to establish.

Who was Lobengula? Was he telling the truth about himself? As the sole guarantor of his own identity, he always maintained his version of the facts, even on his deathbed. The Salford vicar remarked, "A man on the point of death would hardly persist in a false statement."[33] Would he? What would he have to gain, at that point, by an invented truth? But also, what had he to lose? The other picture of Lobengula is that of the native who had learned all too well the lesson of colonial forgery and, having also internalized the laws of modern show business, used this knowledge to "answer back," thus beating the empire at its own game. As an inauthentic primitive, a barbaric prince in disguise, a gentleman who becomes a miner, and a miner who cannot be a British proletarian because he is not white, Lobengula could be best defined as a man ... who is not. As pure image, contrived by himself and by the media at the same time, he is constructed as an absence. The absence of the other refracts and confirms also the absence of the western self, that very subjectivity that high modernism had been trying to reconstruct through the "authenticity" of the native body.

Yet at a certain point in his story, the impulse to self-effacement that Lobengula used to forestall the essentialist expectations of his audience became inextricably entangled with the empire's own strategies of erasure. Lobengula's absence was produced both by his own camouflages and also by his very condition as a colonized. In this last role he was rejected by the miners of Salford—who claimed they did not want to be equated with a member of an inferior race—and by the British government itself. The empire had the last word. In January 1913 the British South Africa Company, asked by the Colonial Secretary to investigate Lobengula's identity and eligibility for a pension, replied that the man's story had no foundation: His name was not listed among the known sons of King Lobengula. Having contacted the organizers of the 1899 exhibition, officials produced the evidence to show that the theatrical Lobengula had been engaged in Natal and knew nothing of Matabeleland. The troublesome case of this histrionic native was resolved: Peter Lobengula had never existed.

If the savage prince had no identity in official records, his multiple travesties became a disturbing memory for Edwardian England, a telling dent in the colonial imaginary of the period. With Lobengula's performances on stage, in the Kaffir kraal, and at his scandalous wedding, the male black body was placed in a position traditionally occupied by women, that of the object of the gaze. Inasmuch as Lobengula contributed to make a spectacle of the male body, his personae were doubly transgressive: Whereas in his "short jacket and straw hat" the colonial subject performed as a white man, his body, painted with tribal decorations and scantily clad, made an erotic display of masculinity. In these displays Lobengula was the perfect replica of the "Papuan native" whom Adolf Loos critiqued in two of his essays, "Ladies' Fashion" (1898) and "Ornament and Crime" (1908). For Loos, the ornamented, tattooed, and scarified body of the native represents a threat to western civilization. By foregrounding the nexus between primitivism, crime, ornament, and femininity, his attack on decoration not merely as an antimodern, antiefficient phenomenon but also as a barbaric, uncivilized practice brings into focus how the anxieties about gender were worked out upon the spectacle of a body such as Lobengula's in Britain in the same period.

These anxieties symptomatically indicated an ongoing crisis in hegemonic definitions of masculinity and sanctioned the search for new criteria for stabilizing gender categories. The modernist "puritan" rejection of ornament became one of these new criteria, further degrading the feminizing effects of ornamentation as a form of savagery; as Loos observes, "The lower the culture, the more apparent the ornament. … The bicycle and the steam engine are free of ornament. The march of civilization systematically liberates object after object from ornamentation."[34] Modernity, epitomized by the sleek functionality of the machine, must do away with the ornament: Decoration, for Loos, threatens progress. Further, decoration is degenerate precisely because of its erotic value, so that the decorative practice par excellence, art itself, is suspect: "The urge to decorate one's face and everything in reach is the origin of the graphic arts. It is the babbling of painting. All art is erotic."[35] Although Loos insists that his rejection of ornament is not a self-sacrifice but free choice, his indictment of decoration as primitive and criminal implies, from the point of view of the masculine subject, a renunciation of the display of his sexuality. This ascetic gesture, mirrored in the sartorial drabness of modern urban men (here the black-coated clerk stands as a culmination) is what characterized "authentic" masculinity and what, for Loos, distinguished the individual from the mass: "The herd must distinguish themselves by the use of various colors, modern man uses his clothes like a mask. His individuality is so strong that he does not need to express it any longer by his clothing. Lack of ornament is a sign of spiritual strength."[36] For Loos, ornamental clothing is acceptable in European culture only when worn by women, precisely because of their dependence on men. Only when women, Loos prophesies, are economically independent from men and do not need to attract attention through an exhibitionist display of their bodies, will "velvet and silk, flowers and ribbons, feathers and paints … fail to have their effect."[37] Until then, these elements will continue to signal women's primitive and backward qualities as well as their proximity to the savage and the criminal.

In the light of Loos's critique of decoration, one can more fully understand the transgressive quality of Lobengula's masquerades. His use of clothes, of both the gentleman's attire and the native's garb, turned his body into a liminal territory where savagery and civilization, masculinity and femininity, had to forgo their stability. Like the western woman or the Papuan male of Loos's example, Lobengula fails to attain the "spirituality" and sobriety that distinguishes modern masculinity—and yet he seems to aspire to it. In other words, he fails to make the "Great Masculine Renunciation," that act of sartorial streamlining of the civil servant, clerk, or businessman, through which modern middle class masculinity and its desexualized sobriety were most plainly exemplified.

The British psychologist J. C. Flugel wrote of the "Great Masculine Renunciation" in 1930. In his *Psychology of Clothes,* on the psychological and social value of dress, he devoted a chapter to the way dress serves to map sexuality onto the body and how it produces and signifies sexual difference. Until the eighteenth century, Flugel claims, men and women used ornament both as a means of erotic exposure and as a way of signaling social status, wealth, and rank. With the postrevolutionary impulse to equality, masculine attire became simpler, functioning as a means of social uniformity rather than distinction. The ethos of the middle class that had come to power with the revolution became visible in the sobriety of masculine clothing. Throughout the nineteenth and early twentieth century, as Flugel affirms, "Modern man's clothing abounds in features which symbolize its devotion to the principles of duty, renunciation and self-control. The male relatively 'fixed' system of clothing is, in fact, an outward and visible sign of the strictness of his adherence to the social code (though at the same time, through its phallic attributes, it symbolizes the most fundamental features of his sexual nature)."[38] Flugel insists that the vertical line that the tie, for instance, inscribes on the masculine body is a stylized visual signifier of the penis. With the turn that Flugel calls the "Great Masculine Renunciation," masculine sartorial flamboyance, together with the pleasure of exhibiting one's body, was superseded by a new chastened uniformity. In this regime of sartorial austerity, which prohibited masculine sexual exposure, the phallus came to be signified by the very minimization and invisibility of sexuality and by the virtues of morality and propriety that this very invisibility signified.

Since the moment when men gave up the sartorial display of their bodies, their exhibitionist desire—the desire to be seen—was displaced onto the desire to see, that is, onto scopophilia, as Flugel defines it, "erotic pleasure in the use of vision."[39] From being the object of another's voyeurism, man became the bearer of the gaze and came to express his desire for exhibitionism only vicariously, by projecting it onto women. This displacement can take place in various degrees, more or less acceptable socially, from the masculine pride at accompanying a beautiful and elegantly dressed woman to the panoply of masculine perversions linked to the identification with woman, such as transvestism. Flugel's reflections prove useful to the feminist critic of masculinity because they provide instruments for critiquing the naturalization of phallic masculine identity. As Kaja Silverman points out, "Flugel ... seems to imply that exhibitionism plays a fundamental part within the constitution of the male subject as it does within that of the female subject—that voyeurism, which is much more fully associated with male subjectivity than is exhibitionism, is only a secondary formation, an alternative avenue of libidinal gratification."[40] In other words, male subjectivity depends on specularity as much as on female subjectivity. The masculine role as bearer of the gaze—he who sees and is not seen—is itself a construct that has been historically and culturally produced.

This "unnatural" quality of masculinity is what Peter Lobengula's case affirms. His African body, whether wearing London wedding clothes or displayed semi-naked in a "tribal" costume, was doubly transgressive. As a native wearing the costume of the gentleman, he reminded the white man of the ephemeral quality of his own identity as a civilized and respectable individual; as a man in the crowd watching Lobengula on his wedding day observed, "Loben is a presentable looking gentleman," literally, a man made by his clothes. As a man displaying his body, he performed an act that was considered proper only if referred to the female body; his staging of the body represents a return to masculine exhibitionism.

Within the historical and cultural context of his time, Lobengula used clothes in a feminine way, not as a form of parade but rather as masquerade. In the parade, a notion that Jacques Lacan opposed to Joan Rivière's model of feminine masquerade, the male subject uses his clothes prosthetically to show off his sex and his phallic masculinity. In the words of the French feminist critic Eugénie Lemoine-Luccioni, "Masquerade ... helps women to show what they have not (the penis), while flaunting something else. ... Men parade what they have (the male organ) while showing off what is not really proper to the male sex (feathers and ornaments). ... But why parade, if one has the penis?"[41] If, with Flugel, one acknowledges that the male subject is as exhibitionistic as the female and that his identity is decentered, depending on the gaze of the other—in other words, if one posits that both feminine and masculine identities are founded on lack, that they both lack the phallus even though one has the penis—then what separates the parade from the masquerade is indeed a very thin line. Both processes are forms of fetishism, ways of flaunting what was never there. Lobengula's self-fashioning is a form both of parade and of masquerade. As a man playing at masquerading what he has (the penis but not the phallus)—in fact, what he is supposed to have as a man but what is denied to him as a colonial subject—he shows that savagery, whiteness, and masculinity are all props, nothing but ornaments. Ultimately, he demonstrates that the phallus is not a natural presence, something one is born with, but rather, like the mask itself, an artifice, an acquired art. The story of Lobengula implies that for the modern western subject, "savagery" represented much more than a nostalgic return to nature, authentic feelings, and unbridled sexuality. Primitive ornamentation and nakedness allowed a return to a premodern practice of masculine exhibitionism; as such, in modernist primitivism, they became the venue of a largely unexplored and taboo staging of gender transgression.

## LEIRIS'S "MANHOOD": WEARING WOMAN

In contemplating the possibility of abolishing sartorial differences between the sexes, Flugel explains the heterosexual's disgust at this idea as "the fear of regressing to the ambisexual state, or even, in the case of men, to a stage at which homosexuality predominated."[42] This threatening regression must be guarded against through the constant enforcement of heterosexuality: "It is as though a mistake must be avoided at all costs; and this can best be done by a sex differentiation of such a kind that we can see at a glance whether or no a given individual falls within the category of permissible sexual objects."[43] The desire to "see at a glance" invokes castration anxiety and the need to have an object on which the masculine scopophilic obsession can focus; the same desire points to the need to establish fixed boundaries, recognizable "at a glance," between clearly defined categories of sexual difference that are permissible within heterosexual logic. The sartorial and implicitly gender and sexual transgressions of the native body displayed in the European metropolis at the exhibitions, in the music hall, or in the jazz bar could be celebrated by the modernist without upsetting heterosexuality. As such, this body served as a site where traditional definitions of gender could be contested and where a perverse masculinity, female-identified and caught in exhibitionist specularity, could be expressed.

In the work of both Leiris and Lawrence the attempt to resexualize the male body through the mediation of the primitive is also a means of affirming this perverse masculinity; in Lawrence's texts it also serves as a covert means of signifying homoerotic desire. The display of the masculine body, modeled on the uncovered body of the native, was not, as in the case of the dandy's fashionable excess, a form of intentional exposure, meant to reveal while disguising. For both Leiris and Lawrence perverse masculinity and homoeroticism are occluded truths, with merely the status of fantasy, unraveled in front of the reader's eyes and denied at the same time. The reinscription of the erotic on the male body through the fetishistic rhetoric of clothing and nakedness stands as a key metaphor for the modernist's double gesture of sexual self-display and occlusion. Clothes can function as a revelatory fiction, as in Leiris's text, or as a form of protection, an ambiguous disguise for the masculine desire for the same, as in Lawrence. Although Lawrence's novel *The Plumed Serpent* predates Leiris's autobiographical writing in *Manhood* (the novel was published in 1926, and the autobiography in 1946, based on material written between 1931 and 1933), I will consider *Manhood* before *The Plumed Serpent* because it stands as the first term of this modernist dialectic of masculinity. Whereas Leiris, through his identification with the female body, opens a rift in the heterosexual discourse of gender by subverting traditional definitions of sexual difference, Lawrence's ambiguous costuming of the male body serves the purpose of suturing Leiris's subversive gesture into an image of phallic masculinity. The veiling and disclosing of the male body through clothing, which both authors enact in their texts, again highlights the elusiveness of the phallus and the dramas of intermittent veiling and exposure that structure its presence.

As a man of letters and an art critic, Michel Leiris came of age in the mid- to late 1920s, writing for the journal *Documents* and gravitating into the cultural orbit of Surrealism and of Georges Bataille, to whom *Manhood* is dedicated. As a student of Marcel Mauss and Marcel Griaule at the Institut d'Ethnographie in Paris, Leiris imbibed the cultural and intellectual climate created by the avant-garde interest in the primitive; from the perspective of these ethnographers, Africa was not simply a colonial possession to subjugate and exploit but an assemblage of different and mysterious cultures to be studied as objects of scientific knowledge. Leiris left for Africa in 1931 on the Dakar-Djibouti mission, sponsored by the Institut d'Ethnographie and organized by Griaule; the expedition was financed by Parisian high society, the group that admired Picasso's and Vlaminck's paintings and cheered the dances of Josephine Baker and Jo Alex. In three years, Griaule's group collected a vast amount of material: photographs, written ethnographies, and over 3,000 objects destined to enrich the collections of the Musée d'Ethnographie—soon to be renovated and transformed into the Musée de l'Homme.

For Leiris, who was Griaule's secretary-archivist, the expedition marked a high point in his life. The African experience was extensively reworked in all his writing, particularly in *L'Afrique fantôme* (1934), as well as in the many volumes of his autobiography. Throughout, the author's perspective is that the primitive did not work as a means of escape from civilization and the individual self but rather as a means of returning the subject to himself. Such a journey into the exotic, recommended by Leiris's own psychoanalyst, produced in him "an emotional void of growing proportions,"[44] where the *promesse de bonheur* of native life opened a space for masculine introspection. Instead of investigating the other, he started to keep notes on himself, collecting the data and the "evidence" he used later in *Manhood*.

From the start Leiris turned this study of the male self into a narrative: "But the voyage must be told. It cannot be a heap of observations, notes, souvenirs. ... A journey *makes* sense as a 'coming to consciousness'; its story hardens around an identity. ... But what if one refuses to tell?"[45] This passage testifies to a double movement toward and away from the self; the formless, experiential bundle of facts must be made sense of, straightened into a narrative. At the same time, the "refusal to tell" amounts to a disavowal of the very notion of a solid, steady identity on the author's part. In Leiris's words, the identity seems to preexist the story; in fact, his "hard" identity, as I will show, is a function of the story, fashioned through a narrative that is simultaneously open and reticent ("What if one refuses to tell?"). His attempt to sincerely and transparently reveal his self is continually undermined by his elliptical way of proceeding in the narrative through dreams, images, and mental associations—opaque devices that contradict the author's claim to "telling all." At the same time, he engages in a coquettish game of disclosure: He lets us see more than what he says and unclothes himself to the reader in a revelatory way, letting his corporeal obsessions run free while he seems to be coolly analyzing them in his rational commentary. *Manhood* is a Surrealist Bildungsroman, written under the aegis of psychoanalysis and primitivism, its aim to recount the passage "from the miraculous chaos of childhood to the fierce order of virility."[46] The means by which masculine corporeal identity gets articulated in the course of the story, however, sanctions the failure of this transformation: No change from chaos to order takes place. Leiris's choice of words is important here: The religious-magical credulity of childhood produces not manly rationality but "fierceness." The definition of masculinity as wildness not only refers to the Nietzschean blond beast but also underlies the central role of primitivism in Leiris's imaginary.

The sexualization of the male corporeality in *Manhood* is predicated on the impulse to expose the body and on the contradictory attempt to protect it from the reader's gaze. The book itself stands as a naked body that Leiris tries (or at least feigns to, given the author's pleasure in producing the spectacle of male nudity) unsuccessfully to dress up. Introducing himself, for example, Leiris shows that his identity as a man is threatened, rather than enhanced, by mirrors: "I like to dress with the greatest possible elegance; yet, due to the defects I have just described in my physique and in my financial means ... I usually consider myself profoundly inelegant; I loathe unexpectedly catching sight of myself in a mirror, for unless I have prepared myself for the confrontation, I seem humiliatingly ugly to myself each time" (Leiris, 4). Leiris hates the look of himself in the mirror because what is reflected there is an image of lack. Thus the pleasure in looking at his own body is quickly converted, in the text, into the pleasure at being looked at *like a woman*, masochistically offering himself to the gaze and identifying with the abjection and "dirt" of the female body.

This identification with the feminine position as the object of the gaze takes place for the first time when he is eleven through his theatrical staging of a masturbatory scene. In a moment of solitary fantasy he unclothes his body ("slipping my nightshirt down over my shoulders in order to free the upper part of my body, and having no material anywhere except around my hips, like a loincloth"), identifying with a courtesan, "one of those undoubtedly marginal figures who still had something royal about them" (Leiris, 27). By simultaneously playing the role of both the subject and the object of the gaze, Leiris defies the exclusionary oppositions of Cartesian subjectivity and comes to occupy the position of the abject, a figure in which debasement and aristocracy (and later, sacredness) clash without a mediation. This ambivalent position fascinated and repelled the author: Although he secretly enjoyed, while masturbating in the secrecy of his room, his imagined identity as a courtesan, he openly admits to a deep hatred and disgust with the maternal body as well as with the female genitals. Through his simultaneous disgust with and desire for the female body, Leiris comes to occupy a liminal position between Oedipal and pre-Oedipal identifications, desiring and rejecting the phallus at the same time and alternately attributing it to the maternal and paternal figure, with whom he identifies in turn.

This hatred for the female body is reinforced by a childhood memory of a game during which the author encountered for the first time the horror of the female sex. In the game "eyes put out," the eye, the organ of masculine scopic power, is transformed into what he imagines as "the female dirt," and the act of gazing turns into one of blind touching. In the game, which his sister and her husband made him play as a child, Leiris, blindfolded, was made to push his index finger into an egg cup filled with wetted bread crumbs and was told that he was blinding somebody. The game left an indelible impression on him: "The significance of 'eyes put out' is very deep for me. Today I often tend to regard the female organ as something dirty, or as a wound, no less attractive for that, but dangerous in itself, as everything mucous, bloody and contaminated" (Leiris, 46). In this scene, the act of blinding, of violently denying the gaze, is associated with the act of penetration, which is in turn "punished" by the dangerous and contaminating contact with what appears to Leiris as the female substance par excellence, blood. By perpetrating both acts and by "rationalizing" them as a means to violate and "become" the violated female body, Leiris becomes a split subject, subject and object at the same time.

Horror, blood, and femininity, as well as the pleasure of disgust, branded on his mind an image that Leiris recognized as central to his identity, Lucas Cranach's painting *Lucrece and Judith* (Figure 5.2). This double image of two female nudes, the first of a raped woman, Lucrece the victim, the second of the castrating and vindictive figure of Judith carrying Holofernes's head, visually represent Leiris's duplicity as a subject. The painting functions as a mirror image for the writer, more acceptable to him than the loathed mirror image of the inelegant man with which the book opened. The two women—the Roman virgin raped by Tarquin and the Jewish widow who took revenge on another rapist, her captor, Holofernes—repropose the nexus between eroticism and pain, pleasure and punishment, that stand for Leiris as a site of abject arousal. The image of Lucrece "pressing to the center of her white chest, between two marvelously hard, round breasts ... the narrow blade of a dagger, whose tip is already beaded, like the most intimate gift appearing at the end of the male member, with a few drops of blood"

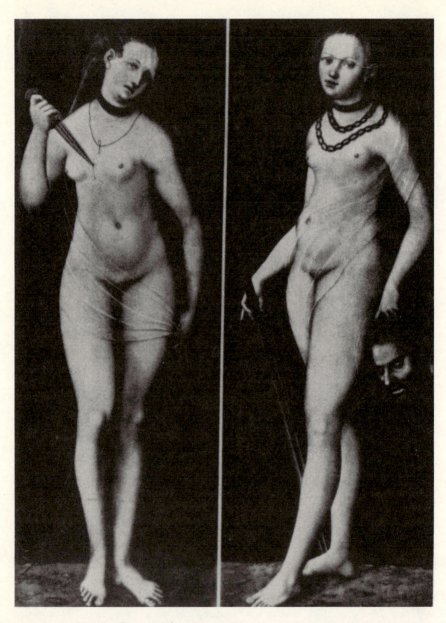

*Figure 5.2   Lucas Cranach the Elder,* Lucrece and Judith. *Frontispiece to Michel Leiris's* Manhood.

(Leiris, 94) evokes the same image of penetration and blinding, the same juxtaposition of the feminine and the masculine, that characterized the game "eyes put out." The abjected mixture of blood and sperm, which metonymically refigures Leiris's split gender and sexual identity, stands as a foil to the counterimage of eroticized horror, that of the castratrix Judith holding the sword in one hand and the head of Holofernes in the other. Judith appears to Leiris as a monstrous and powerful woman, cannibalistically enjoying the body of a man that is already marked as abject: "The bearded ball she holds like a phallic glans she could have sundered merely by pressing her legs together when Holofernes' floodgates opened; or which, as ogress at the height of her madness, she might have cut from the powerful member of the drunken (and perhaps vomiting) man with a sudden snap of her teeth" (Leiris, 94–95). Cranach's painting of female bodies provides Leiris with the perfect scenario to "play out" his identificatory fantasies—a mobile theater of the self in which he can be both the body punished and the body administering the punishment; an object (the dagger-penis) or a body part ("Like Holofernes with his head cut off I imagine myself sprawling at the feet of this idol" [Leiris, 95]) scattered, fragmented, and at the same time on its way to a phallicly reconstituted totality.

For Leiris, Judith and Lucrece represent an image of self-protection and self-annihilation, equally signifying the thrill in hurting and the pleasure in being hurt, in seeing and being seen. Even more, the identification with Cranach's two heroines allows the author to recognize the source of his sexual arousal: the nexus between fear and beauty, horror and pleasure. In turn, his bloody and violent notion of eroticism, the barbaric rituals of love encoded in the image of the two women, provides for Leiris a means of access to "the sacred": "Love—the only possibility of a coincidence between the subject and the object, the only means of acceding to the sacred, as represented by the desired object insofar as it is exterior and alien to us—implies its own negation, because to possess the sacred is at the same time to profane and to destroy it by gradually robbing it of its alien character" (Leiris, 120). The sacred is therefore a state in which the individual is "outside himself" and, by transgressing the psychic and corporeal boundaries that define his individual self, merges with the other. Like Judith "biting off Holofernes' genitals," the sacred is a (metaphorically) cannibalistic moment in which the subject "eats" and ingests the other and, as in ancient and primitive sacrifices, makes it part of himself in an act of fusion that results in the loss of ego and body boundaries. Leiris's "savage" concept of the erotic as a recuperation of a barbaric sacredness was in this historical period being encoded in modern culture through the discourse of primitivism. *L'art nègre* and jazz were seized by Leiris and many others as a language of feelings and physical sensations that, just as Cranach's painting had also done, reflected back as a social mirror his own desires and obsessions.

Leiris relates that the jazz music played in private houses and in bars right after the First World War became for him an intoxicating experience. Jazz, as he describes it, provoked almost a state of possession in its listeners: "It was the element which gave these celebrations [the parties] their true meaning: a *religious* meaning, with communion by dance, latent and manifest eroticism, and drinks, the most effective means of bridging the gap that separates individuals from each other at any kind of gathering" (Leiris, 109). Eroticism and exoticism entered Leiris's life under the sign of jazz: While falling in love with Kay ("the first woman I authentically knew" [Leiris, 109]), Leiris also encountered the "myths of black Edens," which spurred his interest in ethnography and, a few years later, led him to Africa.

At the moment when the author appears to have reached the manhood of the book's title and his masculine identity is confirmed to himself through his heterosexual desire for a woman, the specter of Lucrece and Judith return to haunt him. He decides to punish his self-abandon, his sensuous enjoyment of music, dance, and sexuality, by an act of self-restraint that he perceives as an act of self-preservation. After military service, feeling that he must now achieve something in life, he gives up every form of intoxicating expenditure (except alcohol) and decides to become a man of letters exclusively devoted to his work. During this period he also dedicates extraordinary attention to his appearance. By "affecting the British style" and wearing rigorously cut, somber clothes, Leiris turns his body into the very image of productive and desexualized masculinity. At the same time he seems to be aware that the phallic power these clothes promised is highly unstable. Thus he deploys different stratagems meant to turn his body into a fetish and confer on it a phallic quality that it does not possess. For instance, he describes how, in the attempt to soothe his skin irritated by the razor, he took to powdering his face, as if to hide behind the impassivity of a mask. He regarded the mask (which might remind us of the face powder of the dying Aschenbach in *Death in Venice*) as a means of protection, a way of covering his own weakness: "This corresponded to a symbolic attempt at mineralization, a defense-reaction against my inner weakness and the collapse by which I felt myself threatened" (Leiris, 117). Paradoxically, he tries to "mineralize" and steel his body through a form of decoration (makeup) that for a critic such as Loos marks both the criminal body of the savage and the exhibitionistic corporeality of women. His desire to literally write his masculinity across his face intersects with "savage" practices of body ornamentation that for him expose rather than hide sexuality and gender transgression.

When Leiris looks in the Cartesian mirror of subjectivity he sees double: Not only does he not recognize himself (in fact he rejects and loathes his image) but he sees two female bodies (the figures painted by Cranach). By simultaneously identifying with both, he becomes twice decentered; only in Africa, by recognizing his self-reflection, as he comes to do in the body of the Ethiopian sorceress, can Leiris reestablish a one-to-one relation with his self. Leiris's African trip of 1931 assumed for him a therapeutic value: Through psychoanalysis he wanted to free himself from the desire for self-punishment, which he felt resulted from his Catholic education. Africa was for him a site of self-discovery, but it did not suggest a rational explanation of his will to punishment. His encounter with the Ethiopian woman stabilized his diffracted identity while once again mobilizing his eroticized passion for violence.

The Ethiopian woman, with whom he professed to have fallen in love, appeared to Leiris as the living embodiment of both Lucrece and Judith, that is, of his double desire for subjectivity and abjection. In the author's description the woman is characterized by all the elements of female sexuality that attract and disgust him: dirt, sickness, and the sacred. She smells of sour milk; she looks like a mannequin; her neck is savagely tattooed and marked by blue scars. Above all, she is syphilitic, sexually mutilated (her clitoris has been excised), and, as the daughter of a witch, she performs sorcery herself. What makes Leiris fascinated by her is the sight of the woman sacrificing a lamb to her gods "and drinking, out of a porcelain cup, the blood still hot from the victim's throat" (Leiris, 140). The act of watching the sacrifice establishes for him the most intimate relation with the sorceress. Although touching the "female wound" through a prop (the egg of the game "eyes put out") is the acme of Leiris's fantasy of power and self-abjection, once his fantasy seems to come true with the figure of the Ethiopian woman, the critic refuses "touch" and withdraws into a position of spectatorial distance.

By identifying with her, Leiris is able to experience vicariously a contact with the element that more than any other arouses and terrifies him: the blood of the victim, which points fantasmatically and metonymically to the abjected female body. At the same time, the image of the Ethiopian woman drinking the lamb's blood sutures the split between victim and victimizer, Lucrece and Judith, the outside and the inside of the body, as well as the perverse identification of masculinity and femininity that in Paris could not be realized other than as a secret fantasy. In Africa, Leiris can watch his fantasy become real, although he chooses not to perform it himself and rather takes up the safer stance of the ethnographer-observer: By secretly identifying with the witch, he can inflict the deadly blow on the other's body (and therefore *act* and be an individual subject) and at the same time merge once again with the other by drinking its blood (and therefore renouncing the individuality he has just affirmed). The moment of the sacrifice is the equivalent of Judith drinking Holofernes's blood after having killed him and of Lucrece tasting her own blood flowing from her double wound, that inflicted by the rapist and that she inflicts upon herself with the dagger. The flowing of the lamb's blood out of its throat and into the witch's body is an image of circularity and homogeneity that sanctions the loss of any clear distinction between subject and object.

Africa, for Leiris, allows this climactic encounter with himself and his desires through the body of the Ethiopian woman. Through his voyeuristic experience of the sacrifice he exorcises both his desire to "mineralize" himself into a hard and recognizable identity and the opposite impulse to "melt," to lose his individual self in the body of the female other. After the expedition Leiris returned to France healed: "I am in better health, apparently, and am no longer as continuously haunted by the "tragic themes" (Leiris, 141). Finally capable of facing his split identification with the two feminine figures of Lucrece and Judith, he realizes that what he needs is "finding the way in which the world and myself, object and subject, confront each other on an equal footing, as the matador stands before the bull" (Leiris, 141). His concluding image, once again, is not that of a woman but rather that of the male body of the matador displayed in a bloody ritual—a spectacle of masculine corporeality that fixated two of the male modernists who fretted most over masculine identity, Picasso and Hemingway.

The concluding words of *Manhood* suggest that an identity has finally hardened around the narrative: "I explain to my mistress how necessary it is to construct a wall around oneself by the means of clothing" (Leiris, 146). Once the self has been erected, Leiris's words imply, it needs to be protected, kept untouched, lest it crumble and be lost. There is, however, an alternative reading of this modernist melancholia regarding the self and its masks, a reading in which clothes are not the means of protection but rather the vehicle of a dangerous exposure. In that spirit I propose to read Leiris's concluding clothing advice in the context of one of the last dreams narrated in the autobiography, the dream of the turban-woman.

In this revealing dream Leiris finds himself abroad "in a sordid colonial city." He reaches the city by walking along a narrow path strung with masks and primitive sculptures that he does not bother to pick up (recall that the collecting and cataloguing of African artifacts was his task in the Dakar-Djibouti expedition). After a vision of family and parenthood that repels him (he sees "a huge fat man, with his wife and children, particularly disgusting" [Leiris, 144]), he is sitting at his desk, patiently drawing signs on a piece of paper. The signs resemble Arabic characters and are the result of the careful work of months, perhaps years. At a certain point Leiris realizes that the sheet of paper is a piece of cloth. On a corner near the top there appears a female mouth, "no doubt the accidental configuration of a group of signs." Leiris takes up the cloth and wears it, rolling it around his forehead as a turban. This gesture provokes an ecstatic reaction in him: He feels like a fakir or a rajah, "like the one who stabbed himself after having his wives killed." At this point, Leiris's own wife appears in a ghostly white nightgown and, as if realizing finally what he has been doing for a long time, with an incredible sadness in her voice says: "Oh! That was it!" The protagonist's ecstasy is complete when he reaches for his revolver inside a drawer.

In the dream, under the sign of primitivism—the masks, the sculptures, the degraded colonial city—the denouement is a scene of double exposure for Leiris; it fully contradicts his claim of having been healed of his obsessive identification with the female body. By finally wearing the turban-woman—when he wraps the cloth with the woman's mouth round his head, marked, that is, with the imprint of one female orifice—he "becomes" that abject body. By "wearing woman" as clothing, he assumes upon himself the abjection of femininity. The shocked sadness of his wife at the sight of him as turbaned man confirms that this is a moment of gender and sexual transgression: She is struck and disappointed by the evidence that he is not what she thought he was—a man. Leiris never stops being a split subject: The disgust he feels in the dirty colonial city is, in terms of Flugel's discussion of clothes as markers of gender, the same as the disgust of the heterosexual at the collapse of a clear sartorial distinction between femininity and masculinity. The gesture of wrapping the turban-woman around his head (the seat of reason, of the spirit, and therefore of masculinity) is an act of self-imposed dressing up, of effeminacy. Ultimately, his disgust is the correlative of his ecstasy: The pleasure in the erasure of his masculinity by the wearing of the turban culminates in the ecstasy of his final self-annihilation, the final punishment, death.

Read in the context of the dream of the turban-woman, the conclusion of *Manhood* with its reiteration of the importance of clothing hardly signifies a strategy of self-defense for a solid and well-defined masculine identity. In fact, the idea of wrapping the self in clothes as a way of dispelling identity stands as a final affirmation of feminine exhibitionism and of a masochistic identification with the female body. In the last dream, just before Leiris comes to contemplate the necessity of building a wall around oneself by means of garments, a female figure (perhaps a stand-in for his wife) critiques his way of dressing. Leiris's reaction is one of upset surprise: "I am upset: I think of the hat I'm wearing (whereas so many men go out bareheaded), of the bowler I used to have, of my belted raincoat, my gloves, my mannered look, of all that it represents, of my constraint etc." (Leiris, 146). Leiris's "mannered look" speaks of both proper masculine elegance and effeminate excess at the same time. The gloves and the hat are, like the turban-woman, a form of disguise through which the male subject can display and masquerade his body. Leiris renounces the phallus to dream about it, to dress *like* it. His use of clothes implies that the phallic body of the masculine subject is nothing more than this dissimulation; as Lemoine-Luccioni says, "The penis becomes the phallus only when it is exhibited and hidden."[47] Leiris's illusory masculinity is produced precisely by the liminal alternation of bodily disguise and exposure. Masculinity is nothing but a female garment fastened around his head as a talismanic means of protection and abjection—perversely transforming the garment's apotropaic value into a means of exposure and self-obliteration. The turban, which started out as a signifier of coloniality, has the function of protecting himself from becoming a man—individual, recognizable, *one*. Like the body of the Ethiopian woman, Leiris wants to occupy two positions at the same time, that of the subject and that of the object. The ecstatic exposure of his sartorial femaleness allows him to experience the pleasure of liminality and the joyous disgust of abjection.

## "DOES IT FEEL QUEER?" PRIMITIVISM AND THE HOMOEROTIC IN LAWRENCE

For D. H. Lawrence, as for Leiris, a strategic fascination with an overdetermined primitive was a means of transgressing the norms of the primary institution of western rationalism, individual identity. Through a return not only to the body itself but also to its barbaric sensations, both writers attempt to dissolve the self in order to reconquer a primordial and pre-Symbolic state of being. In this, the mediation of a faraway, exotic culture is instrumental: Whereas Leiris used Africa and the image of the Ethiopian woman to vicariously experience his erotic fantasies, Mexico in the 1920s became for Lawrence the setting of a subversive cult of masculine corporeality invested with protofascist political meaning. In *The Plumed Serpent* (1926), the dissolution of individual ego boundaries as a prelude to a return to the body produces a form of what Freud termed the "oceanic feeling," which indicates a relation of pre-Oedipal fusion between two subjects. At the same historical moment when the novel was written, such feelings, as Klaus Theweleit and others have shown, became crucial to the imaginary of fascist totalitarianism, continually enacted in the relation of immediacy and identification that tied the individual to the political leader and the leader to the masses.

Lawrence did not look at natives of the Mexican villages through the lenses of Rousseauean humanism. Rather, through a complex of masochistic relations to the local culture, the figure of the primitive was attractive to him not because of his innocence but because of the cruelty and horror of his barbaric customs. Whereas Leiris's fantasies centered on his relations to women, Lawrence dreams of a brotherhood of men. In early modernist discourse, the scenario of colonial horror par excellence was Kurtz's degradation from explorer-exploiter to enthusiastic participant in Conrad's *Heart of Darkness;* as in Leiris's fantasies of tribal sacrifices and bodily consubstantiation, Kurtz sheds his civilized humanity by participating in "tribal" sacrifices and, it seems, in cannibalism. In Leiris's narrative, the specter of cannibalism is displaced onto the image of the Ethiopian drinking the lamb's blood. The same starred moment of physical fusion between two different bodies represented by the flowing of blood returns in Lawrence's novel, this time translated into the less lurid but similarly highly charged identificatory relationship between the two masculine protagonists. Leiris's ecstatic feeling of intimacy with the sorceress recurs in *The Plumed Serpent* as a moment of orgasmic *jouissance* between two native male bodies touching each other during a climactic ritualistic scene.

Notwithstanding such analogies between the primitivist signifying economy in the writing of each author, Lawrence, despite his at times overbearingly strident prose, is in fact much more reticent than Leiris. His novel elaborates narrative strategies that continually clothe and unclothe the body of the text in an attempt to dissimulate its desire. The pervasive homoeroticism of *The Plumed Serpent* is merely hinted at and affirmed through successive displacements. On one level,

Lawrence removes the European subject's desire for sexual freedom onto the exotic and faraway Mexican native. Furthermore, homoerotic desire for the male body is defused first through the focus on costumes and second through the author's choice of a female character, the Irish (and hence marginally colonial) Kate Leslie, as the embodiment of his own authorial consciousness, with whose point of view the reader is asked to identify.

Thus whereas a narrative of religious-nationalistic revival of rural Mexico becomes the occasion for exposing seminaked "native" male bodies through rituals of clothing and unclothing, by making a woman the bearer of the narrative gaze, Lawrence keeps implicit the suggestion of homoerotic desire. Every time we are asked to admire masculine beauty, we are prompted to do so through what appears to be a female desire. By making the protagonist a western woman, the author manages to turn the homoerotic plot—the central story of the fellowship of Cipriano and Ramón—into a quasi-ethnographic tale of a western traveler going native. At the same time, the colonialist subtext of ethnographic discourse is revealed and comes to crisis in Lawrence's fiction, for his text unveils the parasitical nature of modernism's relation to the native body: The materiality of this body, valorized as "dark" and "earthy" but also considered callow and weak, is used to produce and reinforce a masculine and universalistic mystique founded on the disintegration of otherness.

*The Plumed Serpent's* programmatic mixture of primitivism and protofascism derives from Lawrence's own analysis of what he read as the contemporary decay of the West, which in turn may be traced to his reading of Nietzsche, Otto Weininger, and others.[48] In his narrative of how the civilized subject needs to regain a lost contact with nature and with the body's sensuousness, Lawrence suggests that the reified condition of the individual in modern industrial society, which he himself detested, is the result of an interrupted balance between man and his animal side.[49] This lost relationship of intersubjectivity with nature can be recuperated through sexuality; an unhinibited and phallic sexuality represents for Lawrence, particularly in his later work, the threshold to a sacred dimension to counterbalance modern rationalization and a means of overcoming the freezing of the ego boundaries that such rationalization provoked. The male body as the site of this sexual mysticism is posed as a source both of masculine charismatic authority and of a personal and cultural rejuvenation.

Ϧ    Ϧ    Ϧ

In *The Plumed Serpent* Mexico and its natives represent the medium of an apocalyptic experience, vital and deadly at the same time, through which the heroine Kate Leslie seeks to give a new impulse to her life. The novel opens with a gory description of a bullfight (which takes off, as it were, where Leiris's dream image of the matador leaves off); Kate's Americans are fascinated by its pure sensationalism, but Kate is revolted by what strikes her as a false note in the *urban* spectacle of male violence and hence with its brutalization of the animal itself. She feels claustrophobic in the noisy and dirty crowd of people: In this staged set piece it is as if the feared primitive and the loathed modern have become one. The novel then develops as the story of Kate's vacillating feelings of attraction toward and repulsion against the two specific elements that make her run from the bullfight: the horror of the blood as a spectacle of primitive cruelty and her disgust at the physical contact with masses of others. In her final "submission" to Cipriano Viedma, one of the two male protagonists, there is also implied her acceptance of being "touched," of merging with the body of the other and with those whom Kate considers archaic and inferior, the "dark races": "Ah the dark races! Kate's own Irish were near enough for her to have glimpsed some of the mystery. The dark races belong to a bygone cycle of humanity. ... And on to the particular white man's levels they never will be able to climb. They can only follow as servants."[50] In this characteristically racist passage Lawrence explains Kate's ambiguous attraction to the Mexicans in terms of her own racial identity: He suggests that as an Irishwoman, a Celt, she belongs to an inferior, primitive race herself.

Kate leaves the city and travels alone toward the village of Sayula, intrigued by the rumors about the "men of Quetzalcoatl," acolytes of the ancient god of the Aztec, the Plumed Serpent. In the village she meets Ramón Carrasco, an influential local landowner, and Cipriano Viedma, a general in the Mexican national army, who turn out to be the creators of the myth of Quetzalcoatl. This modern pseudo-mythology has been planned as a means to both inspire and dissimulate an insurrection against the national government. The political dimension of the movement, however, is known only to the leaders and to the higher cadres. To the majority of its adepts it appears as the revival of the ancient, authentic religion of the Mexican people, replacing their modern Catholicism, which is portrayed as sterile and void. As the charismatic leaders of the movement, Ramón and Cipriano claim to be the manifestations of the ancient Aztec divinities Quetzalcoatl and Huitzilopochtli. In Kate's eyes they represent the power of the "dark races," the otherness that can regenerate her existence. Yet although she marries Cipriano in a ritual ceremony created and celebrated by Ramón himself, she refuses to impersonate Malintzi, the mythological bride of Huitzilopochtli. The price of the "magic" and the "mystery" she desires is to be subjected as a wife and a fake goddess; in order to become Malintzi she must cease to be Kate and thus must give up her self and her history.

Woven into the plot of *The Plumed Serpent* are two central issues whose presence contradicts Lawrence's mystique of the native on which the plot revolves: first, the fictitious nature of primitivism as an invented tradition and second, the appropriation of this tradition by male upper class subjects in order to affirm their power over women and over a lower social class. Both issues are foregrounded as if to leave open at all times the possible fictionality and constructedness of versions of gendered subjectivity based on the primitive. Further, through the deployment of costumes, ceremonies, and "savage" rituals invented by the two leaders, these very fabrications provide the occasion for what I suggest is the central event of the book: the display of the sexualized male body as a vehicle of homoerotic desire.

In his representation of the "cruel sacredness" of Mexican culture, Lawrence, despite himself, might seem to debunk the nativist mythology in which he professes to believe by exposing the functioning of primitivism as an ideological construction of protofascist male self-proclaimed leaders. Ramón and Cipriano, through the costumes, the hymns, and the ceremonies, make the peasants simulate the culture of the ancient Indians, which no longer exists. Lawrence, like most of the modernist primitivists, is fascinated by this culture, but only once it is aestheticized. This aestheticization is what the reader is shown being performed by Ramón and Cipriano, so that even as a simulated set of rituals Lawrence can valorize it as a Nietzschean act of will on the part of his admired male leaders. At any rate, like the African carving stared at by Birkin and Gerald in *Women in Love* or the Ethiopian woman with whom Leiris decided he had fallen in love, the spectacle of the primitive turns out to be merely the alibi for an "emancipatory" gesture on the part of those who seem to sympathize with the primitive. The focus appears to be on the "dark bodies" of the natives, whereas it is in fact firmly fixed inward on the "civilized" bodies of the western observers. Lawrence's attribution of the power to fabricate primitivism to his own version of Mexican "leaders" is a ruse whereby the fact that "primitivism" is itself a western creation can be elided. The Mexican native is not aware of his "power of negation" and of his "barbaric" refusal of civilization; it is Lawrence the primitivist who attributes this power *to him*. Throughout the novel the natives are represented as an open text, there to be discovered and interpreted. Their image is only a matter of different readings: For instance, the flat figures in Diego Rivera's murals, which Kate sees at the university in Mexico City, represent the natives as "symbols in the great script of modern socialism … the victims of modern industry and capitalism" (Lawrence, 47). Although "sympathetic," the murals do not represent what Kate wants to see in the Mexicans. In front of Rivera's images, whose crudity reminds her of caricatures, she thinks, with the eye and the mind of the aesthete, of the figures she has seen in the streets; their very poverty constitutes in her eyes a beauty that she feels cannot and must not be touched by any human intervention, particularly a political one.

In Kate's—and the novel's—characteristic scenario of near contact with the natives, Ramón and Cipriano, local leaders as native informants, play a double role as object and subject of the gaze. Whereas they are regarded by Kate as native bodies, specimens of masculine beauty not at all different from the peasants, they in turn exploit Kate's own aestheticized view of the natives to impose a new, fabricated identity on the peons and thus carry on their protofascist program of social renovation. Their "return to the people," their willed identification with the body of the nation, takes place through a transcoding of class categories. The general and the local landowner transform themselves into the symbols of the peasant soul of Mexico by assuming the garb of the lower classes. Their contrived divine and authoritarian identity is presented to the peons as a mirror through which they can reimagine themselves and enjoy a vicarious godhead, but the rituals are in fact staged as a displacement, an arts-and-crafts glorification of the peasants' actual social inferiority.

It is striking that this new divine-popular identity of the two self-proclaimed Mexican modern primitives, Ramón and Cipriano, is affirmed sartorially. The myth of the men of Quetzalcoatl relies from its outset on a symbolic exchange of clothes between upper classes and the peasants. The return of Quetzalcoatl had been entirely orchestrated by Ramón, who, using his knowledge as an amateur archaeologist, decides to impersonate the Aztec god. After emerging naked from the lake in Sayula, Ramón covers himself with the white cotton peasant clothes that some women were washing nearby. Then at sunset, when the laborers return from the fields, he asks one of them to follow him and then gives him, almost in exchange, new, sumptuous clothes: "They gave him new clothing of pure white cotton, and a new hat with star embroidery ... a new blanket with white bars and blue and black, and flowers like stars at the center, and two pieces of silver money" (Lawrence, 53). The exchange of clothes between the god and the human being, the landowner and the peasant, has a high symbolic value. Its ritual quality, however, almost obscures the transaction that accompanies the religious investiture of the Mexican people by the god—the "payment" of the silver coins. The act of dressing up (as the peasant in his new rich clothes) and dressing down (as Ramón in the white peasant cotton) is the equivalent, in a sumptuary key, of the flowing of blood from the body of the sacrificial lamb into that of the Ethiopian woman in Leiris's *Manhood:* It transfigures one subject into another, so that the god and the humble peon become one element. One partakes of the power of the other, and the flesh is displaced onto the garments. A key metaphor of interwar European right-wing nationalism is here reenacted by Ramón: The symbiotic relationship between the political leader and his audience is signified in an exchange of clothes. The monetary exchange in this drama, however, signals that power (particularly economic power) comes from and is upheld by the leader.

The substitution of clothes for blood in Lawrence's representation of the native body makes even more evident the artificiality and theatricality of the discourse of primitivism. In *The Plumed Serpent,* however, the invention of the primitive body is not managed by empire triumphalism, as it was in many late Victorian versions of the colonial encounter, or by the modernist artist interested in tribal artifacts, as in Leiris, but by two educated and westernized natives as a form of ideological interpellation practiced upon the native Mexican population. As a result, the idea of an undifferentiated, homogeneous otherness whose common identity is guaranteed by their common blood is no longer tenable. Hence the Lawrentian opposition between "dark men" and "blond men" as the discourse of race in *The Plumed Serpent* functions to obscure differences of social hierarchy within the "dark race" itself. In this new kind of lesson in applied primitivism, it is the natives who "go native," not in order to resist the power of the colonizer but rather to hegemonize another social class through a ready-made tradition and the elaboration of semireligious rituals. The people of Quetzalcoatl gather in a deconsecrated church to chant Ramón's hymns, wear clothes that he himself has specially designed, and train their bodies, like Baden-Powell's Boy Scouts, in nature.

By recognizing the same "intensity and crudity of the semi-savage ... an intense, unconscious maleness" (Lawrence, 82) both in Cipriano and in the peons even as she also discerns the constructed, theatrical quality of the movement, Kate contributes to the novel's mystifying view of racial homogeneity. She sees in all the men of Sayula the same undifferentiated masculinity, which the peasant costumes further expose. While watching Ramón she thinks that "on his thighs the thin linen seemed to reveal him almost more than his own dark nakedness revealed him. ... She understood why the cotton pantaloons were forbidden in the plaza. The living flesh seemed to emanate through them. ... With the blue sash round his waist, pressing a fold in the flesh ... he emanated a fascination almost like a narcotic, asserting his pure, fine sensuality against her" (Lawrence, 183). The same sensuality is exuded by the bodies of the peasants, who are represented in the novel through Kate's eyes as a catalogue of racial types ("The wild, sombre, erect men of the North! ... The big men of Tlalasca! ... The quick little Indians! ... The queer looking, half-Chinese natives of Vera Cruz!" [Lawrence, 71]) or as a sum of alluring body parts ("the soft, full handsome torsos ... the beautiful ruddy skin ... the strong breast, so male and so deep ... the black moustache ... framing the close silence of the mouth" [Lawrence, 118]). The beauty of the native is summed up in the body of Kate's future husband, Cipriano, upon whom she spies as he takes his bath: "Cipriano was going down [to the lake] to bathe. ... He threw off his wrap and stood dark in silhouette. ... How dark he was! Dark as a Malay, and with that strange archaic fullness of physique, with the full chest and the full, yet beautiful buttocks of men on old Greek coins" (Lawrence, 424). By writing through Kate's eyes, the narrator again and again composes a hymn to the "dark" male body, fetishistically focusing on its most erotically charged parts.

The figure of a woman watching a male body disappears and is replaced by a man, however, at the central moment of the novel, when Ramón and Cipriano engage in a religious ritual that brings their bodies together to touch each other sexually. Kate's absence in this episode makes clear that the spectacle of the magnificent male body is not meant for her but for another man. This is the scene in which Cipriano, in a "trance" induced by Ramón, abandons his own consciousness and literally becomes a body in the hands of Ramón, who guides his journey "far and beyond" toward the introjection of divine power. What Lawrence presents as a moment of divine possession is in fact a scene of seduction: Under Ramón's influence Cipriano becomes a pliable and submissive body ready to be aroused. Blindfolded with a piece of black fur (a classical element in the grammar of sexual fetishism), in bondage, Cipriano is subjected to Ramón and becomes the main actor in a sadomasochistic theater of homoerotic desire. This mise-en-scène culminates in the moment when Ramón seduces Cipriano: "Ramón bound him fast around the middle, then pressing his head against his hip, folded the arms around Cipriano's loins, closing with his hands the secret places" (Lawrence, 367). This scenario of masculine sexual aggressiveness is soon over. The macho attitude at the outset of the god-landowner Ramón gives way to a moment of masculine tenderness, which reveals him as an undefended body: "Then Ramón bound the ankles, lifted Cipriano suddenly … laid him on the skin of a big mountain-lion … threw over him the red and black serape of Huitzilopochtli, and lay down at his feet, holding Cipriano's feet to his own abdomen" (Lawrence, 368). In this gesture of self-abandonment, of entrusting oneself to the other, Ramón is depicted as placing himself in the same subjected position as Cipriano. After recovering from the trance, Cipriano rows across the lake back to Kate to announce to her that he is going to be "the living Huitzilopochtli"—to which she asks, "Does it feel queer?" (Lawrence, 369), not knowing how to interpret his hallucinated appearance.

As soon as the moment of sexuality and male tenderness is over, Ramón and Cipriano's encounter is represented as a rite of religious initiation. During the consubstantiation between man and god experienced by Cipriano, his individual consciousness is dissolved: The hallucinatory trance that seems to seize both characters serves, it is emphasized, as a prelude to a fusion of their selves through the "fusion" of their bodies. The loss of individuality and the waste of the body is eroticized in an episode where a sexual encounter between two men is represented as a mystical experience.

The narrative of *The Plumed Serpent* builds toward this charged moment of homoeroticism from its outset. Yet once this narrative climax is reached, the author makes every effort to normalize the sexual exchange between men. The image of masculine tenderness, the glimpse of the "soft" male body Lawrence offers the reader, is immediately disciplined once again into signifying heterosexuality. The moment of sexual disclosure is followed by a gesture of occlusion aimed at reaffirming phallic masculinity. After the scene of ritual initiation between the two men, the narrative focus quickly and emphatically shifts to Kate and what Lawrence regards as her own failed attempt to relinquish selfhood. It is the sexualized male body that, through a leap into an ecstatic "nothingness," becomes the medium for a contact with divinity. But Ramón's and Cipriano's role-playing, in turn dominant and submissive, is not allowed for a heterosexual couple: To be "in touch" with the divinity symbolized by exotic maleness, Kate alone must submit. She is represented as desiring this contact; at the same time she understands that the "leap into nothingness" that native sexuality promises might be a frightening and destructive experience for her. By asking her to marry him and give up her European, modern identity to impersonate the goddess Malintzi, Cipriano demands from Kate the same submission that Ramón demanded from him. By occupying Ramón's position in a relationship with a woman, Cipriano is safely represented, once again, as heterosexual.

Yet Kate, as the novel depicts her dilemma, is not so ready to lose her self, to fully experience the "nothingness," the personal death that primitive Mexico apparently demands. Lawrence has taken the image of Conrad's abyss (Kurtz's inexpressible vision of "the horror") and turned it into an object of Gothic fascination whose effect changes according to the gender of the observer: The male subject seems to be at ease with it and capable of mastering the "nothingness" he experiences through his body (which would seem inevitable, as it is he who has fabricated it in the first place), but the same nothingness is constructed as a threat for the European woman. In *The Plumed Serpent* the "darkness" of Mexico, together with the myth of Quetzalcoatl, functions on the one hand to interpellate the "native" masses and on the other to master and undo the mollified, decaying western subject. The fact that this subject, the image of the European "going native," is gendered as female is not a secondary detail. Kurtz, the protagonist of *Heart of Darkness,* before going native goes for business: As the entrepreneur of high capitalism, the western masculine prototype of the careerist producer, he goes to the Congo to work and to accumulate company capital. In Lawrence's narrative, almost but not quite an anti–*Heart of Darkness*, the subject who goes to discover an exotic land travels for leisure. As a tourist and a primitivist, Kate is the perfect representative of the modern, emasculated culture of consumption. Hence she finds it impossible to go native: She can neither abandon herself to native nothingness nor can she, like Conrad's Kurtz or like Ramón, impose her power upon the natives by fully joining in the simulated rituals. Rather, her return to a primitive, "original" dimension is articulated as an act of self-renunciation and of submission to masculine power. After much debate, she decides to "make her submission": Without Cipriano she will become a "grimalkin," one of those women (obviously despised by Lawrence) "dressed in elegant clothes," sitting alone in their London apartments.

In the last scene of the book, when she finally goes back to Ramón and Cipriano, she feels strangely out of place between them: "But finding them in their Quetzalcoatl mood, with their manly breasts uncovered, she was not very eager to begin. They made her feel like an intruder. She did not pause to realize that she was one" (Lawrence, 443). Kate's position as an outsider and a spectator of the male body reminds one of another moment of female voyeurism directed at men, the episode of the Kaffir kraal at the Greater Britain Exhibition that I described earlier. This time, however, as a spectator of the sexualized male body, Kate remains only a frustrated voyeuse. As she perhaps not so naively affirms, "A woman is really *de trop* when two men are together" (Lawrence, 443). As a woman between men, she is cast in a subordinate position and not allowed to signify in their mutuality of admiration and desire.

In the protofascist heterotopia dreamed up in *The Plumed Serpent* the discourse of primitivism is used to reveal masculine sexuality through a fetishistic game of masculine clothing and unclothing. Both the white, soft cotton pantaloons of the peons and the hieratic, embroidered costumes of the gods represent a form of sartorial excess that transgresses the laws of propriety and sobriety defining modern European masculinity. The male body—unclothed, decorated, and passionately described by Lawrence—is scandalously resexualized and exposed. Lawrence's depiction of masculine "tenderness" (which would become one of the favorite terms in his subsequent writings) and of pleasure in exhibiting the body reveals that manliness is not a natural property, a fact of "blood," but rather a matter of dressing, or rather of dressing up, for the part. Yet even as it allows this, with the narrator taking the same care with Cipriano's linens as he had with Gudrun's silk stockings in *Women in Love*, the novel systematically tries to reabsorb any moment of gender instability, any representation of the body that seems to jeopardize phallic heterosexual masculinity. Lawrence's attempt to learn from the natives in order to create a new man produces anxieties in the masculine subject himself, which the author displaces onto the female protagonist.

Because of this anxiety—the anxiety of losing individuality and authority, Lawrence continually needs to reclothe and control the bodies he displays. Thus the images of sexual freedom that appear in *The Plumed Serpent*, as well as the costumes and the ritual dances, also function as modes of discipline for both the peons and the leaders: The white pantaloons of the peasants, forbidden in the church square because too revealing, are also a uniform, distinguishing the members of a political organization. Similarly, the war dances performed by the men of Quetzalcoatl to the "blood-rhythm" of barbaric drums are a form of discipline for those the leaders themselves supposedly regard as "the savages." Partly because the distinction between discipline and pleasure is constantly blurred in the novel, the militaristic discipline imposed by Ramón and Cipriano on the natives becomes a device to satisfy their own (and the novel's) voyeuristic desire, as well as a masochistic device for the production of pleasure. Cipriano, for example, uses the discourse of hygiene as an excuse to display and watch the beauty of his men: "And my men must be clean. On the march they would stop by some river, with the order for everyone to stop and wash, and wash his clothing. Then the men, dark and ruddy, moved about naked, with the white clothing of strong white cotton dried on the earth" (Lawrence, 365). In such tableaux of enforced freedom, discipline becomes the occasion for a spectacle of eroticized masculinity. Cipriano's militaristic order, that of an officer to his troop, invites the reader to be the spectator of a titillating scenario. What is arousing for both Cipriano and the narrative generally in this sadomasochist fantasy of body exposure is the possibility of playing a number of different sexual roles at the same time: that of the disciplined subject—Cipriano undresses the peon body, as his own had been previously undressed by Ramón—and that of the disciplinarian, engineering arousing tableaux of masculine nakedness.

In *The Plumed Serpent* the corporeality of the native, like that of the Nietzschean blond beast of prey or of the fin de siècle aesthete's extravagantly clad body, is yet another costume through which modern masculinity was fashioned and explored. Lawrence, through the "earthy" but in fact uniformed body of the native, and Leiris, through the body of the Ethiopian woman read in the same terms as the Christian artwork, negotiate existing definitions of gender and of masculine sexuality. With his simultaneously candid and theatrical "confession," Leiris affirms that clothes cannot be a form of self-protection. Rather, he uses clothing in a strategy of social and symbolic ornament to pin to his Bildungsroman a profusion of his fantasies and desires. Leiris wears his body as a suit, as the emperor of the fable wears his clothes; whether clothed or naked, each has an extraordinary awareness of his ostentatious declaration of his personal status. Leiris's narrative makes clear that under the clothes there is no-body and that masculinity is nothing more than what was signified by the clothes themselves— the female mouth mysteriously appearing in a corner of the fabric of the turban.

Lawrence carries his reader to the same conclusion as Leiris: His writing uncannily reveals that, like the ideology of primitivism that he details and even celebrates as being masquerade, phallic masculinity is specifically a reality effect produced through elaborated rituals and staged spectacles. In his representation of virility, Lawrence uncannily declares that the phallus exists only when hidden or disclosed—that is, it exists in the very act of hiding or disclosing, and it is this act that produces its claimed aura. Under the suit, nothing. Ultimately there is no "it" to be revealed; rather it is the very act of displaying and veiling that stands as a proof or an intimation of the existence of the phallus. Leiris seems to be fully aware of the phantasmatic quality of masculine power: His dreams show us that masculinity, like femininity, is founded on an absence, and he is happy to identify with this nothingness, with the dangerous lack of a subjectivity in the making (or in the process of being wasted) through which he can affirm the disastrous and pleasurable ruination of masculinity. Lawrence, however, appears to be much more reticent to admit the same catastrophe and rather retrenches behind a contradictory staging of his own desires. On the one hand he defuses homoeroticism by dissimulating himself through a female character and her desire; on the other, he denies pleasure, sexual and voyeuristic, by turning it into a form of discipline. And yet he manages to impose discipline on the body as a form of *jouissance*.

This masochistic *jouissance* is the chief form of gratification that the modernist male writer allows himself. Caught between his search for an authoritative, if not authoritarian, identity and his desire to dissolve the self between the phallic hardness of the body and the homoerotic tenderness of the non-Oedipal, he is trapped between the extremes of functionality and ornamentation. Through the theatrical garb that he designed for the characters of *The Plumed Serpent*, Lawrence tried to simultaneously show off and cover homoerotic "softness": His fantastic clothes, his white pantaloons, the embroidered tunics, as well as "the red trousers and white little jackets" in the passage from *Lady Chatterly's Lover*[51] quoted at the beginning of the chapter, are prosthetic devices that eroticize the male body while disciplining it—more precisely, insofar as they discipline it. Worn by the members of a religious-political sect or regarded, as Mellors considers them, as the garb of a universal phallic masculinity, Lawrence's costumes are uniforms—an element of visual and ideological order suggesting regimentation and the masochistically enacted eroticism of discipline. Thus his desire to resexualize the male body and to reaffirm the natural authenticity of masculinity through theatrical props is a contradiction in terms. Lawrence's tale of the body ends with a masochistic gesture, an act of masculine self-sacrifice: The only way to affirm homoerotic desire is to display and at the same time to discipline the sexualized male body, thus mortifying what Lawrence wants to depict as triumphant virility. The only way for the male subject to endure the simultaneous exposure and occlusion of his sexuality—a trick that Lawrence tacitly performs in his narrative—is to train the subject to take pleasure, obviously a masochistic one, in the disciplining of his body.

# CONCLUSION

WHILE SEEKING WAYS to signify homoeroticism and make queerness socially visible, the fin de siècle aesthete produced the blueprint for a counternormative masculinity capable of putting into question established definitions of gender. In early twentieth century European culture this other masculinity—edging on the as yet unthinkable and semiotically opaque territory of homosexuality and on the degraded otherness of femininity—took part in the dramatic reconfiguration of male corporeality, now modeled on the image of the Nietzschean superman. The male bodies that I have studied here, although claiming self-sufficiency, autonomy, and singularity, show that masculinity as well as femininity is a speculary structure of gender identity founded on lack and haunted by its excluded others—in fact, uncomfortably incorporating them.

By deploying representational strategies that resexualize male bodies, the aesthete helped precipitate a crisis of referentiality and of signification that worked to denaturalize the phantasmatic totality of phallic masculinity. The spectacle of strength, sentimentalized suffering, and pleasure registered by these male bodies transgressed the boundaries of proper bourgeois masculinity, crossing over onto the realm of sexualized femininity and of the spectacularly masochistic gay body. For the muscled bodies of popular culture, shown either in action or in pain, the signifier, the name of gender—"man"—does not refer to a steady, fully recognizable referent but rather is destabilized, complicated, and "led astray" by the very sexualities that this name appears to comprehend. The fictitiousness of masculinity, as revealed by the unmanageable sexuality that marks these male bodies, disrupts the semiotic boundaries of gender and exposes the mechanism of signification through which both masculinity and its corporeality are naturalized. The masculinity that the bodies of Sandow, of Tarzan, or of the modern clerk invoke (and ruin at the same time) is antiphallic insofar as it occupies a liminal position in the field of signification dominated by the phallus. The instability that characterizes these masculinities implies that signification is never fully controlled by the subject of reason; rather, desire and the excess signaled by consumer culture, class aspirations, and, above all, sexuality play an equally determining role in its operations. The male hyperbodies that I have examined, apparently heterosexual, powerful, self-managed, and at the same time docile and useful to the state in interpellating its subjects into obedience, designate in fact an unsutured masculinity, open to a semiotic and libidinal indeterminacy that leaves the work of gender signification suspended and necessarily unfinished.

Confronted with this crisis of gender signification inaugurated by fin de siècle aestheticism, early twentieth century European culture displayed signs of an anxious desire to reestablish self-exclusive and fixed norms of masculinity aimed at making outlaw the desires—for expenditure, spectacular self-exposure, and abjection—that had been signaled by the suffering body of the aesthete. As this book has shown, these troubling desires were simultaneously being put in place, and at play, in the male bodies that the dominant culture represented as phallic: Desire is always already inscribed in the new early twentieth century icons of normative masculinity. In the Nietzschean body of the athlete, the warrior, the boy scout, and the strongman the marks of eroticism and expenditure continually contradict the impulse to discipline and self-restraint. These were bodies capable of making virtue out of necessity and of harnessing modern cultural imperatives—imperatives that contradictorily invited the subject both to desire, spend, consume, *and* to produce and ascetically "save" both libidinal and economic capital—to their own potentially deviant desires. For example, the aesthete grafted his impulse to expenditure onto the excesses of conspicuous consumption, and the Lawrentian revolutionary went on to eroticize discipline and the regimented soldierly male body.

Paradoxically, the hypermasculinity of the Nietzschean male body short-circuited the teleological narrative of phallic manliness to meander instead into a number of semiotic detours—"inexpedient" strategies, to use Freud's term—that oppose the logic of heterosexuality while enacting and reiterating it. The strategy that most prominently appears in the images of masculinity that I have examined is the unclothing and dressing up performed by numerous male bodies. These representations of masculine corporeality deploy the logic of striptease, a performance that has been considered almost exclusively in relation to the female body. In Roland Barthes's words, striptease "works by establishing *right from the start* the woman as an object in disguise."[1] During the performance the disguise will be relinquished layer by layer to reach an illusory nakedness claiming to represent "a perfectly chaste state of the flesh." As Barthes points out, the striptease does not culminate in the total exposure of the body, but rather it stops at a final garment, the G-string covered in diamonds and sequins: "The ultimate triangle, by its pure and geometrical shape, by its hard and shiny material, bars the way to the sexual parts like a sword of purity, and definitely drives the woman back into the mineral world, the (precious) stone being here the irrefutable symbol of the absolute object, that which serves no purpose."[2] Barthes's description of striptease as the arch-fetishistic disclosure and occlusion of the phallus is very relevant to my argument about the performance of the male body in early twentieth century culture. The female stripteaser's body-as-jewel recalls on the one hand André Marcueil's transformation into a pearl-tear in Alfred Jarry's novel *The Supermale;* on the other, the same image points to Leiris's attempt to turn himself into a mineral, a precious object, by covering his face with white powder in *Manhood*. Both images are examples of failed phallicization of the male body and at the same time of the elaboration of an antiphallic masculinity through a process of spectacularization and masochization of that body. The transformation of the all-powerful phallus into the useless and decorative jewel, marking the trajectory from masculine authenticity and the natural "hardness" of the male body to the artificiality of the fetish, is a highly appropriate image for the masculinity I have described throughout this book.

What are the effects of this exchange between the hardness of the steeled, exercised male body and the languid solidity of the jewel? At stake in this exchange, at work in all the images of male bodies that I have examined, is the tension between the functional and the ornamental, duty and pleasure, productivity and consumption, that haunts and jeopardizes the claim to order and streamlining of modern masculinity. In Lawrence's writing the conflict between decoration and use, expenditure and willed self-control over one's excess, already predicated by the figure of the Nietzschean superman, comes to a climax. Phallic masculinity is affirmed through "feminine" theatrical props such as costumes and makeup. In turn, these fictional signifiers of gender are used by Lawrence to harden the body and to turn it into a monument, a projectile, and a weapon. The colorful clothes that are supposed to subvert the sartorial precepts of bourgeois masculinity turn into a military uniform.

The exchange between the useful and the superfluous, the functional and the ornamental, that characterizes Lawrence's critique of gender, and modernist discourse generally, comes to a momentary stop with the arresting image of "the legs close bright scarlet, and buttocks nice and showing under little white jackets" on which Mellors's sartorial fantasy centers in *Lady Chatterley's Lover*. Lawrence concludes this passage with even more striking words: "Then women 'ud begin to be women. It's because th'men *aren't* men that th'women have to be." These phrases strike a tone of complaint and reproach against the emasculating culture of modernity. At the same time, in the light of Lawrence's depiction of male masochism and exhibitionism, his statement has an affirmative value: He is stating something his texts have discovered through their narrative construction of the male body: "Men aren't men." Even though mediated and mitigated by the claim to heterosexuality ("Then women 'ud begin to be women"), Lawrence's taboo representation of masculinity announces, like that of Leiris, that manhood cannot be reached, and further implies that a perverse form of pleasure is ingrained in this unreachability, in this continuous postponement of the phallus. It is this supplementary quality of "real" masculinity that testifies on the one hand to the impossibility of fully inhabiting the normative definitions of gender circulated by modern culture, and on the other to the opportunity to transgress and potentially revise these definitions themselves.

This book records the continuous slippage between a call to virility, represented, for example, by the colonial-military uniform of the Boy Scout designed by Baden-Powell, and the impulse to dissolve, figuratively, one's body boundaries into the danger of sexual expenditure—a danger projected onto the phobias of the modern feminine masses and channeled into the pleasures of consumption and the *promesse de bonheur* of the commodity. In the culture of early twentieth century Europe this second impulse took two directions: On the one hand the gender instability of the erotic male body designated a structure of affect useful to commodity fetishism and later, via the discourse of nationalism, to totalitarianism. On the other hand, the improvisations on the theme of Nietzschean masculinity that popular figures such as Sandow or writers such as Leiris and Lawrence proposed, deliberately or uncannily, had the effect of resexualizing the male body and of turning its spectacularity (particularly in the case of Leiris and Lawrence) into the means of embodying abjected femininity and homoerotic desire.

To become bodies "beyond recognition" and to refigure heterosexual norms of masculinity outside the logic of the phallus, the male figures that I have studied deployed, besides costuming, another tactic, that of orgasmic fusion. By claiming to embody two ancient Aztec gods, the two protagonists of Lawrence's *The Plumed Serpent* experience a form of oneness in the moment when they abandon their selves to "melt" and dissolve into each other. This fantasy of fusion, of losing the contours of the body and the ego through a scene of orgiastic unselfconsciousness, had been anticipated, for example, by Wilde's Dorian Gray (who "becomes" his portrait), by the young soldier of the First World War (who was asked by the ideology of nationalism to forget his individuality in order to help constitute the body of the nation), and by the macho technophilia of the Futurists (who fantasized about "man multiplied by the motor"—the perfect interfacing between flesh and metal, that, as Klaus Theweleit has argued, could only explode and release itself in the violence of war).

Both strategies of modern male embodiment, costuming and the act of bodily fusion, work to enact and contest existing norms of masculinity. Just as the sartorial flamboyance and the sexualized exposure of male flesh reenacted forms of exhibitionism that, since the eighteenth century, European culture had categorized as feminine, so also the moment in which the male subject relinquishes his individuality to be absorbed into the body of the other has the effect of destabilizing his claimed hypermasculinity. Continually hailed by the "manly" culture of the early twentieth century, the culture that prefigured the fascist imaginary, men were called to occupy a gender position that proved uninhabitable. The impossibility of fully conforming to the imperatives of phallic masculinity as it had been shaped by the image of the Nietzschean superman and its mass culture, avant-garde, and primitivist doubles is signified by what remains as excess in these representations of the male body: erotic desire. Continually displaced and dissimulated, this desire becomes fully legible, in a flash, in the sexualized and masqueraded Lawrentian body: The "legs close bright scarlet" and the "buttocks nice" stand as a fetishistic substitution for something that does not exist; the body itself becomes a form of clothing. Modern masculinity, its early twentieth century representations suggest, is not written on the body; rather, like the phallus itself, it can be worn and made visible only through a fetishistic game of gender striptease. The superman wears his muscles as a suit, and the modern male body is a new costume of masculinity, a fashionable yet far-reaching style in clothing.

# Notes

## Introduction

1. See Elaine Showalter, *Sexual Anarchy: Gender and Culture at the Fin de Siècle* (New York: Viking, 1990).

2. Norbert Elias, *The Civilizing Process* (New York: Urizen Books, 1978); Mikhail M. Bakhtin, *Rabelais and His World*, trans. H. Iswolsky (Cambridge: MIT Press, 1968). See also Fernand Braudel, *Civilization and Capitalism: 15th–18th Century*, vol. 2, trans. S. Reynolds (New York: Harper and Row, 1982).

3. See Michel Foucault, *History of Sexuality, I: An Introduction*, trans. R. Hurley (New York: Random House, 1978); Francis Barker, *The Tremulous Private Body: Essays on Subjection* (London: Methuen, 1984); Peter Stallybrass and Allon White, *The Poetics and the Politics of Transgression* (Ithaca: Cornell University Press, 1986).

4. See Kathy Peiss, "Making Faces: The Cosmetic Industry and the Cultural Construction of Gender, 1890–1930," *Genders* 7 (Spring 1990).

5. See Robert Gildea, *Barricades and Borders: Europe 1800–1914* (Oxford: Oxford University Press, 1987); Eric Hobsbawm, *Industry and Empire* (Harmondsworth: Penguin Books, 1978), and *The Age of Empire* (New York: Vintage Books, 1987); Karl Polanyi, *The Great Transformation: The Political and Economic Origins of Our Time* (Boston: Beacon Press, 1957); and S. B. Saul, *The Myth of the Great Depression 1873–1896* (1969).

6. Kaja Silverman, *Male Subjectivity at the Margins* (New York: Routledge, 1992); Paul Smith, "Action Movie Hysteria, or Eastwood Bound," *differences* 1, 3 (Fall 1989), pp. 88–108, now in Paul Smith, *Clint Eastwood: A Cultural Production* (Minneapolis: University of Minnesota Press, 1995); Gilles Deleuze, *Masochism* (New York: Zone Books, 1991); Gay Lynn Studlar, *In the Realm of Pleasure: Von Sternberg, Dietrich and the Masochistic Aesthetic* (Urbana: University of Illinois Press, 1988).

7. Silverman, *Male Subjectivity*, p. 62.

8. Ibid., pp. 189–190.

9. Ibid., p. 206.

10. Smith, "Eastwood Bound," p. 102.

11. See Judith Butler, "Imitation and Gender Insubordination," in *Inside/Out*, ed. Diana Fuss (New York: Routledge, 1991); and Jonathan Goldberg, "Recalling Totalities: The Mirrored Stages of Arnold Schwarzenegger," *differences* 4, 1 (Spring 1992).

12. Butler, "Imitation and Gender Insubordination," p. 27.

13. Ibid., p. 17.

14. Ibid., p. 21.

15. Ibid., p. 23.

16. Michel de Certeau, *The Practice of Everyday Life* (Berkeley: University of California Press, 1984); Dick Hebdige, *Subculture: The Meaning of Style* (London: Methuen, 1979); Tania Modleski, *Feminism Without Women: Culture and Criticism in a Postfeminist Age*

(New York: Routledge, 1991); Angela McRobbie, *Postmodernism and Popular Culture* (New York: Routledge, 1994); and Mike Featherstone, *Consumer Culture and Postmodernism* (London: Sage, 1991).

17. Theodor Reik, *Masochism in Sex and Society*, trans. Margaret H. Beigel and Gertrud M. Kurth (New York: Stein and Day, 1962); Leo Bersani, *The Freudian Body: Psychoanalysis and Art* (New York: Columbia University Press, 1986). Silverman includes Bersani's theory among the "utopian" readings of masochism, together with Gayle Rubin's and Gay Lynn Studlar's, implicitly because of his choice of disanchoring masochism from the structure of both Oedipal and pre-Oedipal identifications to present it rather as constitutive of sexuality, infantile and adult alike.

18. "Suffering, discomfort, humiliation and disgrace are being shown and so to speak put on display. ... In the practices of masochists, denudation, parading with all their psychic concomitant phenomena play such a major part that I feel induced to assume a constant connection between masochism and exhibitionism." See Reik, *Masochism in Sex and Society*, p. 72.

19. Sigmund Freud, "The Economic Problem of Masochism," in *The Standard Edition of the Complete Psychological Works of Sigmund Freud*, vol. 19, trans. and ed. James Strachey (London: Hogarth Press, 1954), pp. 169–170.

20. Bersani, *The Freudian Body*, p. 34.

21. "Male Subjectivity," special issue of *differences* 1, 3 (Fall 1989); "The Phallus Issue," *differences* 4, 1 (Spring 1992); "Male Trouble," special issue of *Camera Obscura* 17 (May 1988); Eve Kosofsky Sedgwick, *Between Men* (New York: Columbia University Press, 1985), and *Epistemology of the Closet* (Berkeley: University of California Press, 1990); Jonathan Dollimore, *Sexual Dissidence: Augustine to Foucault* (Oxford: Clarendon Press, 1991); Jeffrey Weeks, *Coming Out: Homosexual Politics in Britain from the Nineteenth Century to the Present* (London and New York: Quartet Books, 1983); Alan Sinfield, *Cultural Politics: Queer Reading* (London: Routledge, 1991); Lynne Joyrich, "Critical and Textual Hypermasculinity," in *Logics of Television*, ed. Patricia Mellencamp (Bloomington: Indiana University Press, 1990); Sharon Willis, "Disputed Territories: Masculinity and Social Space," *Camera Obscura* 19 (January 1989); Maurizia Boscagli, "A Moving Story: Masculine Tears and the Humanity of Televised Emotions," *Discourse* 15, 2 (Winter 1992–1993).

22. Teresa de Lauretis, "The Technology of Gender," in *Technologies of Gender* (Bloomington: University of Indiana Press, 1987).

## Chapter 1

1. Walter Pater, *The Renaissance: Studies in Art and Poetry* (1893 ed.) (Berkeley: University of California Press, 1980), p. 156. Further references to this work are given in the text.

2. The cultural resonance and press attention that the trials of Stella and Fanny, the two transvestites Ernest Boulton and Frederick Park, received in 1871, as well as the publication of the novel *Teleny* (1893), to which Oscar Wilde may have contributed, show, as Alan Sinfield points out, that "concepts of homosexuality were well enough developed in certain quarters" during the late Victorian period. See *The Wilde Century: Effeminacy, Oscar Wilde and the Queer Moment* (New York: Columbia University Press, 1994). However, a queer identity was only in the making at the time of Wilde. It was produced through a process of cultural bricolage of elements as different as sexology, medical and juridical discourse, and

existing homosexual subcultures: "The dominant twentieth century queer identity ... has been constructed in this kind of process—mainly out of elements that came together at the trials [Wilde's]: effeminacy, leisure, idleness, immorality, luxury, insouciance, decadence and aestheticism" (p. 12).

3. See Jonathan Dollimore, *Sexual Dissidence: Augustine to Wilde, Freud to Foucault* (Oxford: Clarendon Press, 1991); Eve Kosofsky Sedgwick, *Between Men* (New York: Columbia University Press, 1985); Jeffrey Weeks, *Coming Out* (London: Quartet Books, 1977); Moe Meyer, ed., *The Politics and Poetics of Camp* (New York: Routledge, 1994); Ed Cohen, *Talk on the Wilde Side* (New York: Routledge, 1993); Ellen Moers, *The Dandy* (London: Secker, 1960).

4. Regenia Gaigner studies the aesthete's self-marketing and self-packaging in *Idylls of the Marketplace: Oscar Wilde and the Victorian Public* (Stanford: Stanford University Press, 1986). The assonance and "relative convergence" of aestheticism and consumerism is also explored by Rachel Bowlby in "Promoting Dorian Gray," in *Shopping with Freud* (Routledge: New York, 1993). Thomas Richards's *The Commodity Culture of Victorian England: Advertising and Spectacle 1851–1914* (Stanford: Stanford University Press, 1990) provides important insights into the system and the cultural effects of early consumerism in England.

5. Max Nordau, in the new German edition of *Degeneration* (1896), seized the opportunity to refer to Wilde as "the most unfortunate embodiment of a mentality [*Denkweise*] which has played a part in modern spiritual life and which is still embraced by no small number of degenerates and their imitators." *Degeneration* (New York: Appleton, 1985), p. 320. Further references to this work are given in parentheses in the text.

6. For an exhaustive discussion of the culture and the literature of decadence, see Jean Pierrot, *The Decadent Imagination 1880–1900* (Chicago: University of Chicago Press, 1981).

7. This is, of course, the bourgeois culture that Max Weber studies in *The Protestant Ethic and the Spirit of Capitalism.* For the "effeminacy" of literary culture and the middle class cult of manliness in the late nineteenth century see J. A. Mangan and James Walvin, eds., *Manliness and Morality* (Manchester: Manchester University Press, 1987); Robin Gilmour, *The Idea of the Gentleman in the Victorian Novel* (London: Allen and Unwin, 1981); G. J. Barker-Benfield, *The Culture of Sensibility* (Chicago: University of Chicago Press, 1992); and Christine Heward, *Making a Man of Him* (London: Routledge, 1988).

8. Labouchère is quoted by Richard Ellmann, *Oscar Wilde* (London: Hamish Hamilton, 1987), p. 149.

9. For a discussion of Winckelmann's interest in classicism and the male body see Alex Potts, *Flesh and the Idol: Winckelmann and the Origins of Art History* (Oxford: Oxford University Press, 1980), p. 150.

10. Richard Jenkyns, *The Victorians and Ancient Greece* (Oxford: Oxford University Press, 1980), p. 150.

11. Eve Kosofsky Sedgwick, *Epistemology of the Closet* (Berkeley: University of California Press, 1990), p. 136.

12. In the words of Eve Sedgwick, "Modern homosexual panic . . . represents not a temporal imprisoning obstacle to philosophy and culture, but, rather, the latent energy that can hurtle them far beyond their own present place of knowledge." See *Epistemology of the Closet*, p. 139.

13. For an informed discussion of Pater's role in the intellectual scene at Oxford see

Richard Dellamora, *Masculine Desire: The Sexual Politics of Victorian Aestheticism* (Chapel Hill: University of North Carolina Press, 1990), especially Chs. 2 and 5.

14. See Dollimore, *Sexual Dissidence;* Sinfield, *The Wilde Century;* and Gaigner, *Idylls of the Marketplace.*

15. Dellamora, *Masculine Desire*, p. 210.

16. Oscar Wilde, *The Picture of Dorian Gray* (Harmondsworth: Penguin Books, 1983), pp. 131–132. Further references to this work are given in parentheses in the text.

17. See Gilmour, *The Idea of the Gentleman,* p. 8.

18. Jules Barbey d'Aurevilly, *Of Dandyism and of George Brummell,* trans. Douglas Ainslie (London: J. M. Dent, 1897), p. 102.

19. Georges Bataille, *La part maudite,* introduction by Jean Pielm (Paris: Éditions de Minuit, 1967), vol. 7, p. 16.

20. Georges Bataille, "The Notion of Expenditure," in *Visions of Excess: Selected Writings 1917–1939,* ed. Alan Stoekl (Minneapolis: University of Minnesota Press, 1985), p. 118.

21. Bataille, *La part maudite,* pp. 35–36.

22. Michèle Richman, *Reading Georges Bataille: Beyond the Gift* (Baltimore: Johns Hopkins University Press, 1982), p. 18.

23. Sedgwick, *Epistemology of the Closet,* p. 164.

24. Moe Meyer, "Under the Sign of Wilde: An Archaeology of Posing," in *The Politics and Poetics of Camp,* ed. Moe Meyer. See also Jonathan Dollimore, "Different Desires: Subjectivity and Transgression in Wilde and Gide," in *The Lesbian and Gay Studies Reader,* ed. H. Abelove, M. Barale, D. Halperin (New York: Routledge, 1993).

25. Ellmann, *Oscar Wilde,* p. 208.

26. Meyer, "Under the Sign of Wilde," p. 81.

27. Ibid. p. 83.

28. Ibid. p. 88.

29. Bowlby, "Promoting Dorian Gray," p. 16.

30. Jean-Joseph Goux, "General Economics and Postmodern Capitalism," *Yale French Studies* 78 (1990), p. 220.

31. Bataille, "The Notion of Expenditure," p. 117.

32. Ibid., p. 124.

33. Bataille, *La part maudite,* p. 71.

34. Wilde's Dorian Gray reminds me of Gabriele D'Annunzio, whose flamboyant decadence was displayed, for instance, in his own home, Il Vittoriale, on Lake Garda. Today a museum, Il Vittoriale—its rooms cluttered with collectibles, art, and kitsch objects—is probably the best illustration of chapter 11 of *The Picture of Dorian Gray.* As a decadent and an aesthete, D'Annunzio was also interested in St. Sebastian; see *Il martirio di San Sebastiano* (Milan: Fratelli Treves Editori, 1911), which was set to music by Claude Debussy in his *Martyre de Saint Sebastien, Mystère de Gabriele D'Annunzio* (Paris: Durand & Fils, 1912).

35. The book can be identified as Karl Joris Huysman's *A rebours* (Against nature), and the protagonist is Des Esseintes.

36. This was the time when advertisement and the display of goods became particularly lavish at the exhibitions, in the windows of individual shops, and in quickly developing department stores. See Michael B. Miller, *The Bon Marche: Bourgeois Culture and the Department Store, 1869–1920* (Princeton: Princeton University Press, 1991).

37. Rupert Hart-Davis, ed., *Selected Letters of Oscar Wilde* (New York: Harcourt, Brace and World, 1962), p. 352.

38. Sedgwick's commentary on Wilde's physique points to the "transformative power" and "uncanny courage" of his flaunting of his difference: "As a magus in the worship of the 'slim rose-gilt soul'—the individual or generic figure of the 'slim thing, gold-haired like an angel,' that stood at the same time for a sexuality, a sensibility, a class, and a narrowly English national type, whose own physical make was of the opposite sort and (in that context) an infinitely less appetizing, desirable and placeable one, showed his usual uncanny courage . . . in foregrounding his own body so insistently as an index to such erotic and political meanings." See Sedgwick, *Epistemology of the Closet*, pp. 175–176.

39. As Meyer affirms, the Marquess of Queensberry's attack on Wilde, accusing him of being a "posing sodomite," provoked not only a sexual but also a class exposure: "By accusing him of being a posing sodomite, not only did Queensberry intimate that it was Wilde who was being inscribed, thus removing the social protections enjoyed by the inscriptor [penetrator], but it acted as an insult to Wilde's self-defined class standing, reminding him of the more common heritage he had labored to overcome during his rise to the top." *Poetics and Politics*, p. 90.

40. Charles Baudelaire, *Mon coeur mis a nu*, quoted in Gaigner, *Idylls of the Marketplace*, p. 213. See also Jean-Joseph Marchand, *Sur "Mon coeur mis a nu" de Baudelaire* (Paris: l'Herne, 1970).

41. Rachel Bowlby points out the commercial possibilities implied in modern masculine beauty: "The implicit convergence of the ideals of advertising and aesthetics can be further suggested by the growing habit during this period of commissioning famous artists to design advertisements. The first and best known of these, Millais' *Bubbles* (1886) was an ad for Pears' Soap, showing a beautiful curly-haired boy who might have been a prefiguring type for Dorian Gray himself." See Bowlby, *Shopping with Freud*, p. 13.

42. For an analysis of Wilde's trials see Montgomery Hyde, *The Trials of Oscar Wilde* (London: William Hodge, 1948); and Cohen, *Talk on the Wilde Side*.

43. Two useful critical discussions of the novella are Rolf Gunther Renner, *Das Ich als aesthetische Konstruktion: "Der Tod in Venedig" und seine Beziehung zum Gesamtwerk* (Freiburg: Roembach, 1987); and Eric Lawson Marson, *The Ascetic Artist: Prefigurations in Thomas Mann's "Der Tod in Venedig"* (Bern: Lang, 1974).

44. See James Steakley, *The Emancipation Movements in Germany* (New York: Arno Press, 1975).

45. Thomas Mann, *Letters* (New York: Knopf, 1975), p. 103.

46. Ibid., pp. 103–104. Mann is here implicitly critiquing the late nineteenth century representation of homosexuality by sexology and its claim that the homosexual belonged to a third sex.

47. Mann, *Letters*, p. 104.

48. Sedgwick, *Epistemology of the Closet*, p. 145.

49. Thomas Mann, *Death in Venice*, in *Death in Venice and Other Stories*, trans. David Luke (New York: Bantam Books, 1988), p. 220. Subsequent references to the novel are given in parentheses in the text.

50. See Sedgwick, *Epistemology of the Closet*, p. 140.

51. F. Holland Day's career and involvement in the aestheticist movement is studied by Estelle Jussim, *Slave to Beauty: The Eccentric Life and Controversial Career of F. Holland Day Photographer, Publisher, Aesthete* (Boston: David R. Godine, 1981).

52. One of the most famous visual examples of this homoerotic algolagniac drive is Aubrey Beardsley's production, for instance, in the tables he drew to illustrate Wilde's play *Salome.*

53. Julia Kristeva, *Powers of Horror,* trans. Leon S. Rudiez (New York: Columbia University Press, 1982).

## Chapter 2

1. Robert Gildea, *Barricades and Borders: Europe 1800–1914* (Oxford: Oxford University Press, 1987), p. 355.

2. See Eric Hobsbawm, *The Age of Empire* (New York: Vintage Books, 1989); Lucio Colletti, *Il marxismo e il crollo del capitalismo* (Rome: Laterza, 1975); Ernest Mandel, *Late Capitalism* (London: NLB, 1975); and Karl Polanyi, *The Great Transformation* (Boston: Beacon Press, 1957).

3. James Walvin, *Leisure and Society 1830–1950* (London: Longman, 1978), p. 62.

4. See Garry Leonard, "Molly Bloom's 'Lifestyle': The Performative as Normative," in *Molly Blooms: A Polylogue on "Penelope" and Cultural Studies,* ed. Richard Pearce (Madison: University of Wisconsin Press, 1994), p. 196.

5. Quoted in Walvin, *Leisure and Society,* p. 81.

6. Jonathan Rose, *The Edwardian Temperament* (Columbus: Ohio University Press, 1986).

7. Sources for a discussion of the social and cultural meaning of the employee are David Lockwood, *The Black-coated Worker* (London: Allen and Unwin, 1958); Adrian Forty, *Objects of Desire* (New York: Pantheon Books, 1986); F. D. Klinger, *The Conditions of Clerical Labour in Britain* (London: M. Lawrence, 1935); and Siegfried Kracauer, *Die Angestellten aus dem neuesten Deutschland* (Frankfurt am Main: Frankfurter Societatis Druckerei, g.m.b.h., 1930).

8. Forty, *Objects of Desire,* p. 121.

9. Lockwood, *The Black-coated Worker,* pp. 25–30.

10. "[The employee's work] was clearly subaltern and remunerated in wages ... but ... was also clearly non-manual, based on formal educational qualifications, if modest ones, and above all carried on by men—and even some women—most of whom ... aspired, often at great material sacrifice, to the style of life of middle class respectability." Hobsbawm, *The Age of Empire,* p. 172.

11. Ibid., p. 186.

12. Antonio Gramsci, "Subversive," in *The Prison Notebooks* (New York: International, 1971), p. 273.

13. "There exist two distinct strata of *morti di fame:* the day labourers and the petty intellectuals [among whom is the clerk]. ... Many petty clerks in the town originate socially from these strata, and conserve the arrogant mentality of the impoverished nobleman, of the landowner who endures work under compulsion. The 'subversiveness' of these strata has two faces, one turned to the left and one to the right, but the left face is only a means of blackmail; at the decisive moment they always turn to the right, and their desperate 'courage' always prefers to have the *carabinieri* on their side." Gramsci, *Prison Notebooks,* p. 274.

14. Hobsbawm elucidates the relation between nationalism, class mobility, and petty bourgeois ressentiment: "Patriotism compensated for social inferiority. ... As the war was to show, even clerks and salesmen in the service of the nation could become officers and—

in the brutally frank terminology of the British upper class—'temporary gentlemen.'" *The Age of Empire*, pp. 160–161.

15. T. S. Eliot, *Selected Poems* (London: Faber and Faber, 1976).

16. Naomi Schor, *Reading in Detail: Aesthetics and the Feminine* (London: Methuen, 1987), p. 4.

17. For a discussion of the feminization of mass culture see Andreas Huyssen, "Mass Culture as Woman: Modernism's Other," in *After the Great Divide: Modernism, Mass Culture, Post-Modernism* (Bloomington: University of Indiana Press, 1986).

18. Ibid., p. 53.

19. See Raymond Williams, *The Long Revolution* (New York: Harper and Row, 1966), pp. 263–264.

20. Michel Foucault, "Of Other Spaces," *Diacritics* (October 1984).

21. Walvin, *Leisure and Society*, p. 87.

22. For a discussion of the social effects of sports during the early twentieth century see Walvin, *Leisure and Society*; John Hoberman, *Sport and Political Ideology* (Austin: University of Texas Press, 1984); H. E. Meller, *Leisure and the Changing City, 1870–1914* (London: Routledge, 1976). Specifically on English football, see O. L. Owen, *The History of the Rugby Football Union* (London: Playfair Books, 1955); and J. Arlott, ed., *The Oxford Companion to Sports and Games* (Oxford: Oxford University Press, 1976).

23. Walvin, *Leisure and Society*, p. 63.

24. "The numbers of firms providing holidays with pay steadily grew, though usually linked to an insistence on prompt and regular attendance throughout the rest of the working year. ...The Manchester engineers Mater and Platt set up L.10,00 of company shares for one such scheme. 'It has occurred to me [wrote the chairman in 1910] that the annual holiday might be thoroughly enjoyed as a means of healthy recreation out of town.'" See Walvin, *Leisure and Society*, p. 80.

25. In England "the safe and clean home" and the family became during the 1910s and 1920s the target of strong government propaganda as the most important place for the construction of the healthy body of the nation. As the contemporary social critic Alice Ravenhill affirmed, "Parental care and intelligent home management are thus intimately concerned with the physical evolution of the race, as well as with its moral development." A. Ravenhill, "Some Relations of Sanitary Science to Family Life and Individual Efficiency," in A. Ravenhill and C. S. Schiff, eds., *Household Administration: Its Place in the Higher Education of Women* (New York: Henry Holt, 1911). Quoted in Forty, *Objects of Desire*, p. 117.

26. E. M. Forster, *Howard's End* (New York: Vintage Books, 1956). Subsequent references to this edition are cited in parentheses in the text.

27. See Peter Widdowson, *E. M. Forster's Howard's End: Fiction as History* (London: Chattoo and Windus, 1977); and Nigel Rapport, *The Prose and the Passion: Anthropology, Literature and the Writing of E. M. Forster* (Manchester: Manchester University Press, 1994).

28. Gustave Le Bon, *Psychology of the Crowd: A Study of the Popular Mind* (London: Ernest Benn, 1930).

29. Ibid., p. 36.

30. Ibid., p. 40.

31. "With social mobility and the decline of traditional hierarchies establishing who belonged and who did not belong to the 'middle rank' or 'estate' of society, the boundaries of

this intermediate social zone ... became hazy." Hobsbawm, *The Age of Empire,* p. 170. See also Thorstein Veblen, *The Theory of the Leisure Class* (1899) (New York: MacMillan, 1953).

32. Francis Galton, "Eugenics, Its Definition, Scope and Aims," *Nature* 70 (1904), p. 82.

33. See Michael Rosenthal's excellent study *The Character Factory: Baden-Powell's Boy Scouts and the Imperatives of Empire* (New York: Pantheon Books, 1984), pp. 130–160.

34. C.F.G. Masterman, *The Heart of Empire* (London: T. Fisher Unwin, 1901), p. 8.

35. See G. R. Searle, *Eugenics and Politics in Britain 1900–1914* (Leiden: Noordhoff International, 1976).

36. Rosenthal, *The Character Factory,* p. 147.

37. Quoted in Searle, *Eugenics and Politics,* pp. 26–27.

38. Ibid., p. 34.

39. William C. Dampier Whetham and Catherine Durning Whetham, *The Family and the Nation* (London: Longmans, Green, 1909), p. 9.

40. Rosenthal, *The Character Factory,* p. 147.

41. Arthur Moeller van den Bruck, *Die italienische Schonheit* (Berlin and Leipzig: J. C. Cotta, 1930), p. 240.

42. Graham Dawson shows how different images of masculinity produced Britishness in this period in *Soldier Heroes: British Adventure, Empire and the Imagining of Masculinities* (London: Routledge, 1994).

43. For an account of Brooke's life see Christopher Hassall's biography *Rupert Brooke* (London: Faber and Faber, 1964).

44. Virginia Woolf, "Rupert Brooke," *Times Literary Supplement,* August 8, 1918, p. 371.

45. "Brooke had long been fascinated by the vagabond and the wanderer as human types. The spiritual vagabond, he had observed while still at Rugby, was a rebel 'against the safeties and little confines of our ordinary human life.' ... Now Brooke began to think and write of himself increasingly in these terms—as an adventurer out of Conrad and Kipling. ... In Samoa and Tahiti he experienced great contentment and was captivated by the romance of living with people ... who were simple rather than complex." Robert Wohl, *The Generation of 1914* (Cambridge: Harvard University Press, 1979), p. 88.

46. Ibid., p. 91.

47. Ibid., pp. 86–92.

48. Stephen Ascheim, *The Nietzsche Legacy in Germany 1890–1990* (Berkeley: University of California Press, 1992), p. 75.

49. Émile Zola, *La bête humaine* (Harmondsworth: Penguin Books, 1977). Further references to the novel are given in parentheses in the text.

50. Friederich Nietzsche, *On the Genealogy of Morals,* trans. and ed. Walter Kaufmann (New York: Vintage Books, 1969); *Twilight of Idols,* in *The Portable Nietzsche,* trans. and ed. Walter Kaufmann (Harmondsworth: Penguin Books, 1983); and *Thus Spoke Zarathustra,* trans. and ed. R. J. Hollingdale (Harmondsworth: Penguin Books, 1986).

51. Nietzsche, *Twilight of Idols,* p. 549.

52. Nietzsche, *On the Genealogy of Morals,* p. 40.

53. Ibid.

54. Nietzsche, *Thus Spoke Zarathustra,* p. 62.

55. Ibid.

56. As Stephen Ascheim points out, "About 150,000 copies of a specially durable wartime *Zarathustra* were distributed to the troops. Even Christian commentators were struck that *Zarathustra* had taken its place alongside the Bible in the field. Indeed, this very

combination was a key way for the interpreters to integrate the notorious author of the *Antichrist* into respectability." See Ascheim, *The Nietzsche Legacy*, pp. 135–136.

57. Nietzsche, *Twilight of Idols*, p. 511.

58. "Just look at these superfluous people! They acquire wealth and make themselves poorer with it. They desire power and especially the lever of power, plenty of money. These impotent people! ... Leave the idolatry of the superfluous! A free life still remains for great souls. Truly, he who possesses little is so much the less possessed: praised be a moderate poverty! Only then, when the state ceases, does the man who is not superfluous begin; does the song of the necessary man, the unique and irreplaceable melody begin. ...Do you not see it: the rainbow and the bridge to the Superman?" Nietzsche, *Thus Spoke Zarathustra*, pp. 77–78.

59. For the relation between movement, speed, and physical efficiency in the early twentieth century see Stephen Kern, *The Culture of Time and Space 1880–1918* (Cambridge: Harvard University Press, 1983).

60. Hoberman, *Sport and Political Ideology*, p. 130.

61. See Stefan Zweig, *The World of Yesterday*, Ch. 4, "Universitas Vitae" (London: Cassel, 1943).

62. Gildea, *Barricades and Borders*, p. 377.

63. Quoted in Hoberman, *Sport and Political Ideology*, p. 77. In *The Political Training of the Body* (1937), Baumler anthropomorphizes the state into a giant athlete representing the "collective body" of the *Volk*. Thus society is seen as an organized and trained body.

64. Walter Lacqueur, *Young Germany: A History of the German Youth Movement* (London and New Brunswick: Transaction Books, 1962), p. 18.

65. Ascheim, *The Nietzsche Legacy*, p. 115.

66. Lacqueur, *Young Germany*, p. 7.

67. Carl Boesch, "Vom deutschen Mannsideal," *Der Vortupp* 2, 1 (January 1, 1913), p. 3; quoted in George L. Mosse, *Nationalism and Sexuality: Middle Class Morality and Sexual Norms in Modern Europe* (Madison: University of Wisconsin Press, 1985), p. 46.

68. Lord Robert Baden-Powell, *Rovering to Success: A Book of Life Sport for Young Men* (London: 1920), pp. 11–28.

69. Rosenthal, *The Character Factory*, is an excellent study of the English scout movement. See also John M. Mackenzie, "The Imperial Pioneer and Hunter and the British Masculine Stereotype in Late Victorian and Edwardian Times," and Allen Warren, "Popular Manliness: Baden-Powell, Scouting and the Development of Manly Character," both in *Manliness and Morality: Middle Class Masculinity in Britain and America 1800–1940*, ed. J. A. Mangan and James Wavin (Manchester: Manchester University Press, 1987).

70. Lord Robert Baden-Powell, *Scouting for Boys* (London: C. Arthur Pearson, 1928), p. 2.

71. C. H. Stigand and Denis D. Lyell, *Central African Game and Its Spoor* (London: H. Cox, 1906), p. 3.

72. Giorgio Triani, *Pelle di sole pelle di luna: Nascita e storia della civilta balneare* (Venice: Marsilio, 1988).

73. Mosse, *Nationalism and Sexuality*, p. 32.

74. Otto Weininger, *Sex and Character* (London: W. Heinemann; New York: G. P. Putnam's Sons, 1907).

75. Baden-Powell, *Rovering to Success*, p. 206.

76. Gabriele D'Annunzio, *Per la piu grande Italia* (1915) (Rome: Per l'Oleandro, 1933); Maurice Barrés, "Young Soldiers of France," in *The War and the Spirit of Youth*, ed. Maurice Barrés, Anne C.E. Allison, Sir Francis Youngshusband (Boston: Atlantic Monthly, 1917); Walter Flex, *Der Wanderer zwischen beiden Welten* (The wanderer between two worlds) (Munich: Becksche Verlag, 1922).

77. "Soltanto la guerra sa svecchiare, accelerare, aguzzare l'intelligenza umana, alleggerire e areare i nervi, dare mille sapori alla vita e dell'ingegno agl'imbecilli." Filippo Tommaso Marinetti, "Guerra sola igiene del mondo" (1915), in Marinetti, *Teoria e invenzione futurista* (Milan: Mondadori, 1968), p. 335. My translation.

## Chapter 3

1. Antonio Gramsci, *Selections from Cultural Writings* (New York: Schocken Books, 1988), p. 335.

2. Ibid., p. 356.

3. Matei Calinescu, *Five Faces of Modernity,* Ch. 4, "Kitsch" (Durham, N.C.: Duke University Press, 1987).

4. "Kitsch is ... what reaches the masses or the middle, low-brow public because it is 'consumed'; it is what gets used-up (and therefore impoverished), because it has been 'abused' by a great number of consumers." Umberto Eco, "La struttura del cattivo gusto," in *Apocalittici e integrati: Comunicazioni di massa e teorie della comunicazione di massa* (Milan: Bompiani, 1964), p. 115. My translation

5. Theodor Adorno, *Aesthetic Theory* (London: Routledge and Kegan Paul, 1970), p. 340.

6. See Andreas Huyssen, *After the Great Divide: Modernism, Mass Culture, Postmodernism* (Bloomington: University of Indiana Press, 1986), p. 22.

7. Ibid., p. 24.

8. Eco, "La struttura," p. 115.

9. Adolf Loos, *Spoken into the Void: Collected Essays 1879–1900*, trans. Jane O. Newman and John H. Smith, with an introduction by Aldo Rossi (Cambridge: MIT Press, 1982). For a feminist critique of Loos's attack on the ornament and on kitsch as a decadent and "feminine" style, see Naomi Schor, *Reading in Detail: Aesthetics and the Feminine* (New York: Methuen, 1987).

10. The social and cultural scene of turn of the century Vienna, in which Loos operated, is well illustrated by Carl Schorske, *Fin de Siècle Vienna* (Princeton: Princeton University Press, 1987); and Allan Janik and Stephen Toulmin, *Wittgenstein's Vienna* (New York: Simon and Schuster, 1973).

11. "The barriers erected by the nobility against the high nobility, ... and by the lower nobility against the bourgeoisie had collapsed, and everyone could furnish his home and dress according to his own taste. ... It would be wrong, however, to see progress in this situation. For princely furniture ... cost great sums of money. But since this kind of wealth was not available to the general public, they therefore copied at the expense of material and execution. As a result, superficiality, hollowness, and that horrible monster, imitation, which threatens to suck the marrow out of the bones of our crafts, have made their entry." Loos, *Spoken into the Void*, p. 92.

12. For a history of the zoo see Richard D. Altick, *The Shows of London* (Cambridge: Harvard University Press, 1978), in particular the chapter "Zoos and Pleasure Gardens."

13. John Berger, *About Looking* (New York: Pantheon Books, 1980), p. 19.

14. "A peasant becomes fond of his pig and is glad to salt away its pork. What is significant, and is so difficult for the urban stranger to understand, is that the two statements in that sentence are connected by an *and* not by a yet." Berger, "Why Look at Animals?" in Berger, *About Looking,* p. 5.

15. Eugen Sandow, *Strength and How to Obtain It* (London: Gale and Polden, 1897), p. 1.

16. My sources for Sandow's autobiography also include Frank W. Lane, "Sandow the Strongman," *Saturday Book* 24 (1964), pp. 140–147; and R. Brandon Kershner, "The World's Strongest Man: Joyce or Sandow?" *James Joyce Quarterly* 30, 4 (Fall 1993), pp. 667–691.

17. Cheryl Herr mentions Sandow's theatrical fame in her study of popular culture inside and outside Joyce's *Ulysses* in *Joyce's Anatomy of Culture* (Urbana and Chicago: University of Illinois Press, 1987). See also Ernest Short, *Fifty Years of Vaudeville* (London: Eyre and Spottiswoode, 1946); Archibald Hadon, *The Story of the Music-Hall* (London: Fleetway Press, 1930); and Peter Bailey, ed., *Music-Hall and the Business of Pleasure* (Milton Keynes: Open University Press, 1986).

18. David Willoughby, *The Super-Athletes* (New York: A. S. Barnes, 1970), p. 61.

19. The film *Strongman Poses* was made by Thomas A. Edison in 1896.

20. See R. B. Kerschner, "Degeneration, the Explanatory Nightmare," *Georgia Review* 40 (Summer 1986), p. 420.

21. Ibid.

22. James Joyce, *Ulysses* (New York: Vintage Books, 1986), p. 234.

23. William A. Ewing, *The Body: Photographs of the Human Form* (San Francisco: Chronicle Books, 1994), p. 168.

24. Allen Ellenzweig, *The Homoerotic Photograph* (New York: Columbia University Press, 1992), p. 14.

25. Joe Laurie Jr. and Gene Fowler, *Vaudeville: From the Honky-Tonk to the Palace* (New York: Kennicot Press, 1953), p. 33.

26. Ellenzweig, *The Homoerotic Photograph,* p. 7.

27. Ibid., p. 15.

28. Altick, *The Shows of London,* p. 335.

29. Ibid., p. 346.

30. Ellenzweig, *The Homoerotic Photograph,* p. 43.

31. Roland Barthes, *Wilhelm von Gloeden* (Naples: Amelio Editore, 1978), p. 11.

32. Scott Long, "The Loneliness of Camp," in *Camp Grounds: Style and Homosexuality,* ed. David Bergman (Amherst: University of Massachusetts Press, 1993), p. 86.

33. Quoted in Jonathan Goldberg, "Recalling Totalities: The Mirrored Stages of Arnold Schwarzenegger," *differences* 4, 1 (1992), p. 176.

34. Ibid., p. 179.

35. Ibid.

36. Bernard Sobel, *A Pictorial History of Vaudeville,* with a foreword by George Jessel (New York: Citadel Press, 1961), p. 51.

37. Sandow, *Strength and How to Obtain It,* p. 110.

38. Eugen Sandow, *The Construction and Reconstruction of the Human Body* (London: John Bale and Davison, 1907).

39. See Gabe Essoe, *Tarzan of the Movies: A Pictorial History of More than Fifty Years of Edgar Rice Burroughs' Legendary Hero* (New York: Citadel Press, 1968).

40. Umberto Eco, *Il superuomo di massa* (Milan: Cooperativa Scrittori, 1976), p. 175.

41. Edgar Rice Burroughs, *Tarzan of the Apes* (New York: Ballantine Books, 1963). Further citations are given in parentheses in the text.

42. Hadon, *The Story of the Music-Hall*, p. 161.

43. Gramsci, *Selections from Cultural Writings*, p. 336.

44. Paul Smith, "Action Movie Hysteria: Eastwood Bound," *differences* 1, 3 (Fall 1989), p. 102.

45. Leopold von Sacher-Masoch, *Venus in Furs* (1870) (New York: Zone Books, 1991).

46. " ... questa macchinetta stridula che pare sul treppiedi a gambe rientranti un grosso ragno in agguato." Luigi Pirandello, *I quaderni di Serafino Gubbio operatore*, in *Tutti i Romanzi* (Milan: Mondadori, 1957), p. 1162. My translation.

47. " ... col tempo, si arriverá a sopprimermi. La macchinetta ... girera da se." Ibid., p. 1111.

48. "L'India sará finta, la jungla sará finta, il viaggio sará finto, finta la *miss* e finti i corteggiatori: solo la morte di questa povera bestia non sará finta. ... In mezzo a una finzione generale soltanto la sua morte sará vera." Ibid., p. 1154. My translation.

49. " ... la qualitá precipua che si richiede in uno che faccia la mia professione e l'*impassibilitá* di fronte all'azione che si svolge davanti alla macchina." Ibid., p. 1111. My translation.

## Chapter 4

1. Stephen Kern's work contains much extremely interesting information on signs of the new order; on the introduction of watches, for example, he relates that at the end of the nineteenth century in Germany "there was a sharp rise in the domestic production and importation of pocket watches ... 12 million imported watches for a German population of about 52 million. ... The new profusion of watches was a response to, as well as a cause of, a heightened sense of punctuality in this period, especially in urban centers." Stephen Kern, *The Culture of Time and Space 1880–1918* (Cambridge: Harvard University Press, 1983), pp. 110–111.

2. See Hillel Schwartz, "Torque: The New Kinesthetic of the Twentieth Century," in *Incorporations*, ed. Jonathan Crary and Sanford Kwinter (New York: Zone, 1992).

3. Jonathan Rose, *The Edwardian Temperament 1895–1919* (Athens: Ohio University Press, 1986), particularly Ch. 4, "The Efficiency Men."

4. See David Harvey, *The Condition of Postmodernity: An Inquiry into the Origins of Cultural Change* (Oxford: Blackwell, 1989), Ch. 8, "Fordism."

5. Georg Simmel, "The Metropolis and Mental Life," in *Sociology of Georg Simmel* (Glencoe, Ill.: Free Press, 1950), p. 438.

6. Ibid., p. 437.

7. The episode is mentioned by Kern, *The Culture of Time and Space*, p. 114.

8. Theodor Adorno, *Minima Moralia*, trans. E.F.N. Jephcott (London: Verso, 1987), p. 19.

9. Robert Hughes, *The Shock of the New* (New York: Knopf, 1991), p. 48.

10. Adorno, *Minima Moralia*, p. 19.

11. "The war had thrust me, as a soldier, into the heart of the mechanical atmosphere. Here I discovered the beauty of the fragment. I sensed a new reality in the detail of the machine, in the common object. I tried to find the plastic value of these fragments in modern life." Quoted in Susan Sontag, *On Photography*, in *A Susan Sontag Reader*, with an introduction by Elizabeth Hardwick (New York: Vintage, 1983), p. 233.

12. For a brief history of the automaton in modernity see Jean-Claude Beaune, "The Classical Age of Automata: An Impressionist Survey from the Sixteenth Century to the Nineteenth Century," in *Fragments of a History of the Body* (New York: Zane, 1989). For a discussion of the body of the modernist automaton in a feminist and postmodern frame, see Rey Chow, "Postmodern Automatons," in *Writing Diaspora* (Bloomington: Indiana University Press, 1993).

13. F. T. Marinetti, *Marinetti: Selected Writings*, ed. R. W. Flint (New York: Strauss, Farrar and Giroux, 1971), p. 41. Further citations to this edition are given in parentheses in the text.

14. Quoted in Reyner Bahnam, *Theory and Design in the First Machine Age* (Cambridge: MIT Press, 1989), p. 121.

15. Quoted in Rose, *The Edwardian Temperament*, p. 160.

16. Klaus Theweleit, *Male Fantasies*, vol. 2 (Minneapolis: University of Minnesota Press, 1989), p. 143.

17. Ibid., p. 199.

18. Ibid., p. 162.

19. *Mafarka le futuriste* was first published in France in 1909. Here I refer to the Italian edition, *Mafarka* (Milan: Edizioni Futuriste di "Poesia," 1910), p. 2, my translation. Further citations of this edition are given in parentheses in the text.

20. Alice Yaeger Kaplan, *Reproductions of Banality: Fascism, Literature, and French Intellectual Life* (Minneapolis: University of Minnesota Press, 1986), p. 76.

21. Paul Virilio suggests an interesting connection between the prosthetic injured body and Futurist prosthesis: "The function of the machine as prosthesis for the (injured) human body is exemplified by the image of the refunctioned body of the WWI 'disabled soldier.' It was discovered that the damage caused by the war machine to the mechanics of the surviving bodies could be compensated by other machines-prostheses. ... In 1914 the German army had few or none exemptions, for it had decided to make physical handicap functional, by using each man according to his specific disability: the deaf will serve in the artillery, hunchbacks in the automobile corps etc. Paradoxically, the dictatorship of movement exerted on the masses by military powers led to the promotion of unable bodies." Paul Virilio, *Speed and Politics* (New York: Semiotexte, 1986), p. 62.

22. Gramsci, *Prison Notebooks* (New York: International, 1971), p. 303.

23. "Taylor is in fact expressing with brutal cynicism the purpose of American society—developing in the worker to the highest degree automatic and mechanic attitudes, breaking up the psycho-physical nexus of qualified professional work, which demands a certain active participation of intelligence, fantasy and initiative on the part of the worker, and reducing productive operations exclusively to the mechanical, physical aspect." Gramsci, "Americanism and Fordism," *Prison Notebooks*, p. 302.

24. Ibid.

25. Ibid., pp. 303–304.

26. In Gramsci's account, the new type of man is produced through a rationalization of sexual instincts inevitably linked to women and expenditure. Gramsci implicitly praises this new sexuality, comparing it to the prebourgeois sexuality of peasants, which he valorizes by imagining it through a primitivist lens. "Womanizing demands too much leisure. The new type of worker will be a repetition, in a different form, of peasants in the villages. ... He [the peasant] loves his own woman ... who is free from affection and doesn't play little games about being seduced and raped in order to be possessed. It might seem that in this way the sexual function has been mechanized, but in reality we are dealing with the

growth of a new form of sexual union, shorn of the bright and dazzling color of the romantic tinsel typical of the petty bourgeois and the Bohemian layout." See ibid., p. 304.

27. Ibid., p. 309.

28. Virilio, *Speed and Politics*, p. 63.

29. "Yes! Power to the artists! The vast proletariat of gifted men will govern. ... The proletariat of gifted men, in cooperation with the growth of mechanized industrialism, will arrive at that maximum of salary and the minimum of manual labor, which, without lessening production, will be able to give any intelligent person the freedom to think, create and enjoy the arts." Marinetti, *Beyond Communism*, 1917; and *Selected Writings*, p. 155. The two previous quotes in the text are from ibid., pp. 155, 301, respectively.

30. "The production process runs its course publicly in secret. Everyone goes through the necessary motions at the conveyor belt, performs a partial function without knowing the entirety. Similar to the pattern in the stadium, the organization hovers above the masses as a monstrous figure whose originator withdraws it from the eyes of its bearers, and who himself hardly reflects upon it." See Siegfried Kracauer, "The Mass Ornament," in *Critical Theory and Society: A Reader*, ed. Stephen Bronner and Douglas Kellner (New York: Routledge, 1989), pp. 145–154, esp. p. 148.

31. Theweleit, *Male Fantasies*, vol. 2, p. 153.

32. Kracauer, "The Mass Ornament," p. 152.

33. Ibid.

34. Ibid., p. 158.

35. Ibid., p. 148.

36. Ibid., p. 152.

37. Andreas Huyssen dedicates a chapter to the femme fatale motive in *Metropolis*. See "The Vamp and the Machine: Fritz Lang's *Metropolis*," in *After the Great Divide: Modernism, Mass Culture, Postmodernism* (Bloomington: Indiana University Press, 1986). Two other analyses of *Metropolis* that I find useful are Mary Ann Doane, "Technophilia, Technology, Representation and the Feminine," in *Body Politics: Women and the Discourse of Science*, ed. Mary Jacobus, Evelyn Fox-Keller, and Sally Shuttleworth (New York: Routledge, 1990); and Roger Dadoun, "*Metropolis*, Mother-City, 'Mittler'-Hitler," in *Close Encounters: Film, Feminism and Science Fiction*, ed. Constance Penley, Elizabeth Lyon, and Janet Bergstrom (Minneapolis: University of Minnesota Press, 1991).

38. The dialogue between Fredersen and Rotwang, from the American version of *Metropolis*, is quoted by Enno Palatas in "*Metropolis*, Scene 103," in *Close Encounters: Film, Feminism and Science Fiction*, p. 161.

39. Palatas, "*Metropolis*, Scene 103," p. 166.

40. Doane, "Technophilia, Technology, Representation," p. 167.

41. On the financing of *Metropolis* and its political implications, see Dadoun, "*Metropolis*, Mother-City," p. 231.

42. Roger Shattuck and Simon Watson Taylor, eds., *Selected Works of Alfred Jarry* (New York: Grove Press, 1965), p. 9.

43. Roger Shattuck, *The Banquet Years: The Origins of the Avant-Garde in France 1885–1914* (New York: Vintage Books, 1955).

44. Alfred Jarry, *The Supermale* (New York: New Directions Books, 1964), p. 1. Hereafter page references to this edition are given in parentheses in the text.

## Chapter 5

1. The phrase "the Great Masculine Renunciation" was used for the first time by J. C. Flugel in *The Psychology of Clothes* (London: Hogarth Press, 1930). The same concept has been elaborated and illustrated more recently by Quentin Bell, *On Human Finery* (London: Hogarth Press, 1948); Ann Hollander, *Seeing Through Clothes* (New York: Viking, 1975); Diane de Marly, *Fashion for Men: An Illustrated History* (New York: Holmes and Meier, 1985); Kaja Silverman, "Fragments of a Fashionable Discourse," in *Studies in Entertainment*, ed. Tania Modleski (Bloomington: Indiana University Press, 1986), pp. 139–155; and Jennifer Craik, *The Face of Fashion* (New York: Routledge, 1994). On the question of clothing and the cultural representation of gender see Marjorie Garber, *Vested Interests: Cross Dressing and Cultural Anxiety* (New York: Routledge, 1992); and Valerie Steele, *Paris Fashion: A Cultural History* (New York: Oxford University Press, 1988).

2. For a comprehensive discussion of the political and anticolonialist meaning of primitivism as a new aesthetic during the first decade of the twentieth century in France see Patricia Leighten, "The White Peril and *L'art nègre*: Picasso, Primitivism and Anticolonialism," *Art Bulletin* 72, 4 (Winter 1990), pp. 609–630.

3. See Henry Gates Jr., ed., "'Race', Writing, and Difference," special issue of *Critical Inquiry* 12, 1 (Autumn 1985); and Patrick Brantlinger, *Rule of Darkness: British Literature and Imperialism, 1830–1914* (Ithaca: Cornell University Press, 1988). For discussions of the relation between primitivism and twentieth century ethnography see James Clifford, *The Predicament of Culture: Twentieth Century Ethnography, Literature and Art* (Cambridge: Harvard University Press, 1988); and Marianna Torgovnick, *Gone Primitive: Savage Intellects, Modern Lives* (Chicago: University of Chicago Press, 1990).

4. Janet Flanner, who in that year, 1925, was an American correspondent in Paris, captured the impact of Baker's entrance on stage in this description: "She made her entry completely nude except for a pink flamingo feather between her limbs; she was being carried upside down and doing the split on the shoulders of a black giant. ... She was an unforgettable female ebony statue. A scream of salutation spread through the theatre." Janet Flanner, *Paris Was Yesterday* (New York: Viking Press, 1972), pp. xx–xxi.

5. André Malraux, *Picasso's Mask*, trans. J. Guicharnaud (Paris, 1974, and New York, 1976), pp. 10–11, quoted in Leighten, "The White Peril," p. 625.

6. D. H. Lawrence, *Women in Love* (Harmondsworth, Penguin Books, 1971), p. 71.

7. Ibid.

8. Ibid.

9. Ibid., pp. 71–72.

10. Robert W. Rydell, "Coloniale Moderne," *World of Fairs: The Century-of-Progress Expositions* (Chicago: University of Chicago Press, 1993).

11. José Ortega y Gasset, *The Revolt of the Masses* (New York: Norton, 1960), p. 12.

12. Walter Benjamin, *Das Passagen-Werk*, V, p. 469, quoted in Susan Buck-Morss, "The Flâneur, the Sandwichman and the Whore: The Politics of Loitering," *New German Critique* 39 (Fall 1986), p. 230.

13. See John Mackenzie, ed., *Imperialism and Popular Culture* (Manchester: Manchester University Press, 1986).

14. See Rydell, "Coloniale Moderne"; and John M. Mackenzie, *Propaganda and Empire* (Manchester: University of Manchester Press, 1984).

15. The image of the "black ruthless warrior" was presented mostly in adventure stories and boys' comics: See Brantlinger, *Rule of Darkness*, Ch. 8, "Imperial Gothic: Atavism and the Occult in the British Adventure Novel"; and Peter Jackson, *Maps of Meaning* (London: Unwin Hyman, 1989). For the outlaw sexuality of the black woman see Sander Gilman, "Black Bodies White Bodies: Toward an Iconography of Female Sexuality in Late Nineteenth Century Art, Medicine and Literature," *Critical Inquiry* 12 (Autumn 1985); and Jost Hermand, "Black Sexuality and Modern Consciousness," in *Blacks and German Culture*, ed. Reinhold Grimm and Jost Hermand (Madison: University of Wisconsin Press, 1986).

16. Richard F. Burton, *Two Trips to Gorillaland and the Cataracts of Congo* (New York, 1867), 2 vols., vol. 2, p. 311. See also the opinion of another Victorian explorer, Samuel White Baker: "The African . . . will assuredly relapse into an idle and savage state, unless governed and forced by industry." *The Albert N'yanza, Great Basin of the Nile and the Exploration of Nile Sources* (London, 1866), 2 vols., vol. 1, p. 211; both quoted in Patrick Brantlinger, "Victorians and Africans," *Critical Inquiry* (Autumn 1985), p. 187.

17. Frederic Jameson, *Modernism and Imperialism* (Derry: Field Day Theatre Company Limited, 1988), no. 14, p. 11.

18. Mackenzie, *Propaganda and Empire*, p. 110.

19. Anne Coombs, "The Franco-British Exhibition," in *The Edwardian Era*, ed. Jane Beckett and Deborah Cherry (Oxford: Phaidon Press, 1987), p. 111.

20. Ibid., p. 153.

21. "He and his wife, a former human cannonball, now an equestrienne, had recruited the Africans mainly from farmers in Natal. ... A number of Africans had been induced to join the party under the impression that they were bound for the diamond fields in Kimberly." See Ben Shepard, "Showbiz Imperialism," in Mackenzie, *Imperialism and Popular Culture*, p. 97.

22. Terence Ranger, "The Invention of Tradition in Colonial Africa," in *The Invention of Tradition*, ed. Eric Hobsbawm and Terence Ranger (Cambridge: Cambridge University Press, 1983), p. 220.

23. Mackenzie, *Propaganda and Empire*, p. 104.

24. Coombs, "The Franco-British Exhibition," p. 163.

25. *The Star*, August 11, 1899; quoted in Shepard, "Showbiz Imperialism," p. 100.

26. *The Sketch*, June 28, 1899; quoted in Shepard, "Showbiz Imperialism," p. 99.

27. "Women, apparently of gentle birth, crowd around the nearly naked blacks, give them money, shake hands with them and then kneel, in order that they may investigate further the interior of the overcrowded huts. ... At night it is even worse, for under the cover of partial darkness, the manners of the Matabele grow very offensive and they are encouraged by the behavior of female visitors whose impropriety is plain, and also shower upon them attentions that were certain to be interpreted in the worst way." *Daily Mail*, May 20, 1899; quoted in Shepard, "Showbiz Imperialism," pp. 102–103.

28. *The Morning Leader*, May 12, 1899; quoted in Shepard, "Showbiz Imperialism," p. 193.

29. Sir Harry Johnston, in *Harmsworth History of the World*, ed. Arthur Mee, J. A. Hammerton, and I. D. Innes (London: Harmsworth, 1909), vol. 7, p. 5548.

30. Shepard, "Showbiz Imperialism," p. 95.

31. *The Evening News*, May 15, 1913; quoted in Shepard, "Showbiz Imperialism," p. 96.

32. Shephard, "Showbiz Imperialism," p. 101.

33. Ibid., p. 106.

34. Adolf Loos, "Ladies' Fashion," in *Spoken into the Void: Collected Essays 1897–1900* (Cambridge: MIT Press, 1982), p. 102.

35. Adolf Loos, "Ornament and Crime," in *Adolf Loos, Pioneer of Modern Architecture,* ed. Ludwig Munz and Gustav Kunstler, with an introduction by Nikolaus Pevsner (New York: Praeger, 1966), p. 226.

36. Loos, "Ornament and Crime," p. 231.

37. Ibid., p. 103.

38. J. C. Flugel, *The Psychology of Clothes* (London: Hogarth Press, 1930), p. 113.

39. Ibid., p. 118.

40. Silverman, "Fragments of a Fashionable Discourse," p. 142.

41. Eugénie Lemoine-Luccioni, *La robe: Essai psychanalytique sur le vêtement* (Paris: Éditions du Seuil, 1983), p. 33.

42. Flugel, *The Psychology of Clothes,* p. 202.

43. Ibid., p. 202.

44. Michel Leiris, *L'Afrique fantôme* (Paris: Gallimard, 1950), pp. 54–55; quoted in James Clifford, *The Predicament of Culture* (Cambridge: Harvard University Press, 1988), p. 166.

45. Leiris, *L'Afrique fantôme,* p. 215.

46. Michel Leiris, *Manhood: A Journey from Childhood into the Fierce Order of Virility,* trans. Richard Howard (New York: Grossman, 1964), p. 6. Further citations are given in parentheses in the text.

47. Lemoine-Luccioni, *La robe,* p. 34.

48. See Kingsley Widmer, "Lawrence and the Nietzschean Matrix," in *D. H. Lawrence and Tradition,* ed. Jeffrey Meyers (Amherst: University of Massachusetts Press, 1985), pp. 115–131; and Émile Delaveney, "Lawrence and Weininger," in *D. H. Lawrence: New Studies,* ed. Christopher Haywood (New York: St. Martin's Press, 1987), pp. 137–156.

49. See Russell Berman, "The Aestheticization of Politics: Walter Benjamin on Fascism and the Avant-garde," in *Modern Culture and Critical Theory: Art, Politics and the Legacy of the Frankfurt School* (Madison: University of Wisconsin Press, 1989).

50. D. H. Lawrence, *The Plumed Serpent* (New York: Vintage, 1992), p. 145. Further citations are given in parentheses in the text.

51. D. H. Lawrence, *Lady Chatterly's Lover* (Cambridge: Cambridge University Press, 1993), p. 219.

## Conclusion

1. Roland Barthes, *Mythologies* (New York: Granada, 1983), p. 85.

2. Ibid., p. 88.

# About the Book and Author

A work of feminist critique of gender articulated at the intersection of materialist criticism, queery theory, and psychoanalysis, *Eye on the Flesh* studies the cultural production of a new male corporeality at the beginning of the twentieth century. From the ephebic, neoclassical body of the fin de siècle aesthete—which describes homoeroticism through the pleasures of consumption—to the hypermasculinity of the bodybuilder on the music-hall stage, to the macho technophilia of Italian Futurism and the self-disciplined body of the athlete–soldier–boy scout, Boscagli shows how the culture of modernity demands and consumes a new type of masculinity modeled on high- and popular-culture versions of the Nietzschean superman. This vitalistic male body, the author argues, represented a coherent signifier of masculinity without a referent: Continually hailed by the "manly" culture of the early twentieth century, men were called upon to occupy a gender position that proved uninhabitable. This body is worn as a suit, and masculinity is the result of a fetishistic game of gender striptease.

A brilliantly compelling work of cultural critique, *Eye on the Flesh* shows how male masochism and the post-Nietzschean male body give shape to an unstable gender formation in which normative masculinity edges on abjection, hysteria, and homoeroticism.

Maurizia Boscagli teaches in the Department of English at the University of California at Santa Barbara.

# Index